"Joe Rigney has written an enga... what C. S. Lewis had to say about living for the glory of Jesus Christ. Drawing upon Lewis's books, essays, and letters, Rigney offers an insightful overview of the author's teaching on Christian discipleship."

Lyle W. Dorsett, Billy Graham Professor of Evangelism, Beeson Divinity School, Samford University

"There may be no more important cultural question today than what it means to be human, and as Joe Rigney says early in this book, C. S. Lewis continues to be refreshing and unique on this question and so many others. Rigney's ability to reintroduce Lewis to readers is refreshing, unique, and on full display in this book."

John Stonestreet, President, The Colson Center; coauthor, *A Practical Guide to Culture*

"C. S. Lewis gets to the heart of the human condition, and Joe Rigney gets to the heart of C. S. Lewis. Here is a much-needed book that offers a clear and concise overview of Lewis's vision for the Christian life. Rigney's take on Lewis is appreciative where deserved, critical where necessary, and always insightful in its application."

Trevin Wax, Bible and Reference Publisher, Broadman and Holman; author, *This Is Our Time*; *Counterfeit Gospels*; *Gospel-Centered Teaching*; and *Holy Subversion*

"A thoughtful, lucid, and beautiful exposition of a magnificent writer. Whether you are relatively new to C. S. Lewis or have read all his books, Joe Rigney will show you ideas and connections that are easily missed, and increase your appreciation for Lewis's insights on the Christian life."

Andrew Wilson, Pastor, Kings Church London; author, *The Life We Never Expected* and *Unbreakable*

"C. S. Lewis's theology is a mix of faithfulness to the creeds, brilliant analogies, rare good sense, and, unfortunately, a few areas of doctrinal weakness. Joe Rigney's book *Lewis on the Christian Life* accurately reports Lewis's theology as it relates to practical Christian living. He does an excellent job of bringing out the good sense and carrying on a respectful but critical conversation with Lewis about those shortcomings. The end result is a book that will help you understand Lewis and practice the Christian life. This is a book I'm glad I read and one that you will want to read. I recommend it with enthusiasm."

Donald T. Williams, R. A. Forrest Scholar, Toccoa Falls College; author, *Deeper Magic: The Theology Behind the Writings of C. S. Lewis*

LEWIS

on the Christian Life

THEOLOGIANS ON THE CHRISTIAN LIFE

EDITED BY STEPHEN J. NICHOLS AND JUSTIN TAYLOR

LEWIS

on the Christian Life

BECOMING TRULY HUMAN IN
THE PRESENCE OF GOD

JOE RIGNEY

CROSSWAY®

WHEATON, ILLINOIS

Cover design: Josh Dennis

Cover image: Richard Solomon Artists, Mark Summers

First printing 2018

Printed in the United States of America

Chapter 10, "Christian Hedonics: Beams of Glory and the Quest for Joy," is based in part on the author's presentation "Christian Hedonics: C. S. Lewis on the Heavenly Good of Earthly Joys," delivered at Bethlehem College & Seminary, Minneapolis, October 8, 2016.

Scripture quotations are from the ESV® Bible (The Holy Bible, English Standard Version®), copyright © 2001 by Crossway, a publishing ministry of Good News Publishers. Used by permission. All rights reserved.

All emphases in Scripture quotations have been added by the author.

Trade paperback ISBN: 978-1-4335-5055-3
ePub ISBN: 978-1-4335-5058-4
PDF ISBN: 978-1-4335-5056-0
Mobipocket ISBN: 978-1-4335-5057-7

Library of Congress Cataloging-in-Publication Data

Names: Rigney, Joe, 1982– author.
Title: Lewis on the Christian life: becoming truly human in the presence of God / Joe Rigney.
Description: Wheaton: Crossway, 2018. | Series: Theologians on the Christian life | Includes bibliographical references and index.
Identifiers: LCCN 2017035074 (print) | LCCN 2018008202 (ebook) | ISBN 9781433550560 (pdf) | ISBN 9781433550577 (mobi) | ISBN 9781433550584 (epub) | ISBN 9781433550553 (tp)
Subjects: LCSH: Lewis, C. S. (Clive Staples), 1898–1963. | Christian life. | Lewis, C. S. (Clive Staples), 1898–1963—Religion. | Christianity in literature.
Classification: LCC BX4827.L44 (ebook) | LCC BX4827.L44 R54 2018 (print) | DDC 230—dc23
LC record available at https://lccn.loc.gov/2017035074

Crossway is a publishing ministry of Good News Publishers.

VP		28	27	26	25	24	23	22	21	20	19	18
15	14	13	12	11	10	9	8	7	6	5	4	3	2	1

The child whose love is here, at least doth reap
One precious gain, that he forgets himself.

William Wordsworth,
The Prelude, *book 5*

———————

To my mom,
who helped me to forget myself
so that I could find Joy

CONTENTS

SERIES PREFACE

Some might call us spoiled. We live in an era of significant and substantial resources for Christians on living the Christian life. We have ready access to books, DVD series, online material, seminars—all in the interest of encouraging us in our daily walk with Christ. The laity, the people in the pew, have access to more information than scholars dreamed of having in previous centuries.

Yet, for all our abundance of resources, we also lack something. We tend to lack the perspectives from the past, perspectives from a different time and place than our own. To put the matter differently, we have so many riches in our current horizon that we tend not to look to the horizons of the past.

That is unfortunate, especially when it comes to learning about and practicing discipleship. It's like owning a mansion and choosing to live in only one room. This series invites you to explore the other rooms.

As we go exploring, we will visit places and times different from our own. We will see different models, approaches, and emphases. This series does not intend for these models to be copied uncritically, and it certainly does not intend to put these figures from the past high upon a pedestal like some race of super-Christians. This series intends, however, to help us in the present listen to the past. We believe there is wisdom in the past twenty centuries of the church, wisdom for living the Christian life.

Stephen J. Nichols and Justin Taylor

ACKNOWLEDGMENTS

The acknowledgments section of a book is where the author attempts to discharge his debts to others. I say "attempts" because no words here can adequately repay the many helps I've had in writing this book. Nevertheless, gratitude is good, however inadequate.

Let me begin with the widest possible angle. One significant aid to this project was the wealth of Lewis resources available in a wide variety of formats. In particular, I've been greatly helped by listening to Lewis on audiobook. *The Great Divorce*, read by Julian Rhind-Tutt, has in many ways set the standard for me for all audiobooks. (I've listened to it half a dozen times in the last year alone.) The same might be said of the Space Trilogy. Of course, I've listened to the audio of The Chronicles of Narnia at least twenty times with my sons in the car over the last few years. The audio edition of *C. S. Lewis: Essay Collection and Other Short Pieces* (forty hours' worth!) proved to be a wonderful way to explore the breadth of Lewis's thought. I came away from listening to these essays with a deep awareness of certain themes in Lewis's thought that recur again and again and again. At the same time, I marvel at the myriad ways Lewis communicated those themes at different times to different audiences. In addition, the C. S. Lewis Collection available through Logos Bible Software proved invaluable for finding particular quotations and linking them with similar thoughts elsewhere in Lewis's corpus. I shudder to think how long it would have taken me to track down certain quotations if I didn't have the excellent searchability provided by the software.

Beyond the resources, I'm grateful for the good people at the Chick-fil-A in Bloomington, Minnesota. They kept my cup filled with Dr. Pepper and my belly filled with waffle fries while I wrote large portions of this book at a table in the back. I'm also grateful to the Lehn family, who allowed me the use of their cabin in Wisconsin for a writing retreat where many threads came together for me.

Narrowing in on specific people, I'm grateful to Justin Taylor and Stephen Nichols for inviting me to contribute to this series. I'm still humbled that they asked me, and deeply thankful for their editorial guidance at various stages of the project. Justin, in particular, was a great help in finding a structure and organization for the tangle of insights I collected during my research.

A number of individuals read various chapters and sections from the book throughout the writing process, improving it every time. I want to acknowledge, in particular, my brother Daniel, who is always a great encouragement and sounding board for me. John Piper, Andy Naselli, Devin Brown, and Rick and Adrien Segal all read through the manuscript with sharp eyes, warm hearts, and a deep love and appreciation for Lewis.

I have the immense privilege of teaching Great Books at Bethlehem College & Seminary in Minneapolis. While writing this book, I was able to teach through the material twice—once to undergraduates and once to seminarians. In both cases, the teaching improved the writing. God has built me to gain clarity through class discussions, and this has proved doubly so when my discussion partners have been students like those at Bethlehem. Special recognition goes to Jesse Albrecht, Zach Howard, Don Straka, and Ross Tenneson, who stayed late after class a few times to help me think through the organization of the book.

Outside my own life and teaching, the primary proving ground for Lewis's insights has been Cities Church, where I am blessed to be a pastor. I'm especially grateful for my fellow pastors—Nick Aufenkamp, David Easterwood, Kevin Kleiman, David Mathis, Jonathan Parnell, and Michael Thiel. It is a true joy to serve with such men. I'm also grateful for my community group, which prayed for me throughout the writing. I have no doubt that some of my key breakthroughs were owing to their intercession.

I don't have words to express my gratitude for my wife, Jenny. This book took a lot out of me, and she picked up the slack. Being the wife of a professor, pastor, and author isn't easy. And Jenny has the amazing ability both to encourage me in my writing and to remind me that real life is more important than books. It's living the Christian life that matters; books exist to serve life, and the only books worth writing are those that emerge from a life that is awake, alert, and engaged with real people.

My first book on Lewis was dedicated to my sons, who are both lovers of Narnia. I'm eager for the day when I can introduce them to some of Lewis's other books. My excitement for that day is fed by my own memories of encountering Lewis when I was young, and from the great joy I've had in writing this book and seeing the many connections within Lewis's writings.

This book is dedicated to my mom. I have three reasons for this. The first is that though I can't remember distinctly my first journey into Narnia, I know it was she who sent me there (it's likely she took me there with her). She had an old set of The Chronicles (the American edition, which orders the books properly, by publication, rather than chronologically). She introduced me to Narnia and, as a result, gave me a tremendous gift.

Second is my mom's encouragement during my first encounter with *Mere Christianity*. I'd somehow acquired a copy when I was about thirteen, and it was like a whole new world had opened before me. What I read thrilled me—the clarity of thought, the vividness of expression, the importance of what Lewis was saying. It churned and churned inside me until I had to get it out. And so I did. I found my mom and dad and tried to reproduce Lewis's moral argument for the existence of God. I remember being frustrated that I couldn't explain it as well as Lewis. But even at that young age, I was discovering that I was a born teacher—I wanted to show people things, just because I liked them and wanted to share them. And my mom was there in the midst of that early stumbling attempt to share what I loved, encouraging me all the way.

Finally, one of the main things I've learned from Lewis is the importance of guileless and self-forgetful enjoyment. In other words, enjoying something simply because you enjoy it—losing yourself in some activity or hobby because it was made for you and you were made for it. In one essay, Lewis describes his delight in seeing a boy on a bus enthralled by a fantasy novel, rapt and oblivious to the whole world. "I should have hopes of that boy," says Lewis.[1] Over the years, I've discovered that some people find this kind of simple and innocent enjoyment difficult. For me, it's always been second nature. And I think I owe that to my mom. She has always joined me in my joy. Whatever excited me excited her. It didn't matter if it

---

[1] Lewis, *Lilies That Fester*, 38.

was baseball or science fiction novels, toy army men or American history. When I found something that captured my attention, she made sure the fire stayed lit. It never occurred to me that I should enjoy something because the "right" people said I should. The ability to enjoy something spontaneously and wholeheartedly is a gift from God. In my case, that gift was passed to me through my mom. And so it is to her that I dedicate this book.

INTRODUCTION

The best way to learn about Lewis "on the Christian life" would be a book club. If I had my druthers, every person reading this book would join me in a small group (about ten or so individuals) to read and appreciate what Lewis can teach us about the life of faith. We'd read *The Screwtape Letters* and *Mere Christianity*, the Space Trilogy and The Chronicles of Narnia, *The Four Loves* and *Letters to Malcolm*, *The Great Divorce* and *Till We Have Faces*. We might read some of the apologetic works, like *Miracles* or the *Problem of Pain*, and we'd supplement it all with some of Lewis's essays, sermons, and letters.

The method would be simple. We'd begin reading a book aloud to one another, and I would periodically interrupt to ask a question or make a comment or a connection to something else in Lewis or the Bible. The interruptions would be prime opportunities to press whatever Lewis is saying into our own lives. After the interruption, we'd resume reading. This rhythm of reading and questioning, reading and application, reading and appreciation, would afford a far richer vision of Lewis on the Christian life. For one thing, you'd be getting it straight from the horse's mouth. More than that, you'd begin to *feel* the organic unity of Lewis's thought, what his friend Owen Barfield meant when he said, "What he thought about everything was secretly present in what he said about anything."[1] Immersing yourself in this sort of Lewis book club would help you to enjoy and not merely contemplate Lewis, and therefore (hopefully) enjoy and contemplate God more deeply.[2]

But, alas, this book club is not to be. Instead, the best I can offer is this

---

[1] Owen Barfield, *Owen Barfield on C. S. Lewis* (Oxford: Barfield Press UK, 2011), 121–22.
[2] "Enjoyment" and "contemplation" are technical terms for Lewis. For definitions and descriptions, see chap. 9.

volume on Lewis on the Christian Life. I wish it were a better book. I wish I were able to do the subject matter justice. I owe Lewis so much, and I have only gone deeper in debt through writing this book.

How the Sausage Was Made

A book like this about a thinker like Lewis immediately presents the author with a structural challenge. Some books on Lewis are organized by topic (Will Vaus's *Mere Theology*, and Donald Williams's *Deeper Magic*). Some are organized biographically (Devin Brown's *A Life Observed*). Some seek to provide an overview of Lewis's major works and are thus organized by his writings (Clyde S. Kilby's *The Christian World of C. S. Lewis*, and Wesley Kort's *Reading C. S. Lewis*). I toyed with each of these approaches at one time or another. One of my editors initially suggested structuring the book as a reverse engineering of *The Screwtape Letters*. At one point I considered trying to root everything in *Mere Christianity*, bringing in other works as they unfolded naturally there. I wrote over thirty-five thousand words structured around the theme of dualisms (see below). But in the end, none of these approaches seemed to work.

Now, most authors do not spend so much time telling you about all the books they didn't write. I doubt many readers are all that interested in how the sausage is made; you've come for the eating. I mention these struggles for two reasons. The first is apologetic, and that in both senses. I want to apologize for failing to do my subject justice, and I want to defend myself against certain accusations. Whatever weaknesses remain in this book, they are not because of laziness. But the second reason is the more important, and it will take some explaining. To understand it, I'll need to tell you something about those thirty-five thousand words that I had to abandon (or rework).

After attempting some of the other structures, I settled on the theme of dualisms as the structure to unpack Lewis. The word *dualism* simply means two-ism. A dualism distinguishes between two things that are not identical. Not all dualisms are created equal. There are what we might call "both–and" dualisms and "either–or" dualisms. In either–or dualisms, the two things in question are mutually exclusive. This usually means that one of them is good, and the other is bad. Thus, we must make a choice between them. Both–and dualisms, on the other hand, identify two good things we may distinguish but must not separate. Instead, we must embrace them both.

These two types of dualism run throughout Lewis's writings; for example, body and soul, enjoyment and contemplation, God and self, pride and humility. Because of our sinfulness, we are constantly mixing up the two varieties. When faced with a both–and dualism, we regularly choose one side over the other; we turn it into an either–or. On the other hand, when faced with a true either–or dualism, we try to keep both things. We refuse to make a choice. Much of Lewis's writings may be seen as an attempt to correct this fundamental confusion. If we are discussing a both–and dualism, Lewis will dissuade us from choosing one and rejecting the other. He will try to keep us from becoming Martin Luther's drunken peasant, who is always falling off one side of his horse or the other. Thus, Lewis will urge the wedding of reason and imagination. If we are discussing an either–or dualism, he will insist that we make a choice. We must not be like the people of Israel, halting between two opinions; or the disciples of Jesus, attempting to serve two masters. Thus, Lewis will write of the great divorce between heaven and hell.

Once you've learned to recognize the two types of dualisms, you will find them everywhere in Lewis's writings. Thus, I initially chose to organize this book around the two types of dualisms. The first part would have been devoted to both–and dualisms. It would have been called "The Givens," since these are the features of reality that are simply there and that we ought to receive as gifts from God. These include reason and imagination, enjoyment and contemplation, nature and arch-nature (or super-nature), Creator and creature, theory and reality, poetry and science, eternity and time, predestination and free will, masculinity and femininity, body and soul, pleasures and Joy (with a capital *J*).

The second part would have covered either–or dualisms, and I would have called it "The Choice." I say "The Choice" and not "The Choices" because Lewis believed that in the end, the Choice is singular, even if it comes to us in a variety of guises. There are many manifestations of the Choice, but at bottom it is the same. This fundamental Choice I call God versus self. Now, in one sense, this is a both–and dualism. Both God and self are good and should be embraced. But the Choice in question is which of these will be at the center? Will it be God, or will it be ourselves? That is the fundamental Choice.

From there, we would have seen how this Choice appears in any number of other dualisms: angels versus demons, pride versus humility, maturity versus autonomy, self-knowledge versus morbid introspection, and beauty versus utility. The Choice appears in our family life, where it becomes affection versus possession. It shows up in our sexual lives, where it is Eros versus lust. And it is in our social lives, where it is friendship versus the "Inner Ring," and membership versus equality. In our pleasures, it is deciding between self-restraint and repeated indulgence (what Lewis called "encore"). In our view of ourselves, it takes the form of good pretending versus bad pretending. And, of course, in the end, the Choice leads us inexorably toward either heaven or hell.

These chapters would have been punctuated by a number of narrative interludes that would have brought together different elements in the book. Ransom, Jane Studdock, Mark Studdock, Shasta and Digory, and Orual all show in clear ways the nature of the Choice that faces each one of us. But that book was not to be. Instead, I wrote this one. The Choice is still central; it appears in almost every chapter. But instead of accenting Lewis's dualisms, I emphasize the end and goal of Lewis's reflections on the Christian life—to help us so encounter the living God that we become our true selves. Becoming fully human in the presence of God—that is what Lewis thought the Christian life is all about.

An Invitation to Explore

As a result of this new focus, I loosened the strictures on organizing the chapters. In some of them, I use *The Screwtape Letters* and *Letters to Malcolm* as the launching point. Given the centrality of the Choice, this is a fitting way to discuss the Devil and prayer and church and so forth. *Screwtape Letters* is the Christian life from the vantage point of the demonic powers that seek to harm us. In it, Lewis shows us the world upside down so that we can better see it right side up. Writing from his basest self, he allowed his imagination to run down the ugly paths and tangled ditches of his heart, giving voice to them through a bureaucratic devil. In the preface, however, he notes that a full treatment of the Christian life would require a similar set of letters from the perspective of a guardian angel. Lewis doesn't think such a book is possible, because there is no answerable style to the angelic vision. Thus, we're left with only one side of the coin. However, I'd argue that, while *Letters to Malcolm* doesn't provide the angelic perspective, it does give us Lewis's vision of the Christian life in the mode he felt was most appropriate to his station. *Letters to Malcolm* is not didactic or instructional. Lewis was not writing to a student who is seeking his advice or to a congregant seeking pastoral care. Instead, it is, in his words, an exercise in "comparing notes"—two (educated and thoughtful) travelers conversing about the way. Lewis is a fellow pilgrim on the road, not an enlightened guru speaking to us from the destination, still less a Moses coming down from the mountain of God with stone tablets.

The Screwtape Letters and *Letters to Malcolm* thus provide a good entryway into Lewis's vision of the Christian life. But once inside the house of Lewis, there are many doors. Almost every chapter furnishes passages that link book to book, essay to essay, novel to novel. A tangential question in one chapter becomes the launching point for another. Hidden passages emerge all the time, and surprising connections draw together themes from multiple chapters.

Think of the chapters of my book, then, as various doorways—wardrobes if you like—into the world that is Lewis. They are not the only doorways. They may not even be the best. All I can say for them is this—they are some of the ones that have helped me the most. And after reading this book, I hope you find them helpful as well. Or, again, think of the chapters as a set of keys that will enable you to explore a great house, unimpaired by locked doors. But hear me when I say that *exploration* is the point. Keys only get you in the door; the rooms themselves are where the magic happens.

A Great Omission?

In the remainder of this introduction, I want to say a word about why I think Lewis is quite effective in writing about the Christian life. But before I do, I need to say something about what some readers may regard as a significant omission in this book. In the chapters that follow, I do not spend much time drawing from The Chronicles of Narnia (though they do show up in a few places). There are two reasons for this omission.

The first is that I've already written a book on Narnia and the Christian life, called *Live Like a Narnian: Christian Discipleship in Lewis's Chronicles*. If I had used all of that material in this book, it would be far too long. Thus, I have been selective in choosing which aspects of Narnia are particularly useful or poignant in this book. To see how Narnia factors into Lewis's vision of the Christian life, you'll have to pick up that book and enter the wardrobe.

The second reason is that the Narnian chronicles are probably the most widely read of all of Lewis's books. Add *Mere Christianity* and perhaps *The Screwtape Letters*, and you have the works of Lewis that most Christians are familiar with. For this book, I want to expand our horizons a bit. I want to expose you to some of Lewis's other writings in hopes that you will get a better sense of the whole of his thought. In particular, I've drawn liberally from the Space Trilogy, *Letters to Malcolm*, *The Great Divorce*, *Till We Have Faces*, *The Four Loves*, and numerous lesser-known essays, as well as some of Lewis's personal letters. My hope is that this book will lead some newcomers to these books and will enrich the rereading of those who are already familiar with them.

Why We Read and Love Lewis

Lewis is a master of the soul. He understands the human heart, in all its deceitfulness and grandeur, both in its good design and in its twisted corruption. He is a master of revealing the secret springs of our actions, of unveiling the true motivations underneath the lies we tell ourselves and others. He knows that our motives are complex; yet he can untangle them and sort through the knottiest bundle with unusual clarity. And because we have the sense that he discovered these secret springs through his own painful introspection (or apocalypses), we are not put out by his candor. Lewis speaks not from abstraction but from experience. He knows that of which he writes. He has had the severe mercy of his insights thrust upon him, so that he knows his matter from the inside and out.

This is what makes Lewis's voice so refreshing and unique. It's why he resonates. His voice is what we would like ours to sound like if we could get outside and speak to our own psyches. He is what one wishes his or her conscience—that great accuser or excuser (for so Lewis is to most of us)—sounded like. He is relentless in his pursuit of the truth. But the relentlessness is coupled with a gentle firmness. It is this combination of contraries that resonates—the willingness to hear our pathetic excuses and dodges and to go on seeing through them, the dogged persistence that won't let us off the hook, the absence of moral hectoring and "putting on airs," the sense of familiarity and friendship that means he won't abandon us when we finally (and inevitably) relent.

I cannot count the number of times I've been reading Lewis and felt as though someone had given him a map of my heart—a map that included all the dark places and black caves, the sordid dens of iniquity beyond the reach of the sun. But despite our being exposed, there is no fear of exposure. If Lewis is our accuser, he is a benevolent one. But *accuser* isn't the right word. More like a surgeon, he sees the cancer—he once had it himself (and it never went fully into remission). He sees the toxic bile flowing in our veins. And he won't stop with merely purifying the blood. No half measures here. We will not be healed by a tea strainer. He will find the tumor, that pulsating and throbbing mass in our chests, the remnants of what God intended to be a heart. And when he finds it, he will cut it out. Or, rather, he will pass the scalpel to the Chief Surgeon, who has been standing behind and guiding him all along. And the Surgeon will look at us and ask the same question that the angel asked the lustful man in *The Great Divorce*: "May I kill it?"[3]

Lewis's ability in this respect is likely unparalleled. Where did he learn to cut through us like that, to tap into our truest desires, our deepest motivations, our ugliest thoughts? He learned it from looking at himself. What he says about how he learned about temptation might equally be said of how he learned of longing:

> Some have paid me an undeserved compliment by supposing that my Letters were the ripe fruit of many years' study in moral and ascetic theology. They forgot that there is an equally reliable, though less creditable, way of learning how temptation works. "My heart"—I need no other's—"showeth me the wickedness of the ungodly."[4]

But introspection was not his only school. Lewis lived in books. They were his constant companions, furnishing him with an iconography through which he interpreted his own experience. "In reading great literature I become a thousand men and yet remain myself. Like the night sky in the Greek poem, I see with a myriad eyes, but it is still I who see. Here, as in worship, in love, in moral action, and in knowing, I transcend myself; and am never more myself than when I do."[5]

My Hope for You

That is my hope for this book. I want you to become more yourself by seeing the Christian life through the eyes of C. S. Lewis. I want to help you to enjoy,

---

[3] Lewis, *The Great Divorce*, 108.
[4] Lewis, *The Screwtape Letters*, xli–xlii.
[5] Lewis, *An Experiment in Criticism*, 111.

contemplate, and appreciate him as an author and spiritual guide. If after reading this book, you say, "Well then, I understand Lewis better now. No need to read him anymore," then I will have failed. Success for me will be when, in the midst of reading this book, you throw it down, rush to your shelves, and pull down your copy of *The Great Divorce* or *Perelandra* and, like a good Berean, examine to see whether what I've said is so. To treat this book as a replacement for reading Lewis would be a disaster. I honestly believe that I've only scratched the surface of Lewis's profundity and wisdom. But if you treat this book not as a substitute but as an aid, a guide, perhaps even a key to understanding some of the hidden pathways in Lewis's works, then I think it may be useful. I've not seen everything there is to see, but what I have seen has been profoundly fruitful in my own life.

But enjoying, contemplating, and appreciating Lewis is not my only aim. Not even my primary aim. My further hope is the same as Lewis's own: I want to help you to love God and love your neighbor. I want to help you become truly human—solid, substantive, stable, full of life and joy, and renewed in the image of Christ. Of course, that is not something I can accomplish. It is the gift of God. And so, to begin, I want to invite you into his presence.

CHAPTER I

THE CHOICE

The Unavoidable Either–Or

"Begin where you are."[1] This little phrase, tucked away in one of the letters to Malcolm, is the right place to begin our exploration of Lewis on the Christian life. Lewis calls this a great principle, and it is implicit in almost everything he writes. Again and again, he wants to bring us back to brass tacks, to awaken us to the present reality, to help us feel the weight of glory that presses on us even now. This is the real labor of life: "to remember, to attend. In fact, to come awake. Still more, to remain awake."[2]

But come awake to what? Ultimately to God. But Lewis knows that we often need a preliminary step. We need to face some sort of "resistant reality."[3] That's what "begin where you are" is meant to accomplish. The exhortation "Begin where you are" gives us a location, an identity, and a time. Let's look at each one in turn.

The word "where" denotes location. We are always in a particular place, and Lewis wants us to be attentive to it. Right now, you're reading this book in a particular place. Take a moment to notice it. The firmness of the chair or the softness of the mattress. The wind in the trees or the smell of the coffee. The noise at the next table or the silence of the living room. There's a realness to these things, what Lewis calls "quiddity" or "what-ness." The

---

[1] Lewis, *Letters to Malcolm*, 88.
[2] Ibid., 75.
[3] Ibid., 78.

world around us is real and objective. It is concrete and particular. It has a determinate quality, shape, and texture. And it is full of "impenetrable mysteries." This world of sights and sounds and smells, "this astonishing cataract of bears, babies, and bananas, this immoderate deluge of atoms, orchids, oranges, cancers, canaries, fleas, gases, tornadoes and toads"[4]— this is what Lewis calls nature. So, to begin where you are means that you begin *here*, in the present location.

Second, the exhortation accents an identity. "Begin where *you* are." But what are *you*? According to Lewis, you are a thinking thing, a rational animal. Part of you belongs to nature—your body with its senses and motions and stubborn limitations. But there is another part of you, what Lewis calls an intrusion of the supernatural into the world of nature. This is the soul, the part of you that thinks and reasons, that imagines and enjoys, that wills and chooses. According to Lewis, the validity of our reasoning depends upon the transcendence of reason itself. Reason must stand outside of nature in order for it to give us truth about nature. Our thinking, if we are to regard it as true or false, must be a shot from Something beyond nature, a beam from the Light beyond the sun, a participation in the eternal *Logos*. And if this were a book on Lewis's apologetics, we'd spend some time exploring this argument.[5] As it is, I'll simply note that the "you" that is here is also an incomprehensible mystery, half spirit and half animal, straddling the line between nature and super-nature.

Third, Lewis's great principle accents time. "Begin where you *are*." Not where you *were*. Not where you *will be*. Where you *are*. Because you are not just here; you're also *now*. You're in the present, that astounding place where time touches eternity, the infinitesimal point where the past meets the future. You have a past. You have a future. But all of your living and thinking and enjoying and willing takes place in the present.

So, to begin a book on Lewis, you must begin where you are. And where are you? You, a thinking, imagining, and willing person, are here and now.

God Is Everywhere

But you're not the only one who is here and now. God also is here and now. God is both omnipresent and in the present. He is present everywhere and everywhen. "We may ignore, but we can nowhere evade, the presence of

4 Lewis, *Miracles*, 105.
5 Lewis offers this argument especially in his book *Miracles*.

God. The world is crowded with Him. He walks everywhere *incognito*."[6] But he is not omnipresent in a pantheistic fashion. Pantheism believes everything is God, or at least, a part of God—who is diffused in all things like a universal gas or fluid. But Christianity views God's omnipresence in a different way. The world is not a part of him, and he is not a gas. Instead, he is *totally* present at every point of space and time, and *locally* present in none.[7] His omnipresence is that of an author with and in his story; it is only his attention that keeps us going moment by moment. What's more, space and time do not constrain or confine him. He is transcendent as well as immanent, high and lifted up as well as near and close at hand.[8]

But we can say more. This God who is here and now is "Unimaginably and Insupportably Other."[9] He is beyond our capacity to understand. Not only our language but also our thoughts are inadequate to fully grasp or comprehend him. But this is not because he is too abstract for human speech and thought. He is not abstract at all. As the source of this world of concrete and individual things, he himself is concrete and individual in the highest degree. He is not an ultimate principle or ideal or value. He is not "universal being" (as though he were a big vague generality), but "absolute Being" (he alone exists in his own right).[10] He is the ultimate Fact, "the opaque center of all existences, the thing that simply and entirely *is*, the fountain of facthood."[11] He is incomprehensible and unspeakable not because he is too abstract, but because he is too definite for words.

Not only is God here and now; not only is he the ultimate, concrete Fact; he is also personal. Indeed, he's more than personal. He is suprapersonal, beyond personality. This too makes him unfathomable to us. He is triune, three-in-one, three persons while remaining one God. We cannot grasp this, any more than two-dimensional beings could grasp what is meant by a cube.[12] But though we may not comprehend him, we can comprehend our incomprehension, and from that beginning, begin to know him.

So, then, to begin to understand Lewis on the Christian life, we must

---

6 Lewis, *Letters to Malcolm*, 75.
7 Lewis, *Miracles*, 134–35.
8 "In Pantheism, God is all. But the whole point of creation surely is that He was not content to be all. He intends to be 'all *in all*'" (Lewis, *Letters to Malcolm*, 70).
9 Ibid., 13. "All creatures, from the angel to the atom, are other than God; with an otherness to which there is no parallel: incommensurable. The very words 'to be' cannot be applied to Him and to them in exactly the same sense" (ibid., 73). In the latter sentence, Lewis is setting for the basic theological principle of analogy: God is both like and unlike his creation.
10 Lewis, *Miracles*, 139.
11 Ibid., 141.
12 Ibid., 135–36.

keep ever in our minds these two truths: (1) you are here and now; (2) God—the eternal, omnipresent, suprapersonal Author of all—is also here and now.

God Demands All of Us

But we must go another step. God is not just here and now. He is here and now pursuing us. This ever-present God makes demands of us. And not just any demands. He is not a tax collector, asking for a percentage of your time and resources and leaving the rest to you. As your Creator and Author, he demands all of you. He is the Maker; you are the made. He is the Potter; you are the pot. He is the Author; you are his character. Therefore, he has all rights and claims to you and yours. The almighty Maker of heaven and earth lays claim to your ultimate devotion and affection.

This total claim again sets Christianity off from pantheism. The god of pantheism makes no demands of us. Believing in such a god is attractive precisely for this reason. We get all the emotional comfort of belief in God with none of the unpleasant consequences.

> When you are feeling fit and the sun is shining and you do not want to believe that the whole universe is a mere mechanical dance of atoms, it is nice to be able to think of this great mysterious Force rolling on through the centuries and carrying you on its crest. If, on the other hand, you want to do something rather shabby, the Life-Force, being only a blind force, with no morals and no mind, will never interfere with you like that troublesome God we learned about when we were children.[13]

This pantheistic life-force is a tame god, giving us all the thrills of religion with none of the cost. He is there if you wish for him, but he will not pursue you.

But some of us wish to go beyond the life-force. We want a personal god, not a mere impersonal force. But we don't go the whole way with Christianity. We want a personal god, but one who won't interfere. We don't want a Father in heaven so much as a grandfather in heaven—"a senile benevolence who, as they say, 'liked to see young people enjoying themselves,' and whose plan for the universe was simply that it might be truly said at the end of each day, 'a good time was had by all.'"[14]

---

[13] Lewis, *Mere Christianity*, 26–27.

[14] Lewis, *The Problem of Pain*, 31. The placement and form of quotation marks within Lewis quotations have been Americanized for consistency of appearance.

But the God who is here and now is neither a tame life-force nor a senile grandfather in the sky. He is alive, pulling at the other end of the cord, perhaps approaching at an infinite speed—the hunter, King, husband.[15] He is not indulgent or soft. He is the Great Interferer, insisting that because he has made us, he knows what is best for us. He pursues and interrupts. He confronts and challenges. He is a lion, and he is not tame. But (and we must never forget) he is also good.

This is why Christianity has an ambivalent relationship with what men commonly call religion. We think of religion as "man's search for God," and we place it alongside other departments of human life—the economic, social, intellectual, and recreational. But the living God, the God who is here and now, will not settle for a portion; he demands all. In this sense, if we are to retain the word *religion*, it must encompass and infuse all our activities. There can be no nonreligious acts, only religious or irreligious ones.

Thus, we begin with these three facts: (1) You are here and now; (2) God is here and now; (3) God demands all of you. These three facts yield a fourth: (4) Every moment of every day, you are confronted with a choice— either place God at the center of your life, or place something else there. Either acknowledge the way the world really is, or attempt to live in a fantasy of your own devising. Either surrender to your Creator and Lord, or rise up and assert your own independence. Reality, Lewis says, "presents us with an absolutely unavoidable 'either-or.'"[16] We live in a world of forked roads, where every path regularly and repeatedly branches in two mutually exclusive directions. Our task is to reject the illusion that, in the end, all paths lead to the same place. We must choose, and our choice will make all the difference.

The Choice in *The Great Divorce*

In *The Great Divorce*, Lewis's imaginary vision of the afterlife, the narrator journeys from the outskirts of hell (the "Grey Town") to the outskirts of heaven (the green plains), meeting and conversing with many departed souls. For much of his journey, he is guided by his mentor, George MacDonald (much as Virgil is Dante's guide in *The Divine Comedy*). Many evangelicals stumble over Lewis's imaginary tour of the afterlife. His dream suggests that damned souls can take excursions—leave hell and journey

---

15 Lewis, *Miracles*, 150.
16 Lewis, *The Great Divorce*, vii.

either to earth or to the doorstep of heaven (what MacDonald calls "the Valley of the Shadow of Life").[17] More than that, Lewis suggests that these damned souls have another chance to repent after death. They can choose to stay in heaven (though we witness only one soul making such a choice). Finally, Lewis suggests that if a ghost on an excursion chooses to stay in heaven, its time in the Grey Town will have really been purgatory.

Holidays for the damned, second chances after death, and purgatory. What are we to do with these? The first thing is that we must not deny them. They are really in the story and, at least in the case of purgatory, seem to represent Lewis's actual beliefs. Having said that, we need to see what Lewis is doing in this book, which does *not* include teaching or speculating about the afterlife. In the preface, he is quite clear that he is offering an "imaginative supposal." The transmortal conditions "are not even a guess or a speculation at what may actually await us."[18] He reiterates this point at the end of the book in the mouth of George MacDonald. When the narrator discovers that he is dreaming, MacDonald says, "And if ye come to tell of what ye have seen, make it plain that it was but a dream. See ye make it very plain. Give no poor fool the pretext to think ye are claiming knowledge of what no mortal knows."[19]

So if Lewis is not trying to give us detailed knowledge of the afterlife, and if he's not attempting to give us a treatise on the relationship between eternity and time, what is he doing? MacDonald tells us plainly: "Ye cannot fully understand the relations of choice and Time till you are beyond both. And ye were not brought here to study such curiosities. What concerns you is the nature of the choice itself."[20]

That is why Lewis has shared his dream: to clarify the nature of the Choice.[21] In the dream, we can see the Choice (in all of its various guises) a bit more clearly than we can see it on earth.[22] The imaginative supposal gives

---

[17] MacDonald's words in the story (Lewis, *The Great Divorce*, 68) demonstrate Lewis's aim. Christianity has traditionally spoken of three realms: heaven, hell, and earth in between. Lewis introduces the Grey Town, which stands between earth and Deep Hell (represented by the fact that it will be dark soon in the Grey Town) and the green plains, which stands between earth and Deep Heaven (represented by the mountains and day breaking). In the supposal, the Grey Town and the green plains are presented as extensions of hell and heaven, but they function as exaggerations of earth in order to clarify the nature of the fundamental choice before us on earth.

[18] Ibid., x.

[19] Ibid., 144.

[20] Ibid., 71.

[21] Here and throughout the book, I will often capitalize the word "Choice" in order to accent its centrality for Lewis. When I do, it's referring to the fundamental either–or that confronts us. On what the Choice is, see the remainder of this chapter.

[22] Lewis, *The Great Divorce*, 144.

us a clearer lens. Thus, we need not accept purgatory or second chances or even Lewis's odd views of eternity and time in order to benefit from the story.[23] The main point lies elsewhere, in the choices made by the ghosts. The damned souls who go on holiday are only slight exaggerations of us. They are, in one sense, caricatures. But a caricature is drawn in order to accentuate real features of a person's face. And the ghosts in Lewis's story—with their sins and excuses and grievances and complaints and justifications—are all too real and reminiscent of the person we see in the mirror every day.

The Centrality of the Choice

I highlight Lewis's purpose in *The Great Divorce* because I believe it is his purpose in all his writings on the Christian life.[24] In everything he writes, his aim is to remind us that we are here and now, that God is here and now, that this God makes total demands of us, and that therefore we must choose to bow the knee or to bow up, to surrender and join our wills to God's or to resist his will and insist on our own way. In short, Lewis is ever and always attempting to clarify for us the nature of the Choice.

This Choice is inherent in the very idea of creation. In creation, God makes that which is not God. Needing nothing, he "loves into existence wholly superfluous creatures in order that He may love and perfect them."[25] Perfecting us means drawing us into his own life, not in pantheistic fashion, as if we are to be melted down and absorbed into God like drops of water into the ocean. Rather, Christianity shows us how human beings can "be taken into the life of God and yet remain themselves—in fact, be very much more themselves than they were before."[26] Like a boomerang, God flings us into existence with his right hand in order that he might receive us back with his left. But—and this is crucial—we boomerangs can choose whether to return or not.

By creating something other than himself—that is, something not God but possessing a mind and a will—God made the Choice (and therefore sin) possible. "From the moment a creature becomes aware of God as God and

---

[23] And, for what it's worth, Lewis doesn't truly believe in a second chance after death. As Orual discovers in *Till We Have Faces*, "Die before you die. There is no chance after" (279).

[24] Lewis was once asked, "Would you say that the aim of Christian writing, including your own writing, is to bring about an encounter of the reader with Jesus Christ?" Lewis responded, "That is not my language, yet it is the purpose I have in view." He went on to note that *Letters to Malcolm* is particularly indicative of this approach (Lewis, "Cross-Examination," in *God in the Dock*, 289–90).

[25] Lewis, *The Four Loves*, 127.

[26] Lewis, *Mere Christianity*, 161.

of itself as self, the terrible alternative of choosing God or self for the centre is opened to it."[27] The creature that is entirely dependent upon God and can only be happy in God can try to set up on its own, to exist for itself. This is the sin of pride, and it lurks behind all other sins.

> [It] is committed daily by young children and ignorant peasants as well as by sophisticated persons, by solitaries no less than by those who live in society: it is the fall in every individual life, and in each day of each individual life, the basic sin behind all particular sins: at this very moment you and I are either committing it, or about to commit it, or repenting it.[28]

This is what confronts us in the here and now. God says to us, "You must be strong with my strength and blessed with my blessedness, for I have no other to give you."[29] This is the only happiness there is. "To be God—to be like God and to share his goodness in creaturely response—to be miserable—these are the only three alternatives. If we will not learn to eat the only food that the universe grows—the only food that any possible universe ever can grow—then we must starve eternally."[30] This is the Choice: God or self. Happiness or misery. Heaven or hell.

Of course, there are many variations of the Choice. MacDonald expresses it this way in *The Great Divorce*:

> "Milton was right," said my Teacher. "The choice of every lost soul can be expressed in the words 'Better to reign in Hell than serve in Heaven.' There is always something they insist on keeping even at the price of misery. There is always something they prefer to joy—that is, to reality. Ye see it easily enough in a spoiled child that would sooner miss its play and its supper than say it was sorry and be friends. Ye call it the Sulks. But in adult life it has a hundred fine names—Achilles' wrath and Coriolanus' grandeur, Revenge and Injured Merit and Self-Respect and Tragic Greatness and Proper Pride."[31]

The Choice always involves clinging to some lesser good instead of clinging to God, putting a second or third thing first, rather than putting God first. We all express this Choice differently. "One will say he has always served

---

27 Lewis, *The Problem of Pain*, 70.
28 Ibid.
29 Lewis, *The Problem of Pain*, 47, quoting George MacDonald.
30 Ibid.
31 Lewis, *The Great Divorce*, 71–72.

his country right or wrong; and another that he has sacrificed everything to his Art; and some that they've never been taken in, and some that, thank God, they've always looked after Number One, and nearly all, that, at least they've been true to themselves."[32]

What's more, this Choice is not a singular event. We don't merely make it one time. Rather, we are always making it. Our little decisions, when gathered together, turn out to be not so little after all. We are always sowing the seeds of our future selves.

> Every time you make a choice you are turning the central part of you, the part of you that chooses, into something a little different from what it was before. And taking your life as a whole, with all your innumerable choices, all your life long you are slowly turning this central thing either into a heavenly creature or into a hellish creature: either into a creature that is in harmony with God, and with other creatures, and with itself, or else into one that is in a state of war and hatred with God, and with its fellow-creatures, and with itself. To be the one kind of creature is heaven: that is, it is joy and peace and knowledge and power. To be the other means madness, horror, idiocy, rage, impotence, and eternal loneliness. Each of us at each moment is progressing to the one state or the other.[33]

This is what really matters—these "little marks or twists on the central, inside part of the soul which are going to turn it, in the long run, into a heavenly or hellish creature."[34]

We end this chapter where we began. "Begin where you are." You are still here and now. But now (I hope) you are more aware of the significance of this present moment than you were before. God also is here and now. And he is pursuing you, hunting you, laying total claim to your life. He is offering you life and joy and blessedness. He is offering you himself. And so the Choice confronts you: receive God, or cling to yourself and try to be God. Surrender and become a son of God, or set up on your own and try to replace him. Be happy with his happiness, or turn inward to the broken cisterns in your own soul.

This is the center of Lewis's vision of the Christian life. In the rest of this book, I hope to fill out Lewis's picture. To do so, we must widen the lens a bit. We must get the bigger picture. And so to this bigger picture we now turn.

---

[32] Ibid., 70.
[33] Lewis, *Mere Christianity*, 92.
[34] Ibid., 119–20.

CHAPTER 2

THE GOSPEL

God Came Down

Before we can look at how Lewis helps us make the Choice, we must first have a fuller understanding of Lewis's view of the gospel. In this chapter, I will try to summarize his understanding of the *facts* of the gospel, what some theologians have called "redemption accomplished." These are the great works of God in history, from creation to the incarnation. A later chapter will focus on "redemption applied," the ways in which God's works in history affect us as individuals.

We begin with something we saw in the last chapter. God is the eternal, omnipresent, suprapersonal fountain of all facthood. He is absolute Being and the source of all other existence. Unlike created things, *what* he is (his essence) and *that* he is (his existence) cannot be distinguished. He simply and absolutely *is*. As he tells Moses, "I AM WHO I AM" (Ex. 3:14). Moreover, he is three persons while remaining one God. And because he is three persons, he himself *is* love.[1] Love is not just something that God does, but is in fact his very being. The Father loves the Son, and the Son loves the Father, and the Holy Spirit is that love, and that love is God himself.

Along with the historical Christian church, Lewis believes that God is "a most pure spirit, invisible, without body, parts, or passions, immutable,

---

[1] "All sorts of people are fond of repeating the Christian statement that 'God is love.' But they seem not to notice that the words 'God is love' have no real meaning unless God contains at least two Persons. Love is something that one person has for another person. If God was a single person, then before the world was made, He was not love" (Lewis, *Mere Christianity*, 174).

immense, eternal, incomprehensible."[2] Now, all of these attributes, while truly applied to God, are in some way misleading. They are essentially negative attributes; they deny that God has certain creaturely limitations. As we saw before, God transcends time and space; he is totally present at every point of space and time, and locally present in none. To say that he is infinite is to deny that he has finitude or limitations. Immutability (along with its cousin, impassibility) denies that God changes or is subject to anything outside himself. He is without passions because "passions imply passivity and intermission,"[3] and God is never passive.

The danger is that we take these negative attributes as the whole story. We strip God of creaturely characteristics, and are left with no positive statements about him at all. But the truth of the matter is that the negative attributes are simply the result of a positive, concrete reality that transcends and excludes the creaturely limitations. The problem is that, as creatures, we have "no resources from which to supply that blindingly real and concrete attribute of Deity which ought to replace it."[4] As a result, our idea of God may become so diminished that we wind up envisioning him as "an endless, silent sea, a sky beyond all stars, a dome of white radiance."[5]

Thus, in denying that God possesses creaturely characteristics, we must take care to remember that God is not *less* than these things but more. The negative attributes suggest that God *lacks* something that we possess; the reality is that God is so full of life and energy and joy and being that we say that "he transcends those limitations which we call personality, passion, change, materiality, and the like."[6] "He cannot be affected with love, because He *is* love."[7]

For example, when we say that God does not change, we are tempted to think that he is static, inert, and unmoving, that the rest and peace which God has (and is) is like the stillness of a mountain lake with no breeze. But in reality, "there is no movement because His action (which is Himself) is timeless. You might, if you wished, call it movement at an infinite speed,

---

[2] Westminster Confession of Faith, 2.1.
[3] Lewis, *Miracles*, 148.
[4] Ibid., 144.
[5] Ibid., 144.
[6] Ibid., 143. In a number of places, Lewis suggests that, instead of speaking of God as "incorporeal," we should say that he is "transcorporeal." At one point (*Perelandra*, 30), in speaking of the biblical teaching about sexuality in the age to come, he suggests that, instead of speaking of the glorified state as "asexual" or "sexless," we ought to say that it is "transsexual" (in that the heavenly experience transcends our earthly one). Given the modern connotations of the prefix *trans-*, perhaps it would be better to do what Lewis does when he replaces "impersonal" with "suprapersonal." Thus, the future state is not "sexless," but suprasexual. God is not atemporal, but supratemporal or omni-temporal (just as he is omnipresent).
[7] Lewis, *Miracles*, 148.

which is the same thing as rest, but reached by a different—perhaps a less misleading—way of approach."[8] In other words, God is so active, so alive, so vibrant, so pulsating with vitality, that we cannot ascribe anything to him so dull and lifeless as "change."

Or, again, we say that God is a spirit and incorporeal; he has no body. But often we confuse being a spirit with being a ghost. Ghosts are half men, shadowy echoes of true men, "one element abstracted from a creature that ought to have flesh."[9] But God is no ghost. He is a spirit, and, according to Lewis, spirit is more solid than body (think of the way he depicts the saints, angels, and even the grass and trees in *The Great Divorce*). "If we must have a mental picture to symbolize Spirit, we should represent it as something *heavier* than matter."[10] God is invisible not because he is a ghost but because, in comparison to him, we are. Here in the Shadowlands, we cannot see the things that are truly real.

The Author and His Story

A moment ago I noted that Lewis believes we have no resources for supplying the blindingly real and positive attributes that leave the negative attributes in their wake. But that is not entirely true. God has not left himself without a witness. For the God who transcends all creaturely realities is also the Creator of all creaturely realities. He is the almighty Maker of heaven and earth. "He is so brim-full of existence that He can give existence away, can cause things to be, and to be really other than Himself, can make it untrue to say that He is everything."[11] God is not, like the gods of paganism, a nature god. He is "the God of Nature—her inventor, maker, owner, and controller."[12] Or, to use an analogy that Lewis is especially fond of, God is an Author, the world is his story or play, and we are his characters. Christianity teaches that "God made the world—that space and time, heat and cold, and all the colours and tastes, and all the animals and vegetables, are things that God 'made up out of His head' as a man makes up a story."[13]

God is Shakespeare; we are Hamlet. He has invented us, made us up

---

8 Ibid., 149.
9 Ibid., 147.
10 Ibid.
11 Ibid., 141.
12 Ibid., 185.
13 Lewis, *Mere Christianity*, 37–38.

out of his own head, imagined us into existence.[14] This is why Christians say that God made the world *ex nihilo*, from nothing. Creation is an act of pure gift.

> Before and behind all the relations of God to man, as we now learn them from Christianity, yawns the abyss of a Divine act of pure giving—the election of man, from nonentity, to be the beloved of God, and therefore (in some sense) the needed and desired of God, who but for that act needs and desires nothing, since He eternally has, and is, all goodness.[15]

But God doesn't just create everything and then leave it to run by its own power. We are not deists, believing that God is a watchmaker who has left his timepiece on the beach.[16] Instead, God sustains everything that exists, upholding the cosmos, as Hebrews 1:3 says, "by the word of his power." "Every faculty you have, your power of thinking or of moving your limbs from moment to moment, is given you by God,"[17] so much so that "every man, woman, and child all over the world is feeling and breathing at this moment only because God, so to speak, is 'keeping him going.'"[18] Just as it is Shakespeare's will that keeps Hamlet in existence, so also it is, Lewis says, "only God's attention [that] keeps me (or anything else) in existence at all."[19]

Elsewhere, Lewis compares the relationship between God and creation to a painter and his picture, or a composer and his music.[20] And as with human authors, painters, and composers, God's work of art reflects his skill and creativity. It shows us what he is like. Creation thus furnishes us with at least some positive conception of God. Or, as Paul says, God's "invisible attributes . . . have been clearly perceived, ever since the creation of the world, in the things that have been made" (Rom. 1:20).

---

[14] In using this analogy, Lewis denies that he is watering down the concept of creation. Rather, he is attempting "to give it, by remote analogies, some sort of content" (Lewis, *Letters to Malcolm*, 72).
[15] Lewis, *The Problem of Pain*, 44.
[16] In *Letters to Malcolm*, 74, Lewis notes that Christianity is always fighting on two fronts. Against the pantheists, we insist on the Creator-creature distinction. Against the deists, we insist on the divine presence in created reality in various ways and senses.
[17] Lewis, *Mere Christianity*, 143.
[18] Ibid., 180.
[19] Lewis, *Letters to Malcolm*, 20.
[20] The analogy of an author or playwright and his story resembles other analogies that Lewis employs frequently. "The Christian idea is quite different. They think God invented and made the universe—like a man making a picture or composing a tune. A painter is not a picture, and he does not die if his picture is destroyed. You may say, 'He's put a lot of himself into it,' but you only mean that all its beauty and interest has come out of his head. His skill is not in the picture in the same way that it is in his head, or even in his hands" (Lewis, *Mere Christianity*, 37).

Space is like Him in its hugeness: not that the greatness of space is the same kind of greatness as God's, but it is a sort of symbol of it, or a translation of it into non-spiritual terms. Matter is like God in having energy: though, again, of course, physical energy is a different kind of thing from the power of God. The vegetable world is like Him because it is alive, and He is the "living God," But life, in this biological sense, is not the same as the life there is in God: it is only a kind of symbol or shadow of it. When we come on to the animals, we find other kinds of resemblance in addition to biological life. The intense activity and fertility of the insects, for example, is a first dim resemblance to the unceasing activity and the creativeness of God. In the higher mammals we get the beginnings of instinctive affection. That is not the same thing as the love that exists in God: but it is like it—rather in the way that a picture drawn on a flat piece of paper can nevertheless be "like" a landscape. When we come to man, the highest of the animals, we get the completest resemblance to God which we know of.[21]

Human sonship is thus an echo and dim reflection of divine sonship, just as human kingship is an echo of God's majesty. I'll return to the idea of nature revealing God later. For now, I'll simply note that because creation bears some likeness to God, Lewis regarded creation as a Great Dance. This is because "in Christianity God is not a static thing—not even a person—but a dynamic, pulsating activity, a life, almost a kind of drama. Almost, if you will not think me irreverent, a kind of dance."[22]

The Great Dance

The Great Dance is Lewis's way of celebrating the patterning and ordering within creation, the union and harmony of things that are so very unlike one another. It refers to the interlocking patterns in creation, the woven web of unity and diversity, the subtle and intricate wedding of order and freedom, of necessity and spontaneity, of value and inequality. It is creation in its totality as a work of God's art, where (to some) everything looks planless, though all is planned. Lewis's most extensive celebration of the Great Dance is near the end of *Perelandra*, when the angelic rulers of Mars and Venus, along with Ransom and the Perelandrian Adam and Eve, speak or sing or chant a hymn of praise to God. Here I'll include a sampling in order to give a flavor of what Lewis means by the Great Dance.

---

21 Ibid., 158.
22 Ibid., 175.

The dance which we dance is at the center and for the dance all things were made. Blessed be He![23]

Never did He make two things the same; never did He utter one word twice. After earths, not better earths but beasts; after beasts, not better beasts but spirits. After a falling, not recovery but a new creation. Out of the new creation, not a third but the mode of change itself is changed for ever. Blessed be He![24]

It is loaded with Justice as a tree bows down with fruit. All is righteousness and there is no equality. Not as when stones lie side by side, but as when stones support and are supported in an arch, such is His order; rule and obedience, begetting and bearing, heat glancing down, life growing up. Blessed be He![25]

In the plan of the Great Dance plans without number interlock, and each movement becomes in its season the breaking into flower of the whole design to which all else had been directed. Thus each is equally at the center and none are there by being equals, but some by giving place and some by receiving it, the small things by their smallness and the great by their greatness, and all the patterns linked and looped together by the unions of a kneeling with a sceptred love. Blessed be He![26]

All that is made seems planless to the darkened mind, because there are more plans than it looked for. In these seas there are islands where the hairs of the turf are so fine and so closely woven together that unless a man looked long at them he would see neither hairs nor weaving at all, but only the same and the flat. So with the Great Dance. Set your eyes on one movement and it will lead you through all patterns and it will seem

---

[23] Lewis, *Perelandra*, 183.
[24] Ibid., 184.
[25] Ibid.
[26] Ibid., 186. Here is how Lewis expresses the same truth in *Miracles*:

Where a God who is totally purposive and totally foreseeing acts upon a Nature which is totally interlocked, there can be no accidents or loose ends, nothing whatever of which we can safely use the word merely. Nothing is "merely a by-product" of anything else. All results are intended from the first. What is subservient from one point of view is the main purpose from another. No thing or event is first or highest in a sense which forbids it to be also last and lowest. The partner who bows to Man in one movement of the dance receives Man's reverences in another. To be high or central means to abdicate continually: to be low means to be raised: all good masters are servants: God washes the feet of men. The concepts we usually bring to the consideration of such matters are miserably political and prosaic. We think of flat repetitive equality and arbitrary privilege as the only two alternatives—thus missing all the overtones, the counterpoint, the vibrant sensitiveness, the inter-inanimations of reality. (Lewis, *Miracles*, 200–201)

to you the master movement. But the seeming will be true. Let no mouth
open to gainsay it. There seems no plan because it is all plan: there seems
no center because it is all center. Blessed be He![27]

For Lewis, the hierarchy and order of the world are essential to its beauty. "I
do not believe that God created an egalitarian world. I believe the authority
of parent over child, husband over wife, learned over simple to have been
as much a part of the original plan as the authority of man over beast."[28]
Whatever egalitarian measures we have invented, they are protections and
remedies owing to the fall, not positive goods in themselves. But the true
hierarchical world is still present, and the order and hierarchy within the
whole do not undermine the value of each individual part. Everything is
necessary in order for the work of art to be itself. The key principle, which
Lewis deploys in a variety of settings, is "the higher does not stand without
the lower."[29]

The Fall

Thus far, we've focused on God and creation. The eternal Artist, who has no
need of his art, nevertheless creates a glorious work that displays what he's
like. What's more, he invites his characters to join him in the Great Dance,
to sing the great song that he is composing. How then did this good world
and this Great Dance go wrong?

The simple answer is that the lower rebelled against the higher. One
of God's greatest creatures, an angel, rejected his rule, stepped out of the
dance, and became bent. He then seduced our first parents, and in them all
humanity joined the rebellion, plunging the rest of creation into disorder
and decay. Creation now has "all the air of a good thing spoiled."[30]

What Satan put into the heads of our remote ancestors was the idea that
they could "be like gods"—could set up on their own as if they had created themselves—be their own masters—invent some sort of happiness
for themselves outside God, apart from God. And out of that hopeless attempt has come nearly all that we call human history—money, poverty,
ambition, war, prostitution, classes, empires, slavery—the long terrible

27 Lewis, *Perelandra*, 186.
28 Lewis, "Membership," in *The Weight of Glory and Other Addresses*, 168.
29 Lewis, *Letters to Malcolm*, 87.
30 Lewis, *Miracles*, 196.

story of man trying to find something other than God which will make
him happy.[31]

The Great Dance was perverted; hierarchical harmony became wicked op-
pression. Dark powers oppressed humanity from above; the lower aspect of
man—the body—rebelled against the spiritual aspect, eventually producing
the great sundering called death.[32] Without God at the center, there came
into each of us "something self-centred, something that wants to be petted
and admired, to take advantage of other lives, to exploit the whole universe.
And especially it wants to be left to itself: to keep well away from anything
better or stronger or higher than it, anything that might make it feel small."[33]

Rebellion against God begat all manner of wickedness and destruction
among men. The horror that we feel at the great evils of the world is an
echo of the greatest evil of turning away from God as the source of life and
joy. Lewis attempts to capture the insanity, absurdity, and heinousness of
evil in Ransom's reaction to the discovery of a maimed animal on the unfallen planet Venus. When he encounters the Perelandrian frog wounded
by the Unman, the small evil hits Ransom "like a blow in the face." The
little wounded creature "was an intolerable obscenity which afflicted him
with shame. It would have been better, or so he thought at that moment,
for the whole universe never to have existed than for this one thing to have
happened."[34] Lewis is attempting to shock us out of the familiar stupor
that has grown over us, because sin and evil seem so natural to the world
in which we live.

Now, because I will later deal extensively with sin and evil and how
good things go wrong in our individual lives, I'll pass by any further comments on Lewis's view of the fall. Instead, I'll turn to God's three initial
responses to our rebellion. The first is that he left us with a conscience,
an internal witness to his own goodness. Second, he "sent the human race
what I call good dreams."[35] This is Lewis's way of referring to pagan myths
and stories. For him, the origin of such stories is complex and not simply
to be dismissed as evil or idolatrous.

---

31 Lewis, *Mere Christianity*, 49.
32 "The Enemy persuades Man to rebel against God: Man, by doing so, loses power to control that other
rebellion which the Enemy now raises in Man's organism (both psychical and physical) against Man's
spirit: just as that organism, in its turn, loses power to maintain itself against the rebellion of the inorganic. In that way, Satan produced human Death" (Lewis, *Miracles*, 209).
33 Lewis, *Mere Christianity*, 178.
34 Lewis, *Perelandra*, 94.
35 Lewis, *Mere Christianity*, 50.

On the one hand, Lewis believed that divine influence lay behind at least some of these myths. Additionally, human beings are able to recognize some of the patterns of the Great Dance and compress them into story form. Thus, the cycles of the seasons and the patterns of seedtime and harvest yielded stories about Ceres, goddess of grain, and Bacchus, god of wine. Myths about the corn-king are derived (at least in part) from human imagination reflecting on the facts of nature.[36] But our reflections on nature are twisted by our own sin and corruption, and by the dark powers that rule the world in this time of rebellion. Fallen humans ascribe to lesser gods the work done by the true God, and the fallen lesser gods receive and encourage this corruption. Nevertheless, because sin and evil can only twist what God has made, there are always elements of truth and reality embedded in those ancient stories, and God, in his great wisdom, uses these stories for his own purposes.

Finally, in addition to conscience and the good dreams, God "selects one family out of all of the families of the earth and spent several centuries hammering into their heads the sort of God He was—that there was only one of Him and that He cared about right conduct."[37] God's revelation given to the sons of Abraham moves a step beyond paganism, clarifying God's character and expectations for humanity, as well as giving pictures and symbols of God's plan for rescuing the world.

The Grand Miracle

The centuries of pagan myths and God's revelation to the Jews culminate in what Lewis calls "the Grand Miracle" of the incarnation. God becomes man. The eternal Son of God becomes human. Myth becomes fact. What had been foreshadowed in the pagan myths about the dying and rising god and the corn-king who multiples grain actually appears in time and space and history. Something greater than Ceres, Bacchus, and Venus is here.

If God created a world in which "the higher does not stand without the lower," and if the fall involved the rebellion of the lower against the higher, the incarnation is the descent of the higher into the lower.[38] The incarnation is like the central, missing chapter of a great book, the missing main theme of a symphony. It is the hinge on which the story turns,

---

36 Lewis, *Miracles*, 185.
37 Lewis, *Mere Christianity*, 50.
38 Lewis, *Miracles*, 178.

and when placed within the story, it illuminates everything. Blurry features in the story snap into focus; seemingly irrelevant details take on grand significance. The incarnation, while itself incomprehensible to the finite mind, gives a coherence and harmony to the whole.[39] It is the mystery at the heart of reality whereby the rest of reality makes sense. Like the sun, we cannot look directly at it, but it enables us to see everything else.[40]

Or, to use Lewis's analogy, the incarnation is as if Shakespeare wrote himself into one of his plays as a character (just as Lewis places himself in a few of his stories). "Shakespeare could, in principle, make himself appear as Author within the play, and write a dialogue between Hamlet and himself. The 'Shakespeare' within the play would of course be at once Shakespeare and one of Shakespeare's creatures. It would bear some analogy to Incarnation."[41]

Now, with a little modification, the analogy becomes even more fruitful. Let us progress in stages. God is God—eternal, self-existent, independent from all need of creation. In a wholly free act, God creates the world and becomes the Author of a grand story. At the same time, he includes himself as a character (indeed, the central character) in the drama. He speaks with Adam and Eve in the garden as a fellow character. He meets with Moses in a burning bush on Mount Sinai. He eventually makes his manifest presence (what we might call his local presence, or God-as-character) to dwell in the temple in Jerusalem. Thus, we have God-as-God, God-as-Author, and God-as-character. The incarnation is a further step, a further descent of the higher into the lower. The Son comes all the way down, not just into time and space, not just into humanity, but into a

---

[39] As examples of these details, Lewis mentions the composite nature of humanity (rational thought in a mortal body), the death and rebirth pattern seen in seeds dying in order to bear fruit, the selectivity and narrowness present in nature, and the principle of vicariousness by which all organisms are dependent on each other (ibid., 176–94).

[40] Ibid., 176.

[41] Lewis, *Surprised by Joy*, 227. Lewis uses the same analogy in "The Seeing Eye," in *Christian Reflections*, 171. "One might imagine a play in which the dramatist introduced himself as a character into his own play and was pelted off the stage as an impudent impostor by the other characters. It might be rather a good play; if I had any talent for the theatre I'd try my hand at writing it. But since (as far as I know) such a play doesn't exist, we had better change to a narrative work; a story into which the author puts himself as one of the characters." Using Dante's *Divine Comedy* as an illustration, Lewis notes that the analogy does break down. "Where the analogy breaks down is that everything the poem contains is merely imaginary, in that the characters have no free will. They (the characters) can say to Dante only what Dante (the poet) has decided to put into their mouths. I do not think we humans are related to God in that way. I think God can make things which not only—like a poet's or novelist's characters—*seem* to have a partially independent life, but really have it." I address the question of divine sovereignty and human freedom in Lewis in chap. 8.

womb as an embryo. The Author becomes not just a character but a *human* character.

This is what the incarnation is. Christ is truly God and truly man, true Author and true character. Indeed, Lewis believed that the incarnation is a microcosm of God's relation to all creation.

> There is an activity of God displayed throughout creation, a wholesale activity let us say which men refuse to recognize. The miracles done by God incarnate, living as a man in Palestine, perform the very same things as this wholesale activity, but at a different speed and on a smaller scale. One of their chief purposes is that men, having seen a thing done by personal power on the small scale, may recognize, when they see the same thing done on the large scale, that the power behind it is also personal— is indeed the very same person who lived among us two thousand years ago. The miracles in fact are a retelling in small letters of the very same story which is written across the whole world in letters too large for some of us to see.[42]

God came down as a character so that we might learn to recognize him as the Author. Christ turned water into wine in an instant so we could know that God has been turning water into wine in every vineyard since the beginning of the world. Christ multiplied bread to feed the five thousand so that we could know that God has been turning a little corn into much corn in every harvest in history. And so on through all of Christ's miracles—the healing of lepers, multiplying of fish, even the virgin birth. For Lewis, these miracles are either pointers backward to God's work in creation or pointers forward to God's future work in the new heavens and new earth. The miracles in the gospel "announce not merely that a King has visited our town, but that it is *the* King, *our* King."[43] The Creator of the interlocking patterns, the Lord of the Great Dance, is *here*.

In addition, the miracles of Christ demonstrate something about his humanity. Christ is not a prodigy; he is a pioneer. "He is the first of His kind; He will not be the last."[44] His miracles anticipate powers and abilities

---

[42] Lewis, "Miracles," in *God in the Dock*, 29. Lewis classifies Christ's miracles in two ways. "The first system yields the classes (1) Miracles of Fertility (2) Miracles of Healing (3) Miracles of Destruction (4) Miracles of Dominion over the Inorganic (5) Miracles of Reversal (6) Miracles of Perfecting or Glorification. The second system, which cuts across the first, yields two classes only: they are (1) Miracles of the Old Creation, and (2) Miracles of the New Creation" (Lewis, *Miracles*, 218–19).

[43] Lewis, "Miracles," in *God in the Dock*, 32.

[44] Lewis, *Miracles*, 221.

that all the sons of God will have in the age to come. We catch a glimpse of this when Christ walks on water.

> God had not made the Old Nature, the world before the Incarnation, of such a kind that water would support a human body. This miracle is the foretaste of a Nature that is still in the future. The New creation is just breaking in. For a moment it looks as if it were going to spread. For a moment two men are living in that new world. St Peter also walks on the water—a pace or two: then his trust fails him and he sinks. He is back in Old Nature. That momentary glimpse was a snowdrop of a miracle. The snowdrops show that we have turned the corner of the year. Summer is coming. But it is a long way off and the snowdrops do not last long.[45]

Of course, this is not just true of Christ's miracles. More importantly for our present purposes, Christ is the first real man in history. He is the pioneer not just in terms of his power but also in terms of his conduct. In the person of Jesus, we see "the Divine life operating under human conditions."[46] His words, his actions, his emotions—this is what humanity was always meant to be.

This last point underscores something about the whole purpose of the incarnation. It is not just the descent of the higher into the lower. "In the Christian story, God descends to reascend. . . . He goes down to come up again and bring the whole ruined world up with Him," like a diver swimming to the bottom of some great sea to retrieve a lost pearl.[47] "Christ, reascending from His great dive, is bringing up Human Nature with Him. Where He goes, it goes too."[48] This pattern of descent and reascent is present in the natural world. "Unless a grain of wheat falls into the earth and dies . . . " (John 12:24). It is the pattern of death and rebirth found in every wheat field, in every act of animal generation. Even more, it is the central theme of the entire story that God is telling. "Death and Resurrection are what the story is about; and had we but eyes to see it, this has been hinted on every page, met us, in some disguise, at every turn, and even been muttered in conversations between such minor characters (if they are minor characters) as the vegetables."[49]

---

45 Ibid., 230–31.
46 Lewis, *The Four Loves*, 6.
47 Lewis, *Miracles*, 179–80.
48 Ibid., 220. For a short synopsis of the central thrust of Lewis's book *Miracles*, see the essays entitled "Miracles" and "The Grand Miracle," in *God in the Dock*.
49 Lewis, *Miracles*, 157.

The Death of Christ

If death and resurrection form the fundamental theme of the entire story, then it is fitting that Christ, in his great descent, goes all the way down. Not only does he empty himself and take "the form of a servant," not only is he, though "in the form of God," "born in the likeness of men," but he goes even further. "He humble[s] himself by becoming obedient to the point of death, even death on a cross" (Phil. 2:6–8).

In the Christian view, death is unnatural; it is alien to God's original design for humanity. "Death is the triumph of Satan, the punishment of the Fall, and the last enemy."[50] But what is from one angle a punitive sentence is from another a safety device. To live unendingly in our rebellion, to wrap the chains of lust and pride and nightmare around ourselves for ceaseless centuries would be to reduce us to fiends and devils. It would place us beyond redemption. Death is both a punishment for sins and a mercy that delivers us from the hell of our own gnawing self-centeredness.

But in the death of Christ, death becomes even more than a safety device. It becomes a means of eternal life. In order to take on this positive function, death must be accepted. "Humanity must embrace death freely, submit to it with total humility, drink it to the dregs, and so convert it into that mystical death which is the secret of life." But only a perfect man could fully embrace death. For him, death would not be a punishment but a weapon. Through his own perfect dying, he would defeat death, disarm death, redeem death. Christ is the "representative 'Die-er' of the universe."[51] His obedience to death is a willing obedience; he is a volunteer. And as a perfect volunteer, his death in some way removes the sting of our deaths.

Now, when it comes to describing *how* the death of Christ accomplishes our redemption, Lewis is somewhat cagey. He holds theories of the atonement very lightly. He is dismissive of what he calls the satisfaction view of Christ's death (which is often called penal substitution). Given that his apparent dismissal of penal substitution is a stumbling block to many readers, I've chosen to devote the next chapter to treating the subject on its own. For now, I'll simply summarize Lewis's theory about how Christ's death redeems man.

Essentially, humankind has dug itself a hole from which it is unable to escape. Having tried to set up on our own, we are now rebels in high treason against God. In order to be put right, we must surrender and lay

50 Ibid., 202.
51 Ibid., 211.

down our arms. This is the only way out of the hole we're in, and the technical term for this is *repentance*. Repentance is hard. "It means unlearning all the self-conceit and self-will that we have been training ourselves into for thousands of years. It means killing part of yourself, undergoing a kind of death."[52] And this creates our dilemma: "Only a bad person needs to repent: only a good person can repent perfectly. The worse you are the more you need it and the less you can do it. The only person who could do it perfectly would be a perfect person—and he would not need it."[53]

This is where Christ comes in. He is the perfect penitent. We cannot get out of the hole of selfishness on our own. So God becomes man and steps into the hole with us. As man, he is able to surrender his will and suffer and die. And because he is also God, he does so perfectly. Then, in a great act of charity, he shares his dying with us. "Our attempts at this dying will succeed only if we men share in God's dying."[54] Through the death of Christ, death in general ceases to be the triumph of Satan and instead becomes "God's medicine for Man and His weapon against Satan."[55]

The Resurrection of Christ

The death of Christ is ineffectual without the resurrection. A descent to death with no reascent back to life would not be good news. It would simply be another tragic story about what happens to good men in an ugly world. But Christ was raised from the dead, and his resurrection is at the heart of the gospel. "The Resurrection is the central theme in every Christian sermon reported in the Acts. The Resurrection, and its consequences, were the 'gospel' or good news which the Christians brought."[56] The resurrection of Jesus is not about survival after death or the immortality of the soul. It is the beginning of the new creation, "the first movement of a great wheel beginning to turn in the direction opposite to that which all men hitherto had observed."[57] Christ does not appear as a phantom up from the realm of the dead; he enacts the great reversal. He returns to earth with a spiritual body, one that is both like and unlike his body prior to his death.

---

[52] Lewis, *Mere Christianity*, 57.
[53] Ibid.
[54] Ibid., 58.
[55] Lewis, *Miracles*, 208.
[56] Ibid., 234. Screwtape (Lewis, *The Screwtape Letters*, 138) says that the early Christians were "converted by a single historical fact (the Resurrection) and a single theological doctrine (the Redemption) operating on a sense of sin which they already had" (owing to the universal, moral law that God built into creation).
[57] Lewis, *Miracles*, 238–39.

On the one hand, Christ is able to eat fish, thus showing continuity with his pre-resurrection life. On the other hand, he is able to enter locked rooms, suggesting that his spiritual body relates differently to space (and perhaps time as well). It can be touched; Thomas dispels his doubts by placing his hands where the nails went in (John 20:24–29). But it can also be masked; the disciples on multiple occasions do not initially recognize their friend and Lord until he opens their eyes to do so (Luke 24:13–35; John 21:4–8). This is not just a resuscitation, such as the one Lazarus experienced. This is the inbreaking of a new nature, the anticipation of the new world that Christ will fully consummate when he returns in glory.

In this sense, Lewis, like the New Testament authors, closely links the resurrection of Christ to his ascension to the right hand of the Father. Because Christ has a body, and that body is no longer accessible to us, he must have gone somewhere. Conceiving of this place (a place which Christ goes to prepare for us) is likely impossible. Lewis suggests that reality has, so to speak, more than two floors. Everyone accepts the notion of a natural floor; this is the world of the senses in which we live. And Christians (and all theists) believe in a supernatural floor, that place beyond nature where God dwells. But given the biblical testimony about the resurrection and ascension (not to mention the fact of angels and demons), Lewis posits other intermediate floors between God and the nature we know. These floors are partially interlocked with each other, though in ways we cannot yet conceive or imagine. "In that way there might be Natures piled upon Natures to any height God pleased, each Supernatural to that below it and Subnatural to that which surpassed it."[58] Moreover, the new nature is not being made out of nothing (as this one was) but is instead somehow being rebuilt out of the old one. We are in the midst of a great renovation project, with all the anomalies, inconveniences, hopes, and oddities that such a project suggests. One day, there will be a great unveiling, and the place prepared for us will be as visible and present to us as our own bodies.

Conclusion

Lewis, of course, says much more about each of these great works of God. And I will say more about some of them as this book progresses. But this will do as a summary of the basic facts of the gospel. The living and tripersonal

---

[58] Ibid., 252.

God has created the world. He is the Author; we are his characters. The world is a Great Dance, a woven web, filled with interlocking patterns that are pregnant with divine meaning. All parts are necessary for the work to be what it is, and yet no two parts are identical. All is righteousness, and there is no equality. The higher does not stand without the lower.

And yet the lower has now rebelled against the higher and disrupted (at least in part) the Great Dance. There is now discord in the symphony. Death, the ultimate unraveling and scattering of mind from body and thought from thought, reigns in this brutal and broken world. The world is now the scene of a great insurrection; our own planet is enemy-occupied territory, claimed and counterclaimed by both God and the Devil. God claims the world and all that fills it on the grounds that he made it; Satan claims that the world belongs to him on the ground of his initial success at conquest. But God has not left the war in a stalemate. He has set out to reconquer his realm. He sends word of the coming invasion to the ancient pagans, but the message is garbled and confused. He sends a clearer signal to the Jews, showing them his plans and making them the staging point for his assault on Normandy.

And then, the invasion. He arrives. The manner of his coming is both an absolute shock and the most fitting climax to his story. Before it happens, no one could have guessed it. After it occurs, no one can gainsay it. The higher descends into the lower, all the way down into a womb, passing through poverty and pain and blood into a tomb, down farther into the realm of the forgetful dead (Ps. 6:5; Eccles. 9:5). And then up and out again, into the blazing light of new life, carrying on his shoulders the whole of humanity and nature. Because of his willing obedience even unto death, God highly exalts him and gives him "the name that is above every name, so that at the name of Jesus every knee should bow . . . and every tongue confess that Jesus Christ is Lord, to the glory of God the Father" (Phil. 2:9–11).

CHAPTER 3

THEOLOGY

A Map to Ultimate Reality

In this chapter, I plan to offer some critiques of and corrections to Lewis. If the aim of this book were simply to unpack Lewis's thoughts on the Christian life, then this chapter might not be necessary. Nevertheless, I have two reasons for including it. The first is that, as much as I love Lewis, I love the truth more. If I believe he is mistaken or misleading on some issue of great importance, then I feel duty bound to address it. Thankfully, I think Lewis would approve of this instinct. He appreciated vigorous debate and certainly did not see himself as above correction. So even the criticisms I offer here are, in their own way, an act of love and charity toward him.

Second, some Christians cannot hear all the good that Lewis has to offer because of what they regard as serious errors on his part. They are unable to enjoy the banquet he has prepared because they believe it is mixed with much poison. They say things like, "If a contemporary theologian said the sorts of things about the atonement that Lewis said, we would treat his writings with great caution. We would not recommend his books; we might not invite him to speak at our conferences. Therefore, we ought to treat Lewis in the same way."

I'm sympathetic to this perspective. Lewis did say some troubling things about substitutionary atonement.[1] He says that before he was a

---

[1] Donald T. Williams's recent book *Deeper Magic: The Theology behind the Writings of C. S. Lewis* (Baltimore: Square Halo, 2016) is an excellent treatment of Lewis's theology as a whole. Like me, Williams

Christian, he regarded that doctrine as immoral and silly. He implies that he still maintains some of that attitude. He's certainly willing to treat penal substitution lightly, telling his readers that if it does not appeal to them, they are free to discard it. Given that many evangelicals (myself included) regard penal substitution as a crucial aspect of the gospel, Lewis's dismissal is deeply troubling.[2] The present chapter is my attempt to understand the reasons for Lewis's cavalier attitude toward the doctrine, and, if possible, to recover the doctrine for him, and him for some of his more skeptical readers. But before we can grapple with Lewis on the atonement directly, we need to understand the way he thought about theology in general.

Speaking about God

Lewis was not a professional theologian. He was an apologist and a scholar of medieval literature. Nevertheless, he was familiar with Christian theology since it served both of those vocations. He viewed his task as translating Christianity into laymen's terms. He thought that this was a much-needed task in the twentieth century, given the widespread ignorance of what Christianity taught. He repeatedly suggested that ordination exams require candidates for ministry to translate some theological topic into the vernacular. Until a minister can do this, he said, he does not understand his subject, nor will he be much help in converting the unbelieving.

Nevertheless, Lewis did write about theology. What's more, he theorized about it and tried to help us understand how theology helps us relate to God. God and theology belong together, but Lewis saw how easy it was for us to pull them apart and set one of them up without the other. To understand their relationship, we must first get a definition. Lewis defines theology as "the systematic series of statements about God and about man's relation to Him which the believers of a religion make."[3] Lewis insists that we distinguish between theology and God, or between doctrine and the Truth. These distinctions are a sub-class of a larger distinction Lewis makes elsewhere—between theory and reality. Reality is reality. Theories are what *we say* about reality.

---

is a conservative evangelical who is sympathetic to and critical of Lewis's theology at a number of key points. His chapter on Lewis's view of the atonement and salvation is particularly good at representing and correcting Lewis's view of the atonement, conversion, predestination and free will, faith and works, and perseverance.

[2] For a clear and accessible treatment of the doctrine of penal substitution, see John Stott, *The Cross of Christ*, 20th anniv. ed. (Downer's Grove, IL: IVP, 2006).

[3] Lewis, "Is Theology Poetry?," in *The Weight of Glory and Other Addresses*, 116.

In the same way, doctrines are explanations of who God is and what he has done, and "no explanation will ever be quite adequate to the reality."[4] Thus, we must not mistake our words about the works of God for the works of God themselves. "Doctrines are not God: they are only a kind of map."[5] Thus, to turn from a real experience of God to a creed or doctrine is to turn from something real to something less real, just as a man who turns from looking at the ocean to looking at a map of the ocean is turning from something real to something less real, "from real waves to a bit of coloured paper."[6]

In making these kinds of distinctions, Lewis is not belittling theology or doctrine; he is seeking to give it its proper place. Theory serves reality; it does not replace it. Theology serves God; it is not his substitute. But how does theology serve God (and through him, us)? Again the map shows the way.

> The map is admittedly only coloured paper, but there are two things you have to remember about it. In the first place, it is based on what hundreds and thousands of people have found out by sailing the real Atlantic. In that way it has behind it masses of experience just as real as the one you could have from the beach; only, while yours would be a single glimpse, the map fits all those different experiences together. In the second place, if you want to go anywhere, the map is absolutely necessary. As long as you are content with walks on the beach, your own glimpses are far more fun than looking at a map. But the map is going to be more use than walks on the beach if you want to get to America.[7]

Theology, in this sense, is practical. It keeps our experiences of God from being fruitless. Vague religion—experiencing God in nature or art—is attractive precisely because it requires little work and no commitment. But "you will not get eternal life by simply feeling the presence of God in flowers or music. Neither will you get anywhere by looking at maps without going to sea. Nor will you be very safe if you go to sea without a map."[8]

So theology serves God (and us), first, by collecting the experiences of thousands of people who were really in touch with God and bringing them together in a (somewhat) unified whole and, second, by giving us guidance

---

[4] Lewis, *Mere Christianity*, 54.
[5] Ibid., 154.
[6] Ibid.
[7] Ibid.
[8] Ibid., 155.

and direction about how we can know, honor, and love God and our neighbor. And it is essential that we attend to it. For there is no question that we will have ideas about God; the only question is whether those ideas will be true. "Consequently, if you do not listen to Theology, that will not mean that you have no ideas about God. It will mean that you have a lot of wrong ones—bad, muddled, out-of-date ideas."[9] This is one reason why good theology exists: "because bad [theology] needs to be answered."

What Kind of Speech Is Theology?

So, then, theology—our speech about God—serves our faith in, love for, and obedience to God. Therefore, we must give thought to *how* we speak about him. In an essay entitled "The Language of Religion," Lewis gives his (tentative) thoughts on language in general and how we speak about our religious lives. He begins by distinguishing between three forms of speech, all existing on a spectrum:

⇐ Scientific — Ordinary — Poetical ⇒

He notes that scientific and poetical speech are both improvements on ordinary speech (ordinary speech is in the middle of the spectrum). Scientific speech improves it through precision and abstraction. It changes an ordinary statement like "it is very cold" into a quantitative statement about the precise temperature ("thirteen degrees below zero").

Poetical speech improves ordinary in a different direction. Its aim is to give the listener a certain quality or sense of an object or event. While poetical speech may arouse the emotions, its purpose is not merely subjective.[10] It seeks to give us real knowledge of an object through ample use of adjectives and descriptions that awaken our senses. Its most remarkable power is the ability "to convey to us the quality of experiences which we have not had, or perhaps can never have, to use factors within our experience so that they become pointers to something outside our experience."[11] Poetical speech, then, is a "real medium of information," as much as scientific is, with the noted difference that testing poetical statements is more difficult (though perhaps more rewarding).

---

9 Ibid.
10 Elsewhere he defines poetry at its most basic as "writing which arouses and in part satisfies the imagination" (Lewis, "Is Theology Poetry?," in *The Weight of Glory and Other Addresses*, 117).
11 Lewis, "The Language of Religion," in *Christian Reflections*, 133.

Lewis places religious language on the spectrum between ordinary and poetical. Religious statements can, he argues, be improved in a scientific direction. This is the language of formal or academic theology, where "I believe in God" is uttered as "I believe in incorporeal entity, personal in the sense that it can be the subject and object of love, on which all other entities are unilaterally dependent."[12] To connect it to the earlier discussion, this is one (very technical) way to draw a map about God. We often draw such technical maps for purposes of "instruction, clarification, controversy and the like." But, as Lewis notes, such abstraction and precision are "not the language religion naturally speaks"[13] (and thank God for that!). Religion, since it deals with the most concrete thing in reality (namely, God), naturally moves toward the poetical.

How Poetical and Scientific Help Each Other

This distinction between scientific and poetical speech is closely related to Lewis's understanding of reason and imagination, as we will see in chapter 11. The language of formal theology, directing itself toward the intellect, speaks with clear definitions, precision, and abstraction. Our sermons and hymns (and indeed much of the Scriptures) employ the more poetical and imaginative language: metaphors, similes, imagery, parables, and illustrations.

It is precisely at this point that we often make a fatal mistake. We assume that because the metaphors and images belong with poetical speech, poetical speech alone is symbolic. Even worse, we often take it to be a symbol of the technical, scientific, or theological language. But this is not so. Let us take two different true statements and try to grasp their relationship:

   A. When God is angry, smoke goes up from his nostrils (Ps. 18:8).
   B. God is absolute Being and all human characteristics are inapplicable to him.

Lewis writes that "we have a tendency to regard B as the literal truth and A either as poetical decoration or as a concession to the 'primitive'

---

[12] Ibid., 135.
[13] Ibid.

mind of the ancient Jews." In this, we are half-right. Statement A cannot literally be true. But neither can B. "B is an abstract construction of our own minds. It represents to us as an abstraction, a mere concept, what must in reality be the most concrete of all Facts."[14] Thus, we must not take either of them literally.[15] "Both are only shadows or hints of the reality. A cannot really imagine, and B cannot really conceptualise, God as He is in Himself." Both the poetical (A) and the scientific (B) are ways of speaking about Something more fundamental than either of them (just as the Atlantic is more fundamental than both an impressionist's painting and a nautical map). But poetical speech has this going for it—it is the language of revelation, of the Scriptures. Both A and B are shadows of reality, but only one is a revealed shadow. Both are symbolic, but the divinely chosen symbol must, in the end, supersede the humanly invented one.[16]

Of course, it is important to remember that prioritizing in this way (from ultimate reality down to revealed poetry down again to theological abstraction) doesn't diminish the abstraction. "The higher does not stand without the lower."[17] Abstract theological statements act as correctives against our tendency to take the images literally and draw false inferences from them. In *Letters to Malcolm*, Lewis discusses the relation between these two types of statements by reflecting on the Bible and divine impassibility—the doctrine, closely related to God's immutability and embraced through history by orthodox Christianity, that God does not suffer change and is not properly affected by creation:

> But you must admit that Scripture doesn't take the slightest pains to guard the doctrine of Divine Impassibility. We are constantly represented

---

[14] Lewis to Gracia Fay Bouwman, July 19, 1960, in *Collected Letters*, 3:1173.

[15] Lewis's use of the term "literal" is plagued by the same confusion that afflicts most uses of the term. At various times, he means something like "historical." Thus, for something to be literally true means that it actually happened that way in history. It also seems to carry connotations of precision and exhaustiveness. Thus, if something is literally true, it is true in a precise, technical, and comprehensive sense. When he insists that neither poetical nor scientific statements about God are "literally" true, he is primarily guarding against this notion of comprehensiveness, as though any of our statements about God could completely and exhaustively comprehend him.

[16] Lewis explains:

> B can make no claim to be a revelation: we have made it. A does make this claim. . . . To prefer B is to think that the symbol we have made is better than the symbol He has made. I think we are right to use B as a corrective wherever A, taken literally, threatens to become absurd: but we must instantly plunge back into A. Only God Himself knows in what sense He is "like" a father or king, capable of love and anger. But since He has given us that picture of Himself we may be sure that it is more importantly "like" than any concept we might try to substitute for it. You'll find this dealt with more fully in chapter XI of my *Miracles*. (Lewis to Gracia Fay Bouwman, July 19, 1960, in *Collected Letters*, 3:1172–73)

[17] Lewis, *Letters to Malcolm*, 87.

as exciting the Divine wrath or pity—even as "grieving" God. I know this language is analogical. But when we say that, we must not smuggle in the idea that we can throw the analogy away and, as it were, get in behind it to a purely literal truth. All we can really substitute for the analogical expression is some theological abstraction. And the abstraction's value is almost entirely negative. It warns us against drawing absurd consequences from the analogical expression by prosaic extrapolations. By itself, the abstraction "impassible" can get us nowhere. It might even suggest something far more misleading than the most naïf Old Testament picture of a stormily emotional Jehovah. Either something inert, or something which was "Pure Act" in such a sense that it could take no account of events within the universe it had created.[18]

Lewis here embraces the classical Christian position that all of our language about God, whether poetical or technical, is analogical. Indeed, it would seem that all our language about anything is analogical: "The very essence of our life as conscious beings, all day and every day, consists of something which cannot be communicated except by hints, similes, metaphors, and the use of those emotions (themselves not very important) which are pointers to it."[19] We never get behind biblical analogies (such as God gathering us under his wings, or God being grieved over our sins) to some pure, ethereal, abstract truth. The abstraction ("God has no body" or "God is impassible") is a guardrail, lest we absurdly imagine God to have physical feathers or wet tears. But our abstractions themselves are also analogical. Lewis illustrates by reflecting on our language about the incarnation:

We are invited to restate our belief [in the incarnation] in a form free from metaphor and symbol. The reason why we don't is that we can't. We can, if

---

18 Ibid., 51–52. Elsewhere Lewis writes:

The mistake is easily made because we (correctly) deny that God has passions; and with us a love that is not passionate means a love that is something less. But the reason why God has no passions is that passions imply passivity and intermission. The passion of love is something that happens to us, as "getting wet" happens to a body: and God is exempt from that "passion" in the same way that water is exempt from "getting wet." He cannot be affected with love, because He *is* love. To imagine that love as something less torrential or less sharp than our own temporary and derivative "passions" is a most disastrous fantasy. (Lewis, *Miracles*, 148)

19 Lewis, "The Language of Religion," in *Christian Reflections*, 140. "All language about things other than physical objects is necessarily metaphorical" (Lewis, "Is Theology Poetry?," in *The Weight of Glory and Other Addresses*, 134)."But it is a serious mistake to think that metaphor is an optional thing which poets and orators may put into their work as a decoration and plain speakers can do without. The truth is that if we are going to talk at all about things which are not perceived by the senses, we are forced to use language metaphorically" (Lewis, *Miracles*, 114–15).

you like, say "God entered history" instead of saying "God came down to earth." But, of course, "entered" is just as metaphorical as "came down." You have only substituted horizontal or undefined movement for vertical. We can make our language duller; we cannot make it less metaphorical. We can make the pictures more prosaic; we cannot be less pictorial.[20]

How then should we navigate this swirl of images, whether in the Bible itself or in our own speech about God? Lewis suggests two rules for interpreting biblical images:

> 1) Never take the images literally. 2) When the *purport* of the images—what they say to our fear and hope and will and affections—seems to conflict with the theological abstractions, trust the purport of the images every time. For our abstract thinking is itself a tissue of analogies: a continual modeling of spiritual reality in legal or chemical or mechanical terms. Are these likely to be more adequate than the sensuous, organic, and personal images of Scripture—light and darkness, river and well, seed and harvest, master and servant, hen and chickens, father and child? The footprints of the Divine are more visible in that rich soil than across rocks or slag-heaps. Hence what they now call "demythologizing" Christianity can easily be "re-mythologizing" it—and substituting a poorer mythology for a richer.[21]

This mutual correction—abstractions preventing us from taking images too literally and images ensuring that our emotions and will are properly moved—is fundamental to Lewis's approach to theology. In fact, all symbols, no matter where they fall on the spectrum of poetry to science, correct each other, including the multiple symbols within the Bible. Take, for example, the various promises of our ultimate destiny as believers. Lewis wonders why we need anything more than the promise that we will be "with Christ." Why does God *also* promise us that we will be "like" Christ, or that we will have "glory," or that we will be "fed or feasted or entertained," or that we will "have some sort of official position in the universe—ruling cities, judging angels, being pillars of God's temple"? Why promise anything more than the first? Is the promise of being "with Christ" not enough? The answer has to do with what we've seen above about poetical and scientific speech (and therefore about reason and imagination).

---

[20] Lewis, "Is Theology Poetry?," in *The Weight of Glory and Other Addresses*, 133. It's worth noting that Lewis seems to use the terms analogical and metaphorical interchangeably. Throughout this chapter, I follow him in this convention.

[21] Lewis, *Letters to Malcolm*, 52.

But my point is that this [image of being with Christ] also is only a symbol, like the reality in some respects, but unlike it in others, and therefore needs correction from the different symbols in the other promises. The variation of the promises does not mean that anything other than God will be our ultimate bliss; but because God is more than a Person, and lest we should imagine the joy of His presence too exclusively in terms of our present poor experience of personal love, with all its narrowness and strain and monotony, a dozen changing images, correcting and relieving each other, are supplied.[22]

This is why the Bible gives us multiple images of what it means to be "in Christ." To be "in Christ" can be conceived in legal terms: God is the Judge, we are guilty criminals, but because of what Christ has done, God finds in our favor and declares us righteous. But lest we imagine God purely as a Judge, we also have familial imagery: we are prodigal sons who come home to our Father. Or we are orphans who are adopted into his family. And Scripture gives us other metaphorical worlds as well. The temple cult with its blood and water and ceremonies of consecration lies behind the biblical language of sanctification. Prisons, shackles, slavery, "more bricks, no straw" all lie behind the biblical language of salvation and deliverance. And so on. God is not just our Judge but our rescuer. Not just our rescuer but our master. Not just our master but our Father. Not just our Father but our husband. God supplies "a dozen changing images, correcting and relieving each other," to move our affections and our wills, so that we can begin to comprehend the incomprehensible, that we might "know the love of Christ that surpasses knowledge" (Eph. 3:19).[23]

Tearing Down Penal Substitution

I find Lewis's distinctions between theory and reality, doctrine and truth, theology and God, poetical and scientific to be very helpful.[24] They show us the right way to speak about God without turning our understanding

---

[22] Lewis, "The Weight of Glory," in *The Weight of Glory and Other Addresses*, 34–35.

[23] Elsewhere, Lewis notes that the real activity of imagination is the churning of these images, "thrown off like a spray . . . all momentary, all correcting, refining, 'interanimating' one another, and given a kind of spiritual body to the unimaginable" (Lewis, *Letters to Malcolm*, 87).

[24] At the same time, Lewis's view of theology is undeveloped. His distinction between God and human statements about God is important. But there are more distinctions to be made, particularly between the authoritative and inerrant statements about God we find in the Scriptures and our fallible reflections on Scripture. Lewis, at times, flattens out this distinction (though in other places he clearly affirms it). For a helpful treatment of Lewis's view of the Bible (and its weaknesses), see Donald Williams, *Deeper Magic*, chaps. 2–3.

of him into an idol. Lewis is particularly attuned to the danger of treating our knowledge of God as though it could completely comprehend him, as though God could be reduced to what we can say about him. We clearly can know God and speak about him; human language is no hindrance to knowing God. As one theologian puts it, God speaks human to humans. Nevertheless, though we can speak truly about God, we must be wary lest our theology usurp his place. God, as Lewis says on a few occasions, is "the great iconoclast."[25] For example: "My idea of God is not a divine idea. It has to be shattered from time to time. He shatters it Himself. He is the great iconoclast. Could we not almost say that this shattering is one of the marks of His presence?"[26]

With Lewis's categories firmly in our minds, we're now in a position to examine his dismissive attitude toward penal substitution. Recall what Lewis said earlier in this chapter about the differences between theories and reality. His larger discussion actually deals with the question of the atonement.

> Now before I became a Christian I was under the impression that the first thing Christians had to believe was one particular theory as to what the point of this dying was. According to that theory God wanted to punish men for having deserted and joined the Great Rebel, but Christ volunteered to be punished instead, and so God let us off. Now I admit that even this theory does not seem to me quite so immoral and so silly as it used to; but that is not the point I want to make. What I came to see later on was that neither this theory nor any other is Christianity. The central Christian belief is that Christ's death has somehow put us right with God and given us a fresh start. Theories as to how it did this are another matter. A good many different theories have been held as to how it works; what all Christians are agreed on is that it does work.[27]

To begin, Lewis's articulation of penal substitution is crude and misleading. His caricature of the doctrine makes it easier for him to dismiss. Nevertheless, Lewis's main point is that the *reality* is more important than

---

[25] "He must constantly work as the iconoclast. Every idea of Him we form, He must in mercy shatter" (Lewis, *Letters to Malcolm*, 82). Screwtape encourages Wormwood to keep his patient praying to his composite idea about God, made up of various images floating in his mind. "Whatever the nature of the composite object, you must keep him praying to it—to the thing that he has made, not to the Person who has made him" (Lewis, *The Screwtape Letters*, 25). The situation is "desperate" if Wormwood allows the patient to pray "not to what I think thou art but to what thou knowest thyself to be" (ibid.).
[26] Lewis, *A Grief Observed*, 66.
[27] Lewis, *Mere Christianity*, 53–54.

our theories about it. "That Christ's death has somehow put us right with God" is the important thing to believe; precisely *how* it has done so is less important. We can be nourished by food even if we are ignorant of nutrition. Medicine can heal us even if we are not doctors. And there's an important sense in which Lewis is right. *That* something works is far more important than *how* it works.

And this reservation about theories is no speculative matter for Lewis. One of the central barriers to his acceptance of Christianity was his inability to understand what the point of Christ's dying was. "You can't believe a thing when you are ignorant what the thing is."[28] In other words, Lewis didn't understand what it meant. To him, the notion of penal substitution was "very silly"[29] (and remained so after his conversion).

But even granting the importance of reality over theory, what are we to do with his dismissive attitude toward what many evangelicals regard as a central aspect of the Christian faith? The first thing to do would be to try and understand the reasons for his attitude. In a letter in which he answers a question about substitutionary atonement, Lewis writes:

> When Scripture says that Christ died "for" us, I think the word is usually *huper* (on behalf of), not *anti* (instead of). I think the ideas of sacrifice, Ransom, Championship (over Death), Substitution etc. are all images to *suggest* the reality (not otherwise comprehensible to us) of the Atonement. To fix on any *one* of them as if it contained and limited the truth like a scientific definition would in my opinion be a mistake.[30]

Notice that the different ideas that Lewis lists are meant to "suggest" the reality of the atonement. This is the language of imagination. These terms are meant to conjure up a whole host of images and narratives that help us to comprehend the incomprehensible. But, and this is important for Lewis, he is adamant that we must not treat the image as though it were a scientific definition. We must not pigeonhole or limit the mystery and glory of the atonement by putting it under a microscope. This danger of fixing on one theory or image is what Lewis is often most concerned about. Instead, we are to use multiple suggestive images to lead us to the reality.

Consider these representative statements:

---

28 Lewis to Arthur Greeves, October 18, 1931, in *Collected Letters*, 1:976.
29 Lewis, *Mere Christianity*, 56.
30 Lewis to Mr. Young, October 31, 1963, in *Collected Letters*, 3:1476.

We are told that Christ was killed for us, that His death has washed out our sins, and that by dying He disabled death itself. That is the formula. That is Christianity. That is what has to be believed. Any theories we build up as to how Christ's death did all this are, in my view, quite secondary: mere plans or diagrams to be left alone if they do not help us, and, even if they do help us, not to be confused with the thing itself.[31]

Of course, you can express this in all sorts of different ways. You can say that Christ died for our sins. You may say that the Father has forgiven us because Christ has done for us what we ought to have done. You may say that we are washed in the blood of the Lamb. You may say that Christ has defeated death. They are all true. If any of them do not appeal to you, leave it alone and get on with the formula that does. And, whatever you do, do not start quarreling with other people because they use a different formula from yours.[32]

And, after describing his own theory of the perfect penitent, he writes: "Such is my own way of looking at what Christians call the Atonement. But remember this is only one more picture. Do not mistake it for the thing itself: and if it does not help you, drop it."[33]

Probing Lewis's View

Now, if I were having a conversation with Lewis about this subject, I would ask him a few questions:

1. "Your attitude toward the theories seems a bit glib. Do you really think that we should just 'drop' the picture if it doesn't help us? If the picture is true, as you say, why not say that we should grow into it? Why not enlarge our minds with the puzzling images rather than retreating from them? This is precisely the method you adopt in 'The Weight of Glory.' Examining the puzzling image of 'being noticed by God' yields all sorts of good benefits there. How can the images of the atonement 'correct and relieve' one another, if we are so quick to throw them away when we don't see their usefulness?"

---

[31] Lewis, *Mere Christianity*, 55–56.
[32] Ibid., 181–82. Within these two quotations from *Mere Christianity*, there is an equivocation on the use of the word "formula." In the first quotation, the formula is Christianity itself. The formula is more fundamental than the theories we build up about how Christ's death saves us. In the second quotation, "formula" appears synonymous with "theories." There are multiple formulas, and we should select the one that appeals to us. This equivocation is most likely the result of Lewis writing to a popular audience.
[33] Ibid., 59.

To this, I suspect he would say that his encouragement to drop theories that don't suit you is an apologetic strategy,[34] that his counsel is to set them aside for now, rather than to drop them forevermore. In other words, don't let complicated theological questions keep people from trusting in Jesus. Don't let discussions of calorie counting hinder hungry men from getting bread. In the larger picture, I suspect he would agree with me. If the images are true to reality, we ought to accept them and benefit from them. But, he would no doubt add, the best way for them to become helpful to someone who currently finds them silly might be for that person to set them aside until he or she has progressed further in the Christian life. Solid food, after all, is for the mature.

2. "Your examples of the formula—his death washed out our sins, by dying he disabled death—are as metaphorical as any theory of penal substitution. 'Washing' is a metaphor, drawn either from the bath or, in the Bible, from the temple and its sacrifices. 'Disabling death' calls to mind an image of either warfare in which an enemy is rendered helpless or, in the modern world, shutting off a dangerous machine (perhaps with a kill switch). The point is that theories and images are embedded in your formula. So the question is, why do those theories get to occupy such a privileged place? Penal substitution may be dropped but not the washing of sin and disabling of death? Does that not seem rather arbitrary?"

Lewis might respond that the language of "washing of sins" and disabling or defeating death is straight from the Bible (1 Cor. 15:26; 2 Tim. 1:10; 1 John 1:7) and thus has a greater weight than theories which we construct. I would grant his point and then move to my third question.

3. "If the Bible is authoritative, are its theories? And if biblical theories and images are authoritative for us, then how can you tell us to leave aside the ones that don't appeal to us? If Paul teaches penal substitution, am I obligated to believe it? Or more basically, if someone tells me that God has forgiven me because of what Christ has done (as in your formula), can I really tell him that I have a different preference for expressing my belief? May we really dismiss the words of an apostle so lightly?"

These would be my questions for Lewis. And in such a conversation,

---

[34] Lewis suggests as much in a letter to Dom Bede Griffiths, December 21, 1941: "I think I gave the impression of going further than I intended, in saying that all theories of the Atonement were 'to be rejected if we don't find them helpful.' What I meant was 'need not be used'—a v. different thing" (in *Collected Letters*, 2:502). He goes on to note that he places theories of the atonement in a different category from beliefs like the divinity of Christ. The latter cannot be denied—it must be believed "whether you find it a help or a 'scandal'"—whereas theories of the atonement need not be believed or understood (or even affirmed?).

my hope would be to demonstrate that his own convictions provide the resources for correcting his imbalance and error. As he himself says, Scripture does give us multiple images of how the atonement works; we should embrace them all. If we struggle to comprehend them, we should follow Augustine and Anselm and "believe in order to know." Embrace the truth, however odd we might think it to be, and then see if it doesn't make more sense as we grow in grace. With penal substitution, we should do a Bible study to see if it really is an account of the atonement endorsed by the apostles. If it is, we should try to swallow it. If we still can't, we must gum it until our teeth come in.

Building Up Penal Substitution

In addition to questioning some of Lewis's claims, I'd also try to show that the substance of penal substitution is present in Lewis's own work. To begin with, Lewis clearly believes in retributive justice; he recoils from modern humanitarian theories of punishment.[35] What's more, he embraces the biblical teaching about the wrath of God. In the same letter I quoted earlier, he writes:

> The wrath of God: "something in God of which the best image in the created world is righteous indignation." I think it quite a mistake to try to soften the idea of anger by substituting something like disapproval or regret. Even with men real anger is far more likely than cold disapproval to lead to full reconciliation. Hot love, hot wrath.[36]

This is consistent with what we saw earlier. The wrath of God should not be reduced to something bland like disapproval or regret. Note how Lewis expands the point in *Letters to Malcolm*:

> I fully grant you that "wrath" can be attributed to God only by an analogy. [Note: by this, Lewis simply means that, because God is God, all his attributes are both like and unlike our limited human experience of these attributes.] The situation of the penitent before God isn't, but is somehow like, that of one appearing before a justly angered sovereign, lover, father, master, or teacher. But what more can we know about it than just this likeness? Trying to get in behind the analogy, you go further and fare worse.

35 Lewis, "The Humanitarian Theory of Punishment," in *God in the Dock*, 287–300.
36 Lewis to Mr. Young, October 31, 1963, in *Collected Letters*, 3:1476.

You suggest that what is traditionally regarded as our experience of God's anger would be more helpfully regarded as what inevitably happens to us if we behave inappropriately towards a reality of immense power. As you say, "The live wire doesn't feel angry with us, but if we blunder against it we get a shock."

My dear Malcolm, what do you suppose you have gained by substituting the image of a live wire for that of angered majesty? You have shut us all up in despair; for the angry can forgive, and electricity can't.[37]

Here we see the same thing we saw earlier. Lewis wants us to remember two things: (1) All talk of God's wrath (like all talk of God's love) is analogical. It is imagery and thus misleading if taken literally (i.e., as if it comprehensively and precisely defines God in terms of human experience). (2) We cannot dispense with the imagery, and we must be wary of substituting our own images for the biblical ones. Turn God's wrath into a live wire that we blunder against, and you turn God's love into a power outlet and extension cord. The wrath of God is the converse of his love. It "is the fluid that love bleeds when you cut it. . . . Wrath and pardon are both, as applied to God, analogies; but they belong together to the same circle of analogy—the circle of life, and love, and deeply personal relationships." The perfect beauty and the consuming fire go together, and they are both designed to "facilitate . . . man's act of penitence and reception of pardon."[38]

Whatever reality the analogy serves, we do not have access to that reality *except through the analogy*. There is no work-around, no side door that gets us into the "real" inside. The image is the only door there is. Or, rather, the images (for they are legion) are the only doors there are. We must put guards around them; this is what our abstract theological statements about God are designed to do. And we can, if we are careful, make our own ways in. But they will be as analogical and metaphorical as the biblical ones. Moreover, they will suffer the defect of being *our* images rather than God's. And woe to us if we shut up God's doors and try to climb in through our own makeshift windows. Adding windows may be justified; they may provide a clearer view inside. But they cannot replace God's doors.

Not only does Lewis believe in God's just and holy wrath; he also regards vicariousness or substitution—understood as "one person profiting

---

[37] Lewis, *Letters to Malcolm*, 95.
[38] Ibid., 97.

by the earning of another person"—as "the very centre of Christianity."[39]
Now, it's true that his view of substitution owes more to Charles Williams
than to Paul. In an essay on Williams, Lewis praises Anselm for "holding to
substitutional . . . Atonement," but believes the medieval theologian made
a misstep by regarding this substitution as "forensic."[40] But this is just another question for our Bible study. What do Paul and Peter and John have
to say about forensic substitution? Isn't this what Romans 5 is all about?
If we really do trust that "Christ will somehow share with [us] the perfect
human obedience which He carried out from His birth to His crucifixion,"[41]
can we not say with the biblical authors that part of this "sharing" is a legal
or forensic one? That because Christ is righteous, and we are in him, we
too are righteous? That we stand in God's courtroom clothed in Christ's
righteousness because two thousand years ago, he hung bleeding on our
judgment tree?

These two themes—the wrath of God against rebels and the principle
of substitution—do come together in *Mere Christianity*, the same book in
which Lewis dismisses his (crude) retelling of penal substitution. Lewis
writes, "[Christians] offer an explanation of how God can be this impersonal mind at the back of the Moral Law and yet also a Person. They tell
you how the demands of this law, which you and I cannot meet, *have been
met on our behalf*, how God Himself becomes a man *to save man from the
disapproval of God*."[42]

Christ has met the demands of the moral law on our behalf. God became a man to save man from the disapproval (i.e., wrath) of God. As we
saw in the last chapter, death is a punishment for our sins, and Christ is
the "representative 'Die-er'" in the universe. Thus, Christ, as our representative, bears our punishment (death) in our place. This may lack the precision of full accounts of penal substitution, but it's certainly a start. And,
of course, when it comes time to imaginatively depict this substitution in
Narnia, we have a beautiful rendering of Christ bearing our penalty.[43]

---

[39] Lewis, "The Grand Miracle," in *God in the Dock*, 85.
[40] Lewis, "A Sacred Poem: Charles Williams, *Taliessin through Logres*," in *Image and Imagination*, 127.
[41] Lewis, *Mere Christianity*, 147.
[42] Ibid., 32.
[43] Williams notes that "Lewis was often better at portraying the atonement than explaining it" (*Deeper
Magic*, 157). He points to both Aslan's death in *The Lion, the Witch and the Wardrobe* and the discussion
of sacrifice in *Till We Have Faces* as examples of Lewis's powerful clarity. I concur wholeheartedly with
Williams's summary:

> Lewis has many good things to say about the atonement and salvation. At his best, he deftly
> depicts the dynamics of how calling, faith, and works interact, and he often admirably cap-
> tures the mystery of divine initiative and human response, divine predestination and human

In *The Lion, the Witch and the Wardrobe*, Edmund is a traitor and a rebel. He stands condemned by the law of God, the Deep Magic that is written on the scepter of the Emperor beyond the sea. An accuser stands in the courtroom, demanding the judicial sentence and calling the justice of the Emperor and Aslan into question if they let the guilty boy go free. To let Edmund off, to forgive his treachery, would upend the entire cosmic order. All Narnia would perish in fire and water. There is no working against the Emperor's magic. The moral law of almighty God must stand.

But then, into this hopeless situation comes another magic, a Deeper Magic from before the dawn of time. A blameless and willing victim "killed in a traitor's stead" cracks the stone table and death starts to work backward. This is the Deeper Magic of substitution, of (dare I say it?) *penal* substitution. For is this not what Aslan takes, Edmund's penalty? In dying on behalf of (*huper*) Edmund, is he not also dying in place of (*anti*) the boy? Granted there are other images in this supposal. The witch has a claim on the boy's blood; thus, the ransom theory. But the witch's claim is rooted in the Emperor's magic, just as the Devil's accusations flow from God's holy law. When our record of debt with its legal demands is canceled, the rulers and authorities are disarmed, and we are forgiven (Col. 2:13–15). Here is a swirl of images—a merciful sovereign forgiving a rebel, a lender canceling a mountain of debt, a judge acquitting a defendant because the legal demands have been met, powerful enemies disarmed and subdued—all because the righteous One was killed in a traitor's stead, because the miracle and magic of substitution is deeply and powerfully *real*.[44]

I don't know that I would be able to persuade Lewis, but the reconstruction offered above shows how I—a Christian who loves the penal substitution of Jesus—can benefit greatly from the writings of a man who treated this precious truth so lightly.[45] And perhaps what I've said can help Lewis skeptics to hear him out in areas where his wisdom is much needed.

---

freedom, just as Scripture presents it. He wisely warns us not to substitute our theories about the atonement for the atonement itself. But he fails to give adequate weight to those explanations of the atonement actually taught by Scripture, and he is sometimes less clear than he might have been about the relation of faith and works. He often portrays the atonement more biblically in his fiction than he explains it in his expositions. (*Deeper Magic*, 171)

[44] For a deeper look at substitution in Narnia, see chap. 1, "Deep Magic, and Deeper," in Joe Rigney, *Live Like a Narnian: Christian Discipleship in Lewis's Chronicles* (Minneapolis: Eyes & Pen, 2013), 35–40.
[45] Another area of theological weakness in Lewis is his doctrine of Scripture. Again, Williams's presentation and criticism of Lewis's view in chap. 3 of *Deeper Magic* is excellent. See also Philip Ryken, "Inerrancy and the Patron Saint of Evangelicalism: C. S. Lewis on Holy Scripture," in *Romantic Rationalist: God, Life, and Imagination in the Work of C. S. Lewis*, ed. John Piper and David Mathis (Wheaton, IL: Crossway, 2014), 39–64.

CHAPTER 4

THE GOSPEL APPLIED

Good Infection and Good Pretending

We've looked at the facts of the gospel, the great works that God has done in history to redeem humanity. We are now in a position to look at how those works "become ours." If the gospel is fundamentally "news," an announcement of something that God has done in history in the person of Jesus, then what does that gospel have to do with us? How do we receive its benefits? How does the process work in our own lives? In one sense, the rest of this book is the answer to that question. After all, we are exploring "Lewis on the Christian life." The aim of the present chapter is to provide an overview, a picture of the whole of the Christian life, as Lewis envisioned it.

Good Infection

So, then, how do the benefits of Christ's work come to us? The simplest answer is "by faith." In *Mere Christianity*, Lewis says that we must leave our own transformation into true humans in the hands of God. Lewis explains:

> The sense in which a Christian leaves it to God is that he puts all his trust in Christ: trusts that Christ will somehow share with him the perfect human obedience which He carried out from His birth to His crucifixion: that Christ will make the man more like Himself and, in a sense, make

good his deficiencies. In Christian language, He will share His "sonship" with us, will make us, like Himself, "Sons of God."[1]

Christ will "somehow" share his perfect obedience with us when we put all our trust in him. This is no mere intellectual assent to certain truths about certain historical events. This is a resting in, a hoping in, a relying on Christ, and Christ alone. This faith "somehow" results in our sharing in Christ's obedience, and in Christ making us more like him. Put another way, through faith we come to share in the life of Christ.

> Now the whole offer which Christianity makes is this: that we can, if we let God have His way, come to share in the life of Christ. If we do, we shall then be sharing a life which was begotten, not made, which always has existed and always will exist. Christ is the Son of God. If we share in this kind of life we also shall be sons of God. We shall love the Father as He does and the Holy Ghost will arise in us. He came to this world and became a man in order to spread to other men the kind of life He has— by what I call "good infection." Every Christian is to become a little Christ. The whole purpose of becoming a Christian is simply nothing else.[2]

Lewis says that we come to share in the life of Christ through "good infection." We catch the Christ-life by being close to him, by drawing near to him, in truth, by being "in him." "Everyone who gets it gets it by personal contact with Him. Other men become 'new' by being 'in Him.'"[3] What's more, this good infection is what Christianity is all about. It's the whole show. There is nothing else.

Good Pretending

Good infection is not the only way Lewis describes the whole of the Christian life. He also says that we come to share in the life of Christ through "good pretending." According to Lewis, there are at least two kinds of pretending. One kind is what we normally call hypocrisy; it's when *our pretense is a substitute for reality*. The other kind, the good kind, is seen in children's games. When they play, children often pretend to be grown-ups. In this case, "the pretense leads up to the real thing."[4] They are *pretending*

---

[1] Lewis, *Mere Christianity*, 147.
[2] Ibid., 177.
[3] Ibid., 221.
[4] Ibid., 188.

their way into reality. The same is true when we act friendlier than we feel and find ourselves becoming friendlier. As the demon Screwtape observes, "All mortals tend to turn into the thing they are pretending to be."[5]

This is Lewis's way of describing the Christian life. We pretend to be sons of God so that we become sons of God in practice. We put on Christ and find that we become like him. We dress up as Jesus and we begin to resemble him. Again, Lewis says that this kind of "good pretending" is "the whole of Christianity." There is nothing else.

I imagine that some will find this to be a shocking claim. At the very least, good pretending is an odd way of speaking of the Christian view of salvation. But in the remainder of this chapter, I'd like to suggest that "good pretending" is Lewis's way of talking about a two-stage process that basically corresponds to the classical Protestant distinction between justification and progressive sanctification. It is his way of translating into laymen's terms our standard theological way of speaking.

God Pretending

Good pretending begins with God "pretending," bringing that which is not into reality. The first and foundational stage of the process belongs not to us but to God. In fact, his work underlies and makes possible all our work. In a real sense, he is the one who does everything.

> The Three-Personal God, so to speak, sees before Him in fact a self-centred, greedy, grumbling, rebellious human animal. But He says "Let us pretend that this is not a mere creature, but our Son. It is like Christ in so far as it is a Man, for He became Man. Let us pretend that it is also like Him in Spirit. Let us treat it as if it were what in fact it is not. Let us pretend in order to make the pretence into a reality."[6]

Here we have "the justification of the ungodly" (Rom. 4:5). Strictly speaking, we are not righteous. We are ungodly, wicked, and rebellious. But by the grace of God and through our faith in Christ, God now treats and regards us as righteous. He acquits us in his courtroom; we plead for mercy and find that we go down to our house justified.

Now, speaking of the justification of the ungodly as good pretending

---

[5] Lewis, *The Screwtape Letters*, 58.
[6] Lewis, *Mere Christianity*, 193.

could be misleading. The Protestant doctrine of justification by faith alone has often been accused of involving a legal fiction: God calls an ungodly sinner "righteous" when he is, in fact, not righteous. The Protestant response to this has always been to point out that, while we are not righteous in ourselves, we are counted righteous *in Christ*. God does not regard us in isolation; we have drawn near to Christ. We have placed our whole trust in Christ and his representative dying and his triumphant resurrection. As a result, we are "in Christ." Thus, what is not true of us in ourselves is true of us insofar as God regards or considers or counts us in his Son.[7]

Our Pretending

God's pretending is the decisive and foundational act in the total process of sharing Christ's life with us. But God's work does not nullify our own; it makes it possible. In response to God's pretending, we ourselves join in. We dress up as Christ as we come into God's presence, and in this case, the clothes really do *make* the man. Lewis sees this act of dressing up in the first words of the Lord's Prayer. When we address God as "our Father," we are placing ourselves in the place of sons of God. Despite the fact that we are "a bundle of self-centred fears, hopes, greeds, jealousies, and self-conceits," we still can dress up like sons in order to enter God's presence. The reason we can do this is simple: we call God "Father," because he has called us sons. And he has called us sons because, by faith, we are "in" the only begotten Son.[8]

Lewis frequently connects his language of "good pretending" to the more standard biblical language of "putting on Christ" or "being born again" or "Christ being formed in us."[9] For him, these are all different and complementary ways of talking about the fundamental reality of sharing in the life of Christ. They are images and symbols that give us a picture of what God is doing to us and for us and in us.

I'm sure some readers will still be skeptical of the notion that we pretend our way into the reality of living as God's sons. And if the image doesn't help you, Lewis would say to put it down. But before you do, consider Paul's flow of thought in Romans 6.

---

[7] J. I. Packer ably summarizes the Protestant view: "[God] reckons righteousness to them, not because he accounts them to have kept his law personally (which would be a false judgment), but because he accounts them to be united to one who kept it representatively (and that is a true judgment)" (J. I. Packer, "Justification," in *Evangelical Dictionary of Theology*, ed. Walter A. Elwell [Grand Rapids: Baker, 1984], 596).
[8] Lewis, *Mere Christianity*, 187.
[9] Ibid., 191, 195.

In this section of his letter, Paul is attempting to show that the gospel of God's grace and the justification of the ungodly do not lead us to continue in our wickedness. Those who have died to sin cannot still live in it (6:2). We have been baptized into Christ and therefore baptized into his death. The whole purpose of this union—signified and represented in our baptismal burial—is that we would be raised to "walk in newness of life" (6:4). Union with Christ in his death will necessarily lead to union with Christ in his resurrection life (6:5). The old man was crucified with him; as a result, we are no longer slaves to sin (6:6). Christ, having been raised from the dead, now has complete dominion over death (6:9). He died to sin, once for all, and he now lives to God alone (6:10). And now here's the kicker: "So you also [note how this exhortation flows from our union with Christ in the preceding verses] must consider yourselves dead to sin and alive to God in Christ Jesus" (6:11). This means that we no longer submit to the dominion of sin. We don't offer our members to our old slave master for his purposes. Instead, we present ourselves to God, to our new master, and we wield our members for his righteous purposes.

Thus, in this passage we see the same movement as in Lewis. Christ is dead to sin and alive to God, period. By the grace of God, we are joined to Christ. Thus, in God's reckoning, Christ's death is our death, and his life, our life. God views us through the lens of his Son. And therefore, as a result of this union, we are to "consider ourselves" in a certain way. We are to treat and regard ourselves as though we are as fully alive to God as Christ is. At present, we are not as fully alive to God as Christ is. Sin is still present in our members. But we are not enslaved to it. It has no dominion or claim on us. And thus what God says about us (what Lewis calls God's pretending) trumps "the facts" (as it were) on the ground. Because of Christ, our sin poses no barrier to God's love and fatherly affection for us. He regards us as his sons. Therefore, we ought to act like it. In other words, even though we are not fully dead to sin (since sin is still present in us), we are to pretend ("consider") that we are fully dead to sin because, as far as God is concerned, we are dead to sin in Christ.

Good Pretending and Moralism

Thus far, the basic picture is this: God's pretending (justification) leads to our pretending (progressive sanctification). But the picture needs more filling out. We especially need to be clear about how good pretending and catching good infection differ from mere morality and obedience.

First, a moralistic person may seek to live righteously on his own, that is, as an individual. He may try to live up to his own standards, to obey his conscience, or even the law of God without the need for any other person. Nothing would prevent someone from attempting to live morally by himself. But catching good infection is not a solo affair; God uses means. God works on us through all sorts of things: nature, our own bodies, books, even unbelievers. But the most important means that he uses to give us the Christ-life is other Christians.

> Men are mirrors, or "carriers" of Christ to other men. . . . That is why the Church, the whole body of Christians showing Him to one another, is so important. You might say that when two Christians are following Christ together there is not twice as much Christianity as when they are apart, but sixteen times as much.[10]

Second, good infection and good pretending are not simply matters of morality and obeying rules. Christ is not merely a good example for us to follow. Jesus is alive, right now, in the room with you, and he is doing things to you. The living Christ comes to you and interferes; he kills "the old natural self in you" and replaces it with "the kind of self He has." He is turning you into a "little Christ, a being which, in [your] own small way, has the same kind of life as God."[11]

Third, good pretending gives our obedience to God a different flavor than the hurried and harried obedience of the moralist. The moralist thinks of God either as an examiner who will grade his essays, or as the opposite party in a sort of bargain. He thinks in terms of claims and counterclaims.[12] He performs his duties in the same way an honest man pays taxes: he is willing to pay his share, but he hopes for something left over that will be fully his own.[13] Thus, two results often follow. On the one hand, when the moralist disobeys God or falls into some sin, he is like the pupil who worries that he will fail the course. His remaining obedience is done anxiously (and thus he often makes more mistakes). Obligations become heavy burdens; the stakes are so high. Despair sets in and the moralist simply quits trying. On the other hand, if the moralist is fulfilling his tasks (at least in his own mind), he feels that God is obligated to

---

10 Ibid., 190.
11 Ibid., 191.
12 Ibid., 145.
13 Ibid., 196.

treat him well. Thus, suffering and hardship leave him feeling put out and confused. He's paid his taxes; why doesn't the King keep his end of the bargain? The result is that the moralist grows angry with God and may quit obeying altogether.

The Christian engaged in good pretending obeys in an entirely different manner. He knows by experience that he has nothing to offer God. Everything he has is a gift from God (1 Cor. 4:7). Even his good works are done "in the strength that God supplies" (1 Pet. 4:11). The first result of real Christianity is to blow to bits the idea of a bargain with God. "If you devoted every moment of your whole life exclusively to His service you could not give Him anything that was not in a sense His own already."[14] The good pretender has discovered the fact of his own natural bankruptcy.[15]

But the good pretender also knows that he is bankrupt in another way. He has discovered the depths of his own sinfulness. He knows that beneath his sinful actions (which he is in some measure able to control) are "the rats of resentment and vindictiveness"[16] in the cellar of his soul.[17] He knows that his best efforts are tainted by wrong motives. And thus he is bankrupt in an additional sense.

The result is that the good pretender has despaired of his own efforts, and yet he has not stopped trying to obey. He has given his whole self to Christ, trusting in him alone, and therefore does his best to obey his Lord.

> But trying in a new way, a less worried way. Not doing these things in order to be saved, but because He has begun to save you already. Not hoping to get to Heaven as a reward for your actions, but inevitably wanting to act in a certain way because a first faint gleam of Heaven is already inside you.[18]

This means that the good pretender is not overthrown by his failures. He knows that God demands perfection and that God will never be satisfied until we are perfect as he is perfect. At the same time, he knows that God is merciful, that he forgives our sins, and that he is pleased with even the feeblest of our attempts at obedience.

---

14 Ibid., 143.
15 Ibid., 145.
16 Ibid., 192.
17 Ibid.
18 Ibid., 147–48.

Reflections on Duty and the Christian Life

Good pretending also gives us a richer perspective on the role of duty in the Christian life. For Lewis, the whole category of duty is a result of the fall.

> If we were perfected, prayer would not be a duty, it would be delight. Some day, please God, it will be. The same is true of many other behaviours which now appear as duties. If I loved my neighbour as myself, most of the actions which are now my moral duty would flow out of me as spontaneously as song from a lark or fragrance from a flower.[19]

The reason our duties do not flow spontaneously is that they are impeded by evil in ourselves and others. Thus, God's original design for us (which makes certain attitudes and actions essential to being truly human) and our sinfulness (which makes the spontaneous and delighted exercise of these same attitudes and actions impossible) create the category of duty and the whole moral realm.

How then does good pretending change our perspective on duty? Good pretending means that we do our duty while knowing that duty exists to be transcended. Take the two great commandments: Love God, and love your neighbor. For Lewis, love in the Christian sense is not merely an emotion. It is a state of the will, one in which we wish the good of others, regardless of whether we like them or approve of their conduct. The pattern that Jesus gives us for loving our neighbor is our love for ourselves. When I love myself, I don't necessarily feel a deep fondness and affection for myself. Sometimes, I even loathe myself and my actions. Nevertheless, however much I might dislike my own cowardice or conceit or greed, I continue to love myself and seek my own good and happiness. Thus, while warm feelings of affection may flow from my desire for my own good or the good of my neighbor, they are secondary and derivative.

This then leads us back to the two commandments. "As practical imperatives for here and now, the two great commandments have to be translated 'Behave as if you loved God and man.'"[20] In other words, when faced with the command to love my neighbors, I must not sit and try to manufacture warm feelings for them. "Do not waste time bothering whether you 'love' your neighbour; act as if you did. As soon as we do this, we find one

---

19 Lewis, *Letters to Malcolm*, 114–15.
20 Ibid., 115.

of the great secrets. When you are behaving as if you loved someone, you will presently come to love him."[21] In other words, if we act as if we love someone, if we sincerely "pretend" to love the person, if we do the deeds of love even when we lack (some of) the substance, we will often find that the warm feelings of affection will follow our actions. We will pretend our way into reality. "The Christian, trying to treat every one kindly, finds himself liking more and more people as he goes on—including people he could not even have imagined himself liking at the beginning."[22]

The same thing is true of our love for God. What should we do if we find that we don't have warm feelings of delight and affection for God? "The answer is the same as before. Act as if you did. Do not sit trying to manufacture feelings. Ask yourself, 'If I were sure that I loved God, what would I do?' When you have found the answer, go and do it."[23] Again, this is good pretending. We picture ourselves in our best moments, filled with the Spirit and sharing fully in the life of Christ, and we ask what we would be thinking and feeling and doing in those moments. Then, even though the feelings may not be there, we do the deeds. We complete the actions. We pray, or read the Scriptures, or worship with God's people, or put to death our lusts, or resist our anxieties. And, wonder of wonders, we often find that in his mercy, God turns our pretense into reality. We behave as sons of God and therefore find that the affections of Christ begin to grow in us.

This whole way of thinking puts duty in its proper place. It is not an ultimate good, but it is an intermediate good. It is a crutch in our pilgrim condition. Some day, God willing, our legs will be whole again. Loving God and neighbor will flow forth from us like water from a mountain spring. But until then, we use the crutch. We pretend that we can walk uprightly, and we find that, by God's grace, our legs grow stronger.

The Forgiveness of Sins

To grasp how Lewis's view of duty works itself out, it's helpful to see it in action. Jesus is unequivocal about our duty to forgive others. Indeed, our own forgiveness hangs in the balance. "If you do not forgive others their trespasses, neither will your Father forgive your trespasses" (Matt. 6:15).

---

[21] Lewis, *Mere Christianity*, 131.
[22] Ibid.
[23] Ibid., 132. Lewis continues, "Nobody can always have devout feelings: and even if we could, feelings are not what God principally cares about. . . . He will give us feelings of love if He pleases. We cannot create them for ourselves, and we must not demand them as a right."

> Forgive us our debts,
>   as we also have forgiven our debtors. (Matt. 6:12)

Forgiveness is offered to us on no other terms. Forgiveness of other people's sins—"however spiteful, however mean, however often they are repeated"—is demanded of us.[24]

Our difficulty in obeying this command is sometimes due to our misunderstanding the nature of forgiveness—whether God's forgiveness of us or God's demand that we forgive others. When we ask God to forgive us, often what we are really asking is for him to excuse us. "But there is all the difference in the world between forgiving and excusing."[25] In fact, "forgiveness and excusing are almost opposites."[26] Forgiveness says, "You have done an evil thing; nevertheless, I will not hold it against you." Excusing says, "I see that you couldn't help it or didn't mean it; you weren't really to blame." Therefore, to excuse someone is to let that person off the hook because he didn't really belong on the hook in the first place. It is a matter of fairness; we refuse to blame someone for something that wasn't his fault to begin with. Under this confusion, "what we call 'asking God's forgiveness' very often really consists in asking God to accept our excuses." We want him to remember the extenuating circumstances that led us to do what we did. We go away "imagining that we have repented and been forgiven when all that has really happened is that we have satisfied ourselves with our own excuses."[27]

This confusion about divine forgiveness spills over into our own efforts to forgive others. We're reluctant to do so because we think forgiving them means acting as though their actions weren't really all that bad. To forgive, we think, means to downplay their wickedness and our pain. And so instead of forgiving, we insist on the gravity of the evil and harm done to us. We say, "But I tell you the man broke a most solemn promise." Lewis replies, "Exactly: that is precisely what you have to forgive."[28] If it were not evil, it would not need to be forgiven.

Additionally, our difficulty in forgiving is compounded by our own personal bias. When it comes to our own sins, we are quick to offer excuses, to justify our actions, to draw attention to the extenuating circumstances.

---

[24] Lewis, "On Forgiveness," in *The Weight of Glory and Other Addresses*, 178.
[25] Ibid.
[26] Ibid., 179.
[27] Ibid., 180.
[28] Ibid., 181.

We're perfectly willing to admit that we aren't perfect, but the whole tenor of our confession testifies to our belief that if we can just explain the situation, everyone will realize that we aren't so bad as all that. Yet, when it comes to sins against us, we rule all excuses and explanations out of court. Every appeal to extenuating circumstances is dismissed as so much blame shifting and avoidance of responsibility. Our oppressor will not get off so easily. "In our own case we accept excuses too easily; in other people's we do not accept them easily enough."[29] When we sin, we have explanations. When other people sin, it's because they are indelibly wicked.

The confusion of forgiving and excusing, coupled with this persistent bias in our favor, means that we feel the intolerable burden of Christ's demand that we forgive others. What then can be done? First, we must correct the confusion. Extending forgiveness is not minimizing the evil or accepting the excuses. "Real forgiveness means looking steadily at the sin, the sin that is left over without any excuse, after all allowances have been made, and seeing it in all its horror, dirt, meanness, and malice, and nevertheless being wholly reconciled to the man who has done it." It means facing the evil and pain squarely and utterly renouncing our desire for revenge. It means we "make every effort to kill every taste of resentment in [our] own heart—every wish to humiliate or hurt him or to pay him out."[30] It does not mean that we necessarily trust him again right away; there may be prudent reasons for regarding his word as suspect. But it's possible to be reconciled to someone whose trustworthiness we still question. Faithfulness over time is the only way for him to regain our confidence. But we will never even begin to trust him if we cannot first forgive him.

Second, we must realize that forgiveness is often more of a commitment than a one-time act. In *Letters to Malcolm*, Lewis rejoices when he finally forgives someone he'd been trying to forgive for thirty years.[31] Every time he thought he'd forgiven the great offense, it would reappear a few weeks later, attended with the same familiar malice, bitterness, and anger. Thus, forgiving someone, especially when that person has committed a great evil against us, means putting down the resentment and hatred and spite every time it rears its ugly head in our memory. It means a deliberate commitment to resist the temptation to fondle and nurse the grievance. (Lewis notes that bitterness and resentment often behave exactly like a

---

[29] Ibid.
[30] Ibid.
[31] Lewis, *Letters to Malcolm*, 106.

lust.) Real forgiveness means not only forgiving someone seventy times for seventy offenses but also forgiving someone seventy times for a single offense.

Finally, the only way we'll be able to face the sin head-on and keep on forgiving day after day, year after year, is if we have a deep grasp of our own true position. We must remember where we stand. We are sinners, and however compelling we find our excuses, underneath them is the real knotted bundle of sin—pride, infidelity, deception, betrayal, murmuring, malice, hatred, and envy. It is hard, throbbing, and bitter, like a cancer. And left untreated, it will grow until it consumes us.

The beginning of the treatment is confessing our sins, acknowledging our iniquity, and receiving forgiveness from God through Christ. Only when we feel the soul-lightening force of God's forgiveness will we be able to offer that same forgiveness to others. Only when we know in our bones that mercy triumphs over judgment will we extend that same mercy to others. This is good pretending—seeing who we are and where we stand before God and living into that vision of ourselves in Christ. It's catching the good infection from Christ, sharing what we have received from him with others. It's hard—harder than many of us care to admit. But it's good, and it's necessary, and God is with us to help us forgive others and love our enemies and pray for those who oppress us so that we may be sons of our Father, who is in heaven (Matt. 5:44).

Finding Our True Selves in Christ

Let me conclude this chapter by underscoring the central theme in this book. We have seen that the grand theme of nature and redemption is death and resurrection. Seeds fall to the ground and die in order to bear much fruit. The sun dies every day, descending below the horizon and plunging the world into a death-like darkness (mercifully lit by the lesser lights). It then comes blazing up out of the east every day, preaching a resurrection sermon with each sunrise. This pattern reaches its historical climax in the incarnation of the Son of God, and in his death and resurrection for sinners. All other variations on the theme are revealed as transpositions into a minor key of the great theme of God's symphony. But the theme of this song doesn't just operate at the historical or even cosmic level. It works its way into the life of every person who responds to the call of the gospel.

The principle runs through all life from top to bottom. Give up yourself, and you will find your real self. Lose your life and you will save it. Submit to death, death of your ambitions and favourite wishes every day and death of your whole body in the end: submit with every fibre of your being, and you will find eternal life. Keep back nothing. Nothing that you have not given away will be really yours. Nothing in you that has not died will ever be raised from the dead.[32]

This is the way to become truly human, to become fully ourselves. "It is when I turn to Christ, when I give myself up to His Personality, that I first begin to have a real personality of my own."[33]

There is so much of Him that millions and millions of "little Christs," all different, will still be too few to express Him fully. He made them all. He invented—as an author invents characters in a novel—all the different men that you and I were intended to be. In that sense our real selves are all waiting for us in Him.[34]

Now we have widened the lens. We've seen the bigger picture. And so we return to where we began, to where you are. You are here and now, confronted by the living God in all his truth, goodness, and beauty. The Choice stands before you. But now, at one ear sits the devil Screwtape, seducing and tempting, cajoling and threatening, obscuring reality and stoking the ungodly fog that so easily surrounds you. At the other ear is Clive Staples Lewis, reasoning and imagining, warning and imploring, showing you his notes and reminding you of what is real. Now we're ready to truly begin.

---

[32] Lewis, *Mere Christianity*, 226–27.
[33] Ibid., 226.
[34] Ibid., 225.

CHAPTER 5

THE DEVIL

The Proud and Bent Spirit

In the opening chapter of *The Screwtape Letters*, Screwtape tells his nephew Wormwood that the aim of demons is not to teach humans but to fuddle them. The demonic strategy is not to argue us into sin or unbelief. Rather it is to confuse and obscure our perceptions of reality. Demons blow certain features of the world out of proportion while minimizing others out of existence.

For example, Screwtape tells Wormwood to fix the attention of his "patient," the person he's tempting, on the stream of sense experience and to divert his attention away from universal issues. The patient is to be taught that "real life" consists merely in the familiar physical objects we encounter; there are no universal truths or invisible realities to be concerned with. The only things that are "real" are the bus going by or the boy selling newspapers or the man walking his dog. Reality is reduced to its physical components.

The proper term for this kind of materialist reductionism is *nothing-buttery* since everything we can see and know is *nothing but* a mixture of matter in motion. Humans are *nothing but* sacks of protoplasm. Love is *nothing but* a chemical reaction in someone's brain. Far from being "man's best friend," a dog is *nothing but* the current product of a random evolutionary process that is leading us *nobody knows where*. And a star is *nothing but* a huge ball of flaming gas.[1]

---

[1] For more on Lewis's war on nothing-buttery, see Joe Rigney, *Live Like a Narnian: Christian Discipleship in Lewis's Chronicles* (Minneapolis: Eyes & Pen, 2013), 67–72.

But this isn't the only way that demons obscure reality. Elsewhere in *The Screwtape Letters*, the elder devil describes the different ways demons confuse us about the meaning of the word *real*. Great spiritual experiences are reduced to the bare physical facts. "All that *really* happened was that you heard some music in a lighted building." On the other hand, we can't know what the high dive is "really like" until we climb the ladder to the top and look down below. Here *real* doesn't mean the physical facts (which can be known from the ground), but the emotional effect those facts have on our consciousness. The demonic strategy is to keep us flitting between both uses of the word *real* without noticing that in both cases we are being reductionistic. The demonic rule is as follows:

> In all experiences which can make them happier or better only the physical facts are "real" while the spiritual elements are "subjective"; in all experiences which can discourage or corrupt them the spiritual elements are the main reality and to ignore them is to be an escapist. Thus in birth the blood and pain are "real," the rejoicing a mere subjective point of view; in death, the terror and ugliness reveal what death "really means." The hatefulness of a hated person is "real"—in hatred you see men as they are, you are disillusioned; but the loveliness of a loved person is merely a subjective haze concealing a "real" core of sexual appetite or economic association. Wars and poverty are "really" horrible; peace and plenty are mere physical facts about which men happen to have certain sentiments.[2]

The essential strategy is to take a part of reality and treat it as the whole of reality, to take a partial truth and make it the total truth. This was the Serpent's strategy when he tempted Adam and Eve. God had given our first parents complete freedom to eat from every tree in the garden, except one. One *no* in a world full of *yes*. The Serpent took the one *no* and magnified it until it encompassed the whole garden. "Did God actually say. 'You shall not eat of *any* tree in the garden'?" (Gen. 3:1). The Tempter turned the *single* prohibition into a *total* prohibition. The single *no* in a world full of *yes* became a world full of *no*, and God, who in reality is a loving Father, became, in the mouth of Satan, the great forbidder. The Serpent created a distorted picture of reality and invited Eve to live in it. When Eve revealed that there was some confusion about God's command (she wrongly suggested that

---

[2] Lewis, *The Screwtape Letters*, 181–82.

God had forbidden touching the tree as well as eating from it), the Serpent moved from magnifying the command to denying the threat. "You will not surely die," he said. Instead of blowing God's command out of proportion, he shrank God's warning out of existence.

In the preface to *Screwtape*, Lewis notes that the demons adopt this strategy even about their own existence. They press us toward two opposite errors—either to disbelieve in them completely or to develop an unhealthy interest in them. They want to turn us into either materialists or magicians, to encourage us to practice either scientism (which is not the same as science) or the occult. Either error will do. Demons are content to shrink themselves into nothingness in our eyes, provided that God shrinks along with them. Conversely, if we are determined to embrace the supernatural, they insist on dominating our spiritual vision. In the modern world, their strategy is almost universally the former; they conceal their own existence in order to make us thoroughgoing materialists, who reject the supernatural altogether. If the supernatural is allowed at all, it is admitted either in some sort of comic fashion (the Devil in red tights with pitchfork) or in the terror and horror of the paranormal (the ghosts, spirits, and monsters that frighten us on the big screen).

Screwtape describes these two demonic strategies as a "cruel dilemma." He laments that demons must either conceal themselves and foster atheism or reveal themselves and encourage paganism and the occult. The demonic ideal would be to "emotionalize and mythologize [our] science" in order to produce "the Materialist Magician, the man, not using, but veritably worshipping, what he vaguely calls 'Forces' while denying the existence of 'spirits.'"[3] (In fact, it's just this sort of materialist magician that Lewis portrays from two directions in the characters of Frost and Wither in *That Hideous Strength*.)

The Bent One

Given the confusion around demons, as well as Lewis's extensive use of them in his writings on the Christian life, an overview of Lewis on the dark powers may prove useful. To begin, Lewis is clear that the Devil or Satan is not the opposite of God. He is a fallen angel and thus, strictly speaking, the opposite of the archangel Michael. Additionally, I (along with Lewis) take

---

[3] Ibid., 40.

it that when we talk about the influence of the Devil, we do not imagine that a single fallen angel, however powerful, is directly responsible for all of the things we attribute to his work. There are many devils and demons, perhaps arranged in some kind of hierarchy (or lowerarchy) as Lewis fictionalizes in *The Screwtape Letters*.

In the Space Trilogy, Lewis depicts Satan as a Bent Oyarsa, a rebellious supernatural being who was once given stewardship over Earth (each of the other planets of the solar system is also overseen by an Oyarsa, though the earthly Oyarsa is the only fallen one). It was at the instigation of the Bent One that Adam and Eve originally fell, bringing ruin on the human race and isolating our planet from the rest of the (unfallen) solar system. Also in *That Hideous Strength*, Lewis provides a kind of scientific analysis of demons, referring to them as Macrobes. Just as we speak of microbes—microscopic organisms, which have had an enormous effect on human health and history, even though we were unaware of them until the invention of the microscope—so also there are Macrobes—organisms of extreme simplicity, above the level of animal life, who do not breed or breathe, who have a permanent existence and great power, and who are more intelligent than humans.

> Though there has been little intercourse [between Macrobes and man], there has been profound influence. Their effect on human history has been far greater than that of the microbes, though, of course, equally unrecognized. In the light of what we now know, all history will have to be rewritten. The real causes of all the principal events are quite unknown to historians.[4]

While we almost certainly cannot discern the precise contribution of demons to any particular sin or behavior, Lewis seems open to the possibility that they are somehow involved in all our sins. At the same time, their present strategy of concealment means that their activities can often be explained in terms of natural factors. Lewis portrays the interplay of demonic and physical explanations in the opening chapter of *Perelandra*.

---

[4] Lewis, *That Hideous Strength*, 254. The narrator in *Perelandra* echoes this explanation. "Like the bacteria on the microscopic level, so these co-inhabiting pests on the macroscopic permeate our whole life invisibly and are the real explanation of that fatal bent which is the main lesson of history" (Lewis, *Perelandra*, 12). Throughout the Space Trilogy, Ransom seeks to scientifically analyze angels, called *eldila* in the stories. "They do not eat, breed, breathe, or suffer natural death, and to that extent resemble thinking minerals more than they resemble anything we should recognize as animal" (ibid.).

Breaking Down the Barrier between Natural and Supernatural

The narrator is journeying to visit his friend, Dr. Elwin Ransom, the Cambridge philologist who had been abducted and taken to Malacandra (the planet we call Mars), where he was caught up in an interplanetary conflict. Now back on Earth, Ransom has let a few friends in on the secret and has invited one of them (the narrator) to his home in the country in order to participate in some endeavor. While walking from the railway station to Ransom's cottage, the narrator passes through various stages.

At first, he feels a bit reluctant about the journey, a sense of malaise settling over him. But as he analyzes it, he realizes that his reluctance is not merely distaste or embarrassment at Ransom's adventures, but rather Fear (with a capital *F*). He discovers that he is afraid, both of meeting an *eldil* (an angel or demon) and of getting "drawn in" to some great interplanetary scheme. He begins to look for any excuse to turn back, and is able to continue only with the greatest effort. Though it is a still evening, the narrator feels as though he "were walking into a headwind." He begins to have doubts about Ransom—what if he is a dupe, a Trojan horse being used by some great evil to assault humanity? Or worse, what if he himself is evil, in league with dark powers? The narrator knows that such doubts are irrational; his reason assures him that Ransom is "sane and wholesome and honest."[5] Nevertheless, his imagination will have none of it, and he is forced to press forward despite his increasing resistance. He begins to wonder whether he is having a breakdown or going mad. Terror fills him, and a persistent inner voice urges him to turn around and go back. He stumbles on toward the cottage, half-mad, half-terrified, his mind playing horrible tricks on him in the dark.

Thus, in this short chapter of *Perelandra* we find ordinary reluctance, then irrational fear, culminating in a hallucinatory terror bordering on madness. How does Lewis account for these phenomena in the next chapter? Upon meeting Ransom, the narrator collapses into him, and Ransom asks: "I say—you're all right, aren't you? You got through the barrage without any damage?"[6] The entire trip, from the railway station to the cottage, was a barrage, an assault on the narrator by bent *eldila*, what we would call demons. The doubts, fears, and anxious thoughts that entered the narrator's head were put there by dark principalities and powers.

---

[5] Lewis, *Perelandra*, 11.
[6] Ibid., 19.

88   THE DEVIL

The important thing for our purposes is what light this sheds on Lewis's depiction of the angelic and demonic realm. One of Lewis's burdens throughout his writings is to tear down the barrier between nature and super-nature, between the scientific and the spiritual. This distinction may be of some use, but only if we recognize that it is a distinction within God's single, unified real world. The narrator in *Perelandra* describes how we tend to turn this distinction into an airtight division:

> We tend to think about non-human intelligences in two distinct categories which we label "scientific" and "supernatural" respectively. We think, in one mood, of Mr. Wells' Martians (very unlike the real Malacandrians, by the bye), or his Selenites. In quite a different mood we let our minds loose on the possibility of angels, ghosts, fairies, and the like. But the very moment we are compelled to recognize a creature in either class as real the distinction begins to get blurred: and when it is a creature like an *eldil* the distinction vanishes altogether. These things were not animals— to that extent one had to classify them with the second group; but they had some kind of material vehicle whose presence could (in principle) be scientifically verified. To that extent they belonged to the first group. The distinction between natural and supernatural, in fact, broke down, and when it had done so, one realized how great a comfort it had been—how it had eased the burden of intolerable strangeness which this universe imposes on us by dividing it into two halves and encouraging the mind never to think of both in the same context.[7]

Tearing down this artificial barrier between the scientific and the supernatural is one of Lewis's main goals throughout his writings. He wants us to experience (and even come to love) the intolerable strangeness of the universe. "Reality, in fact, is usually something you could not have guessed."[8] The modern penchant for safely compartmentalizing the body and the soul, the physical and the spiritual, the natural and the supernatural is artificial and, in reality, false to the nature of things. We separate what God has joined together. This is one of the things Ransom learns on his interplanetary excursions: "The triple distinction of truth from myth and of both from fact was purely terrestrial—was part and parcel of that unhappy division between soul and body which resulted from the Fall."[9]

---

[7] Ibid.
[8] Lewis, *Mere Christianity*, 41. This is one of the reasons Lewis believed in Christianity: it is a religion you could not have guessed.
[9] Lewis, *Perelandra*, 122.

Books could be written (and likely have been written) exploring Lewis's attempt to reunite the spiritual and the physical, the natural and the supernatural. But a book about the Christian life must bring everything down to brass tacks, and so we return to the experience of the narrator of *Perelandra*. Like him, we all suffer under a barrage of influence from supernatural spirits. The principalities and powers really do launch their fiery shafts at us day by day. And the reality of those fiery shafts is not called into question by the fact that we can analyze their effects on the body in terms of hormones and chemical imbalances, or on the soul in terms of anxiety and depression. If the soul is really united to the body, if God has fixed laws that allow our bodily moods to influence our souls (and vice versa), then it should be no surprise that the influence of external agents—devils—can be registered by their effects on our bodies and souls. Nor should it be any surprise that one of the ways to fight the Devil is to get a good night's sleep or a healthy meal.

Devoured by Devils

But let us return to the devils themselves. For Lewis, they are real, they were created, and they fell into sin.[10] What was the nature of this first, primal sin? It was the same as every subsequent sin, the same Choice we noted in chapter 1. "The moment you have a self at all, there is a possibility of putting yourself first—wanting to be the centre—wanting to be God, in fact. That was the sin of Satan: and that was the sin he taught the human race."[11] As Lewis says elsewhere, "In the midst of a world of light and love, of song and feast and dance, [Satan] could find nothing to think of more interesting than his own prestige."[12] From this primal selfishness, the Devil and his fallen angels set out on a crusade of conquest, seducing and ensnaring human beings in their nets. And according to Lewis, they ensnare us for the same reason that fowlers ensnare birds—to devour them.

In the preface to *Screwtape*, Lewis writes:

I feign that devils can, in a spiritual sense, eat one another; and us. Even in human life we have seen the passion to dominate, almost to digest, one's fellow; to make his whole intellectual and emotional life merely an

---

10 While Lewis says quite clearly that he believes in devils, he is also clear that his belief in devils is not a part of his formal creed, and that his religion would not be in ruins if this belief were proved false (*The Screwtape Letters*, xxxii).
11 Lewis, *Mere Christianity*, 149.
12 Lewis, *A Preface to Paradise Lost*, 96.

extension of one's own—to hate one's hatreds and resent one's grievances
and indulge one's egoism through him as well as through oneself.[13]

The apostle Paul suggests precisely this sort of thing in Galatians 5:15: "But
if you bite and devour one another, watch out that you are not consumed
by one another."

Such devouring of another's personality is a "bloated spider parody" of
God's desire for human beings. Satan (along with his demonic followers)
wishes to consume weaker spirits, to "permanently gorge its own being
on the weaker's outraged individuality."[14] He desires to assimilate us into
himself. In this way, what for pantheism and many Eastern religions is the
picture of bliss—the single drop being absorbed into an ocean—is in the
Christian view the very definition of hell.[15] On the other hand, in his unfathomable bounty, God "turns tools into servants and servants into sons,
so that they may be at last reunited to Him in the perfect freedom of a love
offered from the height of the utter individualities which he has liberated
them to be."[16]

Screwtape himself expresses this difference between the outlook of
hell and heaven:

> To us a human is primarily food; our aim is the absorption of its will into
> ours, the increase of our own area of selfhood at its expense. But the obe-
> dience which the Enemy demands of men is quite a different thing. One
> must face the fact that all the talk about His love for men, and His service
> being perfect freedom, is not (as one would gladly believe) mere propa-
> ganda, but an appalling truth. He really does want to fill the universe with
> a lot of loathsome little replicas of Himself—creatures whose life, on its
> miniature scale, will be qualitatively like His own, not because He has ab-
> sorbed them but because their wills freely conform to His. We want cattle
> who can finally become food; He wants servants who can finally become
> sons. We want to suck in; He wants to give out. We are empty and would
> be filled; He is full and flows over. Our war aim is a world in which Our
> Father Below has drawn all other beings into himself: the Enemy wants a
> world full of beings united to Him but still distinct.[17]

---

[13] Lewis, *The Screwtape Letters*, xxxix.
[14] Ibid.
[15] Ransom discovers this in his encounter with Weston in *Perelandra*. "What the Pantheists falsely hoped of heaven bad men really received in hell" as they were "melted down into their Master, as a lead soldier slips down and loses his shape in the ladle over the gas ring" (Lewis, *Perelandra*, 148).
[16] Lewis, *The Screwtape Letters*, xl.
[17] Ibid., 46–47.

And thus we see Lewis clarifying for us the nature of the Choice. Screwtape would have us choose between different parts of reality: nature *or* super-nature; matter *or* spirit; body *or* soul. But this is not the true Choice at all. The true Choice is reality as God made it—including both the scientific and the supernatural, the physical and the spiritual, the visible and the invisible—versus the partial, twisted picture of reality painted by the Enemy. We can either live in God's world, with God at the center, or live in the devilish distortion, with ourselves at the center.

The "All-I-Want" State of Mind

And we must not miss how easy it is for us to put ourselves at the center. Screwtape tells Wormwood how the patient's mother has become a strange kind of glutton. Her gluttony appears not in the excess food she eats but in the delicacy of her tastes. Like the man who gorges himself day in and day out, her god is her belly; it dominates her whole life and, through her resulting impatience, uncharitableness, and self-concern, afflicts her son, her friends, and her servants.

> The woman is in what may be called the "All-I-want" state of mind. All she wants is a cup of tea properly made, or an egg properly boiled, or a slice of bread properly toasted. But she never finds any servant or any friend who can do these simple things "properly"—because her "properly" conceals an insatiable demand for the exact, and almost impossible, palatal pleasures which she imagines she remembers from the past; a past described by her as "the days when you could get good servants" but known to us as the days when her senses were more easily pleased and she had pleasures of other kinds which made her less dependent on those of the table.[18]

The "All-I-want" state of mind is not limited to gluttony; it is the hallmark of all demanding claims that human beings make for themselves, and it is the fountain of immense impatience, frustration, and conflict. Most of our daily disappointments and low-grade unhappiness flows from the "All-I-want" state of mind. Fed by constant comparisons to our past, or to our hoped-for future, or to the blessings of our friends, we live in sullen irritation and annoyance, repeating "All I want" like a mantra: "All I want is a house that's a little better or a little nicer, or has a little more room." "All

---

[18] Ibid., 101.

I want is a little respect, or a little peace and quiet, or a little vacation, or a little appreciation." All we want is a "little" more of whatever isn't making us happy right now. And in truth, some of these things might actually do us some good. A restful vacation might be just the thing the doctor ordered. Being appreciated for our efforts at home or at work or being respected by our families, friends, and coworkers may soothe our souls. But they will help us only if we reject the tyranny of the "All-I-want" state of mind.

The peevishness expressed by the "All-I-want" mentality has an even deeper root. It comes from the false sense of ownership we have about our lives. Most of us are prepared to deal with hardship in life. But we are angered (or at least annoyed) by hardship conceived as injury. And what qualifies as injury depends on the claims we make on life. We make claims about our time, our relationships, and our plans; when hardship comes in any of those areas, we feel that something has been stolen from us. The more claims we make, the more injured we feel. The more injured we feel, the more peevish we become, the more that we find ourselves saying "All I want . . . "

Take time, for instance. We all tend to make claims on our time. "My time is my own," we say. I trade some of my time to my employer for a paycheck. I gift some of my time to others—my family, my friends, my church—in my great generosity. But (and this is the important thing) the total time from which I trade and give belongs *to me*. It is my possession and birthright, and if the unexpected visitor or event interrupts my planned use of time, then someone has stolen something of mine.

In reality, time is a gift from God. Both it and we belong to him. As Christians, we pay lip service to this truth; we embrace it *in theory*. We know that we are committed to total service to God, and if he were to appear bodily and command us to do something, we would obey. But his bodily absence doesn't change the facts on the ground. Our time still ultimately belongs to him, and he has given it to us as a gift and stewardship.

The demonic strategy, as in so many other cases, is to obscure the reality of our situation. Our tempters encourage us to make claims of ownership without realizing we are doing it, the only evidence of these claims being our constant sense of frustration and righteous sense of injury. The devils persuade us to say "my own" about all sorts of things that cannot really be ours in any ultimate, possessive sense—time, our bodies, people, positions, prosperity, even emotions like happiness and bliss. Our tempters obscure the different senses of the possessive pronoun so that all uses of *my* become the *my* of ownership. And the more successful they are, the more vaguely aggrieved we become, living with a perpetual sense that our rights and privileges have been violated by we-know-not-whom.

The temptation to say "mine" and "my own" and "all I want" is at the heart of the demonic assault on our souls. And the dark powers are subtle and patient. They do not attack us all at once. Instead they urge us to make small compromises, to smudge and blur the Choice that confronts us. Then they seek to "harden these choices of the Hell-ward roads into a habit by steady repetition."[19] Isolated choices are pressed into habits. These habits are formed into a principle, an ideal, a creed that we are prepared to defend.

> Thus gradually there comes to exist at the centre of the creature a hard, tight, settled core of resolution to go on being what it is, and even to resist moods that might tend to alter it. It is a very small core; not at all reflective (they are too ignorant) nor defiant (their emotional and imaginative poverty excludes that); almost, in its own way, prim and demure; like a pebble, or a very young cancer. But it will serve our turn. Here at last is a real and deliberate, though not fully articulate, rejection of what the Enemy calls Grace.[20]

But God is patient as well. He intends to turn us into sons, to make us truly human. And he can work with any movement in his direction, no matter how small. A real positive pleasure can pierce the fog of worldliness that hangs about us. Pain can be his megaphone to wake the slumbering soul. God demands perfection, but he is also "delighted with the first feeble, stumbling effort you make tomorrow to do the simplest duty. . . . 'God is easy to please, but hard to satisfy.'"[21]

> If we let Him—for we can prevent Him, if we choose—He will make the feeblest and filthiest of us into a god or goddess, a dazzling, radiant, immortal creature, pulsating all through with such energy and joy and wisdom and love as we cannot now imagine, a bright stainless mirror which reflects back to God perfectly (though, of course, on a smaller scale) His own boundless power and delight and goodness.[22]

---

[19] Lewis, "Screwtape Proposes a Toast," in ibid., 196.
[20] Ibid., 196–97.
[21] Lewis, *Mere Christianity*, 202–3, quoting George MacDonald.
[22] Ibid., 206.

CHAPTER 6

THE CHURCH

Worshiping with Christ's Body

Early in both *The Screwtape Letters* and *Letters to Malcolm*, Lewis addresses the relationship between the individual Christian and the church. In *Malcolm*, Lewis primarily confronts the question of liturgy and corporate worship; in *Screwtape*, the elder tempter instructs Wormwood on how to foster the patient's disillusionment with the church. The present chapter will address both dimensions of the Christian life.

The Danger of the Liturgical Fidget

With respect to liturgy, while Lewis has clear opinions about church music, public prayers, and so forth, his main concern is elsewhere. More than insisting on his preferences as a laymen, his main exhortation is for ministers to avoid constant change and flux in the church's liturgy. His whole position boils down to a plea for permanence and uniformity. He laments the perpetual churning of liturgical novelty—what he calls "the Liturgical Fidget"—the ever-changing "brightenings, lightenings, lengthenings, abridgments, simplifications, and complications of the service."[1] Such novelty inevitably tends to move worship in the direction of entertainment.

In Lewis's view, the worship service is "a structure of acts and words through which we receive a sacrament, or repent, or supplicate, or adore."

---

[1] Lewis, *Letters to Malcolm*, 4.

It's something we use or enact in order to honor God and edify each other. Thus, the best worship service is one we don't have to think *about*. Rather, it's something we think *with*. "As long as you notice, and have to count, the steps, you are not yet dancing, but learning to dance."[2] The best worship service is one in which our attention is fixed on God, not on our steps.

Novelty in the service prevents us from using the service to worship God. Instead, our attention is drawn to the service itself. We must think *about* worshiping, rather than actually worshiping. Or worse, the novelty may draw our attention to the minister (or the musician). This distraction endangers devotion. In fact, Lewis wonders whether much novelty in our worship is driven by "clerical one-upmanship," the desire of a pastor or worship leader to stand out from the crowd. Christ's charge to Peter, Lewis reminds us, was "Feed my sheep, not Try experiments on my rats, or even, Teach my performing dogs new tricks."[3]

Lewis thus encourages churches (and especially pastors) to adopt a liturgy and to stick with it. At the same time, he is not completely hidebound. Updating language for the sake of congregational comprehension will be necessary (even if it ought to be done gradually and carefully). Introducing new songs, prayers, and forms may be appropriate. But the goal should be to create a stable and consistent liturgy that allows Christians to feel "at home" in the service so that they can make progress in the art of worship. In a fixed form of service, the congregation knows what is coming. The challenge of spontaneity is that people must engage their critical faculties as they listen; they can't "Amen" what is said until they've evaluated whether it is true or false, phony or sincere. But it is nearly impossible to carry on this critical activity while engaging directly with God in worship. Ironically, "the rigid form really sets our devotions free," because we've learned what steps come next, we've "gone through the motions" before, and we can keep our thoughts from straying and thus fully focus attention on God. Additionally, spontaneity in the form of worship runs the risk of becoming preoccupied with the present moment—current events, present fads, and so forth. Fixed prayers allow the permanent shape of Christianity to show through.[4]

For my own part, Lewis's commendation of mostly fixed forms has

---

2 Ibid.
3 Ibid.
4 Lewis to Mary Van Deusen, April 1, 1952, in *Collected Letters*, 3:177–78.

proved helpful to me as a pastor. As we've sought to establish the liturgy in our church, we've tried to accent the permanence of Christianity through a mostly fixed order of service and the use of consistent prayers and words at key parts in our service (such as the assurance of pardon). At the same time, we vary the songs and some of the prayers to remind ourselves that God does speak to us here and now, in our present circumstances (another important insight from Lewis). As Lewis says in the second letter to Malcolm, "We ought to be . . . simultaneously aware of closest proximity and infinite distance."[5] In worship, we are mindful of both God's transcendence *and* his immanence, of the permanence of Christianity and its relevance to our own day. In this case, the Choice is not to adopt either complete permanence or total relevance, but to insist on holding both of them, even as they may stretch us in opposite directions.

Worship Music

I mentioned just above that the goal of worship is to honor God and edify each other. It's important to note that both of these purposes are necessary as we consider the question of worship. Any lawful activity can be an occasion to glorify God. Singing, drinking a beer, throwing darts, taking a dip in the sea—all of these can be done unto God. "Whether you eat or drink, or whatever you do . . . " (1 Cor. 10:31). But not everything that glorifies God should be done in a service of worship. "For everything there is a season, and a time for every matter under heaven" (Eccles. 3:1). There are a great many things, good in themselves and in their proper place, that would be inappropriate—out of season—in a worship service. Throwing darts, for instance.

What's more, not everything that glorifies God necessarily edifies your neighbor. And the edification of our neighbors must factor into the decisions we make about our worship services. This is how Lewis navigates the tricky waters surrounding the so-called "worship wars." In his day, this debate centered on whether church music ought to consist of complex musical pieces performed by well-trained musicians and a choir or of the old favorites sung (or shouted) by the untrained masses. Lewis's own preference was with the highbrows; he thought that church music should be a special class of music, excellent in its kind. "In the composition and

---

[5] Lewis, *Letters to Malcolm*, 13.

highly-trained execution of sacred music we offer our natural gifts at their highest to God, as we do also in ecclesiastical architecture, in vestments, in glass and gold and silver, in well-kept parish accounts, or the careful organization of a Social."[6]

I happen to differ with Lewis on this question; in my mind, the primary purpose of singing in church is the expression of congregational praise. The congregation is the main "instrument" in the worship service, and the music and musicians exist to accompany and assist the congregation. Thus, my skepticism of both the highbrow choirs that Lewis loved and the rock-concert-like atmosphere of many contemporary worship services.[7]

But this is not the main thrust of Lewis's counsel. Whatever our preferences, our fundamental call is to love our neighbors. We ought to sacrifice and relinquish our own preferences for the sake of edifying them. Differences of taste and preference provide the opportunity "for mutual charity and humility."[8] When a highbrow sacrifices his own preference for excellent music in service to his unmusical neighbor, and when the untrained congregant listens silently and patiently to music he does not really like and cannot fully appreciate out of love for his musical neighbor, there, we can be sure, the Spirit of God is at work.

And this principle applies to far more than church music. In general, we ought not to be choosy about church. Lewis's attitude is the right one: "The idea of allowing myself to be put off by mere inadequacy—an ugly church, a gawky server, a badly turned-out celebrant—is horrible."[9] And it's precisely these things that Screwtape encourages Wormwood to prey upon. The devils take advantage of the fact that the church as she really is—spread out through all time and space and rooted in eternity, terrible as an army with banners[10]—is invisible to us. Instead, we see a drab building and a gaggle of odd people, both only half-finished. We have difficulty connecting the high biblical language—the body of Christ, the temple of God—with the actual people in the pews, their voices out of tune, their funny clothes, their squeaky boots, their double chins. The apparent incongruity is an obstacle to us, creating disillusionment ("Can this really be

6 Lewis, "On Church Music," in *Christian Reflections*, 95.
7 Lewis's perspective on the question of church music is excellent, and I would encourage pastors and worship leaders to consider well the counsel he offers (ibid., 94–99).
8 Ibid., 97.
9 Lewis, *Letters to Malcolm*, 100.
10 Lewis, *The Screwtape Letters*, 9.

the people of God, the bride of Christ?") and leading us to look down our noses at the sons and daughters of God ("People who look/sing/talk like that must have a ridiculous religion, and aren't I a fine chap to go to church with such as these?").

Here as in other places, Lewis writes so compellingly about our temptations because he writes from experience. When he first became a Christian, he wanted a more or less solitary religion—retiring to his room to read theology and pray. What fellowship he sought was with others like himself—educated, intellectual Christians who recognized how aesthetically pathetic most church services were (he describes the hymns at his church as "fifth-rate poems set to sixth-rate music"). In his autobiography, he notes that, even as an unbeliever, he "hated the Collective as much as any man can hate anything" (though at the time he was also vaguely socialistic, not yet recognizing the connection between socialism and collectivism).[11] Over time, Lewis came to see the dangers in both individualism and collectivism. More importantly, he came to see how the church is the antidote to both. To understand how, we need to look at two essays—"Membership" and "Equality"—as well as "Screwtape Proposes a Toast."

Confusion about Membership

The modern world, writes Lewis, has sought to turn religion into a private affair. Paradoxically, we are privatizing religion at precisely the moment that we are collectivizing our public and secular life. Lewis suggests that this is a part of a demonic strategy for neutralizing Christianity. This two-fold strategy is summed up as follows: "When the modern world says to us aloud, 'You may be religious when you are alone,' it adds under its breath, 'and I will see to it that you never are alone.'"[12] Privatized religion in a world devoid of privacy and solitude is essentially a nonentity.

Many Christians recognize that Christianity knows nothing of a solitary religion and thus resist the forced privatization. However, in resisting solitary religion, they run the risk of falling into another of the Enemy's traps—importing modern collectivism into our religious life. Modern collectivism, Lewis says, "is an outrage upon human nature," and may God

---

[11] Lewis, *Surprised by Joy*, 173.
[12] Lewis, "Membership," in *The Weight of Glory and Other Addresses*, 160.

deliver us from it.[13] The collectivism that Lewis has in mind sees politics and our public lives as ends in themselves. It regards participation in society, in the collective, as a positive and natural good which is the natural end of human life. Collective activities—the things we do in politics, law, and business—are thus our highest activities.

Lewis regards this as a serious error. Secular, public activities are in fact lower than our private, familial ones. "The secular community . . . has no higher end than to facilitate and safeguard the family, and friendship, and solitude."[14] In terms of our natural, earthly lives, there is "nothing half so good as a household laughing together over a meal, or two friends talking over a pint of beer, or a man alone reading a book that interests him."[15] Indeed, the entire purpose for which all economies, politics, laws, armies, and institutions exist is simply to prolong and multiply such scenes. Protecting family, friendship, and solitude may require us to temporarily sacrifice them in order to engage in some great collective activity (such as fight in a war to preserve our freedom). But the collective activity is a necessary evil, not a positive good. It is medicine, not food, and woe to the society that embraces confusion concerning this.

In Lewis's mind, the secular notion of the collective is no antidote to the privatizing of religion. The true antidote to all forms of individualism is not the secular collective but the mystical body of Christ. It is the Christian church that delivers us both from individualism and collectivism. Lewis shows how by exploring the different meanings of the word *membership*. Under collectivism, *membership* refers to interchangeable units, homogenous items in the same class. Thus, identically trained and identically dressed soldiers are "members" of an army, and the interchangeable citizens within a constituency are "members" of the voting public. But this is not what the Bible means by membership in the church. In fact, it is quite near the opposite.

When the apostle Paul speaks of Christians as members, he means that we are more like organs in a body—things essentially different from yet complementary to one another. "Christianity thinks of human individuals not as mere members of a group or items in a list, but as organs in a body—different from one another and each contributing what no other

---

[13] Ibid., 161.
[14] Ibid.
[15] Ibid.

could."[16] True membership, unlike inclusion in the collective, is more like a family. Fathers and mothers are not interchangeable parental units. Still less can you swap a grandfather for a child, or a sister for a dog. The unity of the family (and thus the church) "is a unity of unlikes, almost of incommensurables."[17]

The unity of the family and the church thus has a richness and variety to it, unlike the bland uniformity of the collective, epitomized especially in a prison, where every convict loses his name and is simply given a number. Membership in the body of Christ is not simply massing a group of people together like pennies. Rather, it embraces an "extreme differentiation in harmonious union."[18] This union is, first of all, with Christ himself, and it's impossible to imagine a union of greater unlikes. Christ is immortal, sinless, God himself. We are mortal, sinful, and created. And yet we are members of the same body, with Christ as the Head. He is the dominant factor in all considerations of Christian fellowship. Flowing from this fundamental union with the God-man, there is also the incalculable variety among the saints. This sometimes receives formal embodiment, such as the difference between a minister and a layman. At other times, the differences in ministry are too subtle—the give and take of teaching and learning, forgiving and being forgiven, representing Christ to others and having him represented back to us.

Envy and "I'm As Good As You"

It is here that Lewis insists on something that is radically out of step with the modern world: "I do not believe that God created an egalitarian world. I believe the authority of parent over child, husband over wife, learned over simple to have been as much a part of the original plan as the authority of man over beast."[19] God created a hierarchical world, a world of rich and glorious inequality, of authority and obedience. Political equality, though necessary because of human sin, is artificial. More than once, Lewis wrote that he believed in democracy, not because men are so good that everyone should be a part of ruling, but because men are so bad that none of them can be trusted with unfettered power over his fellows.[20] Thus, the noble root

---

16 Lewis, *Mere Christianity*, 185.
17 Lewis, "Membership," in *The Weight of Glory and Other Addresses*, 165.
18 Ibid.
19 Ibid., 168.
20 Ibid. See also Lewis, "Equality," in *Present Concerns*, 17–20.

of the demand for equality is simply the desire for fair play. But however necessary political equality is, "in the Church we strip off this disguise, we recover our real inequalities, and are thereby refreshed and quickened."[21] Equality, like clothing, is a necessary remedy for the fall. However, behind the facade of equal citizenship, the hierarchical world is alive and well. Or, again, political equality is medicine, not food. It is a protection against cruelty, but not in itself a positive good.

However, modern society has sought to take the necessary political ideal of equality and turn it into a factual belief that all people *are* equals. And, according to Screwtape, it has done so under the influence of demonic propaganda. Words like *democracy* and *equality* have become incantations, used to mask the ugly and degrading feeling expressed by the phrase "I'm as good as you." "I'm as good as you" is Lewis's preferred way of speaking of envy. However, he highlights the phrase to show how the feeling can be present and hidden under seemingly common and innocent expressions. The demonic reasons for encouraging the attitude "I'm as good as you" are legion. To begin with, it's not true. "It is idle to say that men are of equal value. If value is taken in a worldly sense—if we mean that all men are equally useful or beautiful or good or entertaining—then it is nonsense."[22] Lewis even challenges the belief that we are all equally valuable as immortal souls. God did not love or die for people because of some value he perceived in them; in and of ourselves, our value in relation to God is zero. God loves us not because we are lovable but because he is love. If the phrase "God loves all equally" has any meaning, the equality lies in his love, not in us.

But not only is this notion of ultimate equality false to the facts; the man who says, "I'm as good as you" doesn't believe it himself. We know this because the phrase is uttered only by those who feel themselves to be inferior. The scholar never says it to the dunce, nor does the pretty woman say it to the plain. Rather, "I'm as good as you" expresses "the itching, smarting, writhing awareness of an inferiority which the patient refuses to accept."[23] Equality as a human ideal breeds "that stunted and envious sort of mind which hates all superiority."[24] For this is what "I'm as good as you" really reveals—that we are full of resentment and envy. Our awareness of our

---

[21] Lewis, "Membership," in *The Weight of Glory and Other Addresses*, 167–68.
[22] Ibid., 170.
[23] Lewis, "Screwtape Proposes a Toast," in *The Screwtape Letters*, 204. The bulk of Screwtape's toast is devoted to exploring the way demons stoke envy and resentment under the guise of democracy and equality.
[24] Lewis, "Equality," in *Present Concerns*, 18.

inferiority produces in us a deep hatred of all superiority, and eventually a hatred of all differences whatever.[25] To the envious, differences become attempts to stand out from the crowd, and thus the crowd demands that the would-be individual return to the collective.

Screwtape knows that such envy is as old as the fall of man. What's new in the modern world is that an odious vice is now treated as a laudable virtue. Under the guise of "equality" and "democracy," envy is celebrated as respectable and praiseworthy. Screwtape commends the results of this demonic propaganda—it accomplishes the same ends as tyranny and dictatorship, but far more effectively. In a dictatorship, the tyrant must always be on the lookout for upstarts, for men and women under his rule who seek to rise up above their peers and thus challenge his rule. A clever tyrant will cut down any stalk of corn that stands out above the rest of the field. But when equality has been enshrined as an ideal, the tyrant need not cut down anyone; the little stalks will do it themselves. Under the influence of the egalitarian spirit, there is a movement toward the discrediting and eventual "elimination of every kind of human excellence—moral, cultural, social, or intellectual."[26]

In "Screwtape Proposes a Toast," Screwtape celebrates (and we must lament) the disastrous effects this envious, democratic spirit has had on education, where intelligent students are held back lest their less capable peers suffer trauma from being left behind. Lewis links this abolition of education with larger trends in society—the death of the middle class through penal taxes, thus preventing them from sending their children to real schools; the correspondent triumph of state education; and the resulting loss of "great men" in the sciences, arts, and public arena. In the end, the democratic spirit can do no less than suffocate democracy itself.

But Lewis's social vision is not our main concern here. If you wish to read more on that, take and read Screwtape's toast, as well as Lewis's essay "Democratic Education" (and then read a newspaper to see just how true Lewis's words have become). For our purposes, the real point is that the envious attempt to level all superiority and human differences, under the

---

[25] "There is in all men a tendency (only corrigible by good training from without and persistent moral effort from within) to resent the existence of what is stronger, subtler or better than themselves. In uncorrected and brutal men this hardens into an implacable and disinterested hatred for every kind of excellence" (Lewis, "Democratic Education," in *Present Concerns*, 33). Contrast this attitude with what Lewis calls "the humblest, the most childlike, the most creaturely of pleasures . . . the specific pleasure of the inferior" (Lewis, "The Weight of Glory," in *The Weight of Glory and Other Addresses*, 37).

[26] Lewis, "Screwtape Proposes a Toast," 201.

mask of equality, is destined to fail. God made a hierarchical world; therefore, people hunger for hierarchy. If we deny this appetite in the name of
equality and "I'm as good as you," it will simply reassert itself in another
form. "Where men are forbidden to honour a king they honour millionaires,
athletes, or film-stars instead: even famous prostitutes or gangsters. For
spiritual nature, like bodily nature, will be served; deny it food and it will
gobble poison."[27] One has only to consider the heroes and the famous of
the modern world to see how much poison we've gobbled. It would be no
surprise to Lewis that a thoroughly egalitarian society would wish to "keep
up with the Kardashians."

Loving the Inequality of Christ's Body

How can we resist the seduction of the democratic ideal, the lie of ultimate
equality, and the collectivism that they produce? Lewis gives a number of
answers, some of which will be explored in later chapters. The two I'll mention here are both related to the church and its worship. For the church, as
the mystical body of Christ, is one of the primary places where we learn to
joyously accept and embrace our spiritual inequalities. It's in the church
that we learn to kneel and bow, to give honor and obedience, as well as
receive them without shame or embarrassment. When we gather as the
church, we turn from the march of the collective to the dance of God.

In the body of Christ, there are many members, many organs. There are
hands and eyes and feet, all under one Head. But hands are not eyes, and
eyes are not feet (1 Cor. 12:15–16). What's more, God arranges the members
as he chooses (12:18), and as a result, the members differ from each other
in function (12:17), apparent strength (12:22), human honor (12:23), and
height (12:31). We must not miss this; some members seem weaker and are
thought less honorable. Some gifts are higher and others are lower. But according to Paul, all members and all gifts are necessary. None are dispens-
able (12:17, 26). This is the first way we resist the pressure of collectivism.
In the church we return to our deep inequalities and find ourselves refreshed and invigorated. We broaden our minds beyond the provincialism
of envy and "I'm as good as you."

> It takes all sorts to make a world; or a church. This may be even truer of a
> church. If grace perfects nature, it must expand all our natures into the

---

[27] Lewis, "Equality," in *Present Concerns*, 20.

full richness of the diversity which God intended when he made them, and Heaven will display far more variety than Hell. "One fold" doesn't mean "one pool."[28]

The Magic of the Lord's Supper

But even in the midst of the fantastic variety of the saints, we still find all our differences relativized. Standing together before the One in whom we live and move and have our being, how could they not be? All of us stand naked and exposed before him to whom we must give account. Lewis found this to be especially true in relation to the Lord's Supper. "Here a hand from the hidden country touches not only my soul but my body. Here the prig, the don, the modern in me have no privilege over the savage or the child. Here is big medicine and strong magic."[29]

In calling the Lord's Supper "magic," Lewis means no disrespect. Rather, he is attempting to honor the great mystery of the sacrament. While Lewis derives great spiritual nourishment from the Lord's Supper itself, he never finds this same nourishment in any theory or doctrine of the Lord's Supper. He explicitly notes the defects of transubstantiation and the memorial view. His descriptions imply that he is closest to a "real presence" view of the Supper, but he would no doubt disclaim the label. No explanation of the Supper lessens the mystery for him. Thus, he falls back on the language of magic to describe his experience of Holy Communion.

By "magic," Lewis doesn't mean the techniques employed by quacks to control nature. Rather, he means "objective efficacy which cannot be further analyzed." In other words, we know that the Lord's Supper "works," even if we are at a loss to know how. He likens this to the magic of fairy tales: "This is a magic flower, and if you carry it the seven gates will open to you of their own accord."[30] How does the flower open the gates? We cannot know. But open they will.

This kind of magic wins a response from us because it rings true to the world. "Mix these two powders and there will be an explosion. Eat a grain of this and you will die."[31] Of course, in these cases, science can provide some form of explanation. Thus, science, by enlarging its territory, pushes back the realm of magic. But science can only push so far. No matter how

---

[28] Lewis, *Letters to Malcolm*, 10.
[29] Ibid., 103.
[30] Ibid.
[31] Ibid.

many explanations are offered, no matter how many theorems proposed and demonstrated, at bottom there will always be the "brute fact" that this universe exists in just the way it does. And this brute fact—inexplicable, arbitrary, unanalyzable—is as magical as the flower in the fairy tale.

This is the magic that Lewis sees in Christianity, the magic that comes through at the Lord's Table, the magic that magnifies and then relativizes all differences among saints. Not only does it undercut all privileges; it is, as we saw in the last chapter, "a permanent witness that the heavenly realm, certainly no less than the natural universe . . . is a realm of objective facts."[32] At the Lord's Table, the veil between the worlds of nature and super-nature is at its thinnest. When we "take and eat," reality punctures the veil. Super-nature invades nature. Somehow, some way, in this meal God gives us the Christ-life. And in giving us the Christ-life, he binds us to himself and to one another. And in union with Christ and his mystical body, we become our true selves. We become truly human.

---

[32] Ibid., 104.

CHAPTER 7

PRAYER

Practicing the Presence of God

The fourth letter from Screwtape is devoted entirely to the subject of prayer. And *Letters to Malcolm* is chiefly about prayer. For Lewis, prayer is central to the Christian life. Given what we saw in our opening chapter about the Choice, this is no surprise. If the living God is here and now, confronting us with his presence, then prayer is precisely the point where we acknowledge that presence. Prayer, whether it is confession, supplication, thanksgiving, or adoration, always involves a surrender, an embracing of God's ever-present presence. This is why Screwtape tells his nephew Wormwood to "keep the patient from the serious intention of praying altogether."[1] When we pray, there is always the possibility that God will act directly to draw us closer to himself. Thus, in this chapter, we'll explore Lewis's view of prayer.

The Physical Body in Prayer

We could begin with prayer as petition. This presented a problem that occupied Lewis throughout his life. Does God alter the course of events in response to our prayers? If God is all-powerful and all-knowing, why should we pray? Lewis helpfully places this problem in its proper context: the problem isn't simply with prayer; it's a problem with *anything we do.*

---

[1] Lewis, *The Screwtape Letters*, 21.

We are in fact wrestling with the vexed matter of divine sovereignty and human responsibility, of divine action and human action. As I plan to treat this question in the next chapter, I'll leave it aside for now.

Instead, we'll begin with the role of the body in prayer. Human beings are hybrids, what Screwtape calls "amphibians—half spirit and half animal."[2] In other words, we are composite beings, consisting of bodies (like the beasts) and souls or spirits (like angels). It is easy for Christians to forget this. We sometimes adopt either of two attitudes we find among the pagans—body-hating asceticism or body-worshiping indulgence. Christianity rejects both of these. In contrast to the ascetics, Christianity insists that "God never meant man to be a purely spiritual creature. . . . He likes matter. He invented it."[3] In fact, Lewis expresses the amazing dignity of the body when he writes:

> But for our body one whole realm of God's glory—all that we receive through the senses—would go unpraised. For the beasts can't appreciate it and the angels are, I suppose, pure intelligences. They understand colors and tastes better than our greatest scientists; but have they retinas or palates? I fancy the "beauties of nature" are a secret God has shared with us alone. That may be one of the reasons why we were made—and why the resurrection of the body is an important doctrine.[4]

Lewis here suggests that human beings know something about God that angels do not.

> There are particular aspects of His love and joy which can be communicated to a created being only by sensuous experience. Something of God which the Seraphim can never quite understand flows into us from the blue of the sky, the taste of honey, the delicious embrace of water whether cold or hot, and even from sleep itself.[5]

Thus, Christians cannot reject or dismiss the body without rejecting and dismissing the glory of God.

And yet, Christians do not revere or worship the body. They resist the lure of the dark gods that treat the bodily appetites as commands to be obeyed. Instead, Christians ought to regard the body as Lewis, following

[2] Ibid., 45.
[3] Lewis, *Mere Christianity*, 64.
[4] Lewis, *Letters to Malcolm*, 17.
[5] Lewis, "Scraps," in *God in the Dock*, 216.

Saint Francis, did—by calling it "Brother Ass." No one ever worshiped a donkey. Nor did anyone ever completely hate it. An ass "is a useful, sturdy, lazy, obstinate, patient, lovable and infuriating beast; deserving now the stick and now a carrot; both pathetically and absurdly beautiful." One of the primary functions of the body in our lives is "to play the part of the buffoon,"[6] to keep our grandiose visions of ourselves in check. The clumsiness and stubbornness of our bodies is profoundly humbling.

At the same time, we must not blame our bodies for the scrapes and troubles we find ourselves in. The notion that our bodies are the root of our sinfulness is pagan in origin, even if it has found Christian sanction because of a misunderstanding of the Pauline use of the term *flesh*. But, Lewis reminds us, the body is not the primary source of temptation. "If the imagination were obedient, the appetites would give us very little trouble."[7] Lewis humorously expands on the soul's tendency to blame the body for its ills:

> "You are always dragging me down," said I to my Body. "Dragging you down!" replied my Body. "Well I like that! Who taught me to like tobacco and alcohol? You, of course, with your idiotic adolescent idea of being 'grown-up.' My palate loathed both at first: but you would have your way. Who put an end to all those angry and revengeful thoughts last night? Me, of course, by insisting on going to sleep. Who does his best to keep you from talking too much and eating too much by giving you dry throats and headaches and indigestion? Eh?" "And what about sex?" said I. "Yes, what about it?" retorted the Body. "If you and your wretched imagination would leave me alone I'd give you no trouble. That's Soul all over; you give me orders and then blame me for carrying them out."[8]

Christians must not reject the body, worship the body, or blame the body. Instead, we must accept and embrace the body, in all its glory and buffoonery, remembering that whatever our bodies do affects our souls. And therefore, as Lewis says, "the body ought to pray as well as the soul. Body and soul are both better for it."[9] Practically speaking, this means that we ought to sometimes kneel to pray, stand to pray, bow our heads to pray, raise our hands or hold hands to pray, or take some other appropriate physical posture. Likewise, keeping our eyes focused on a particular object

---

6 Lewis, *The Four Loves*, 101.
7 Lewis, *Letters to Malcolm*, 17.
8 Lewis, "Scraps," in *God in the Dock*, 216–17.
9 Lewis, *Letters to Malcolm*, 17.

can promote attentiveness in prayer; visual concentration helps spiritual concentration.[10] It also means that we try to avoid praying when we are extremely sleepy. Lewis says that his own practice is to "seize any time, and place, however unsuitable, in preference to the last waking moment." At the same time, he recognizes that bodily posture is less important than sincere devotion. "Kneeling does matter, but other things matter even more. A concentrated mind and a sitting body make for better prayer than a kneeling body and a mind half asleep."[11]

First Things First

In giving this counsel about prayer, Lewis is very clear that he doesn't wish to lay down rules. Nor does he want his own practice to be set up as a universal model. Yet he does offer a number of helpful practices of prayer that are worth considering.

For example, Lewis squarely faces the question of whether anything is too small for us to pray for. May all our desires be brought before God, or must we forcibly exclude trivial desires from our prayers? Lewis offers a twofold response. First, he notes that we ought to aim for a proper frame of mind. We should seek to have what Augustine called "ordinate loves." We must value things according to their value. This means we ought to put first things first, second things second, third things third, and so on. If we fail to do so, we lose the second things that we elevate above first things. This principle appears again and again in Lewis's writings.

> Every preference of a small good to a great, or a partial good to a total good, involves the loss of the small or partial good for which the sacrifice was made.[12]

> You can't get second things by putting them first; you can get second things only by putting first things first.[13]

> Put first things first and we get second things thrown in: put second things first & we lose both first and second things. We never get, say, even the sensual pleasure of food at its best when we are being greedy.[14]

---

[10] Ibid., 84.
[11] Ibid., 17.
[12] Lewis, "First and Second Things," in *God in the Dock*, 280.
[13] Ibid.
[14] Lewis to Dom Bede Griffiths, April 23, 1951, in *Collected Letters*, 3:111.

Aim at Heaven and you will get earth "thrown in": aim at earth and you will get neither.[15]

This is the frame of mind that we ought to have.

But, second, Lewis wisely notes that we don't always have it. In fact, we may rarely have it. What then? Should we pray even when our desires are "out of joint"? When we regard a fourth thing with a desire that should be reserved for a first thing, may we still ask God for it? Lewis notes that forcibly excluding the trivial desire from our thoughts never works. "It is no use to ask God with factitious earnestness for A when our whole mind is in reality filled with the desire for B. We must lay before Him what is in us, not what ought to be in us." Thus, at the very least, honesty demands that we bring these trivial, inordinate desires to God, no matter how insignificant we may know them to be. "I have no doubt at all that if they are the subject of our thoughts, they must be the subject of our prayers." At the same time, in bringing them before God, we may discover how inordinate our desires are. This is just as well, for then we are able to repent of our excessive desire while still asking for the thing we want. Prayer is the place where we lay all the cards on the table so that God can help us to moderate our excesses. We may be wrong in our desires; but we are more wrong if we try to hide our inordinate loves. There's no use pretending we don't want what we really want. It's childish (and dishonest) to try to somehow trick the all-knowing God. "The ordinate frame of mind is one of the blessings we must pray for, not a fancy dress we must put on when we pray."[16] We make our requests known and leave the results to God. He may grant our desires, or correct our desires, or enable us to endure the frustration of our desires. But it all begins with honesty.

Spontaneous and Ready-Made Prayers

Lewis also helps us to think about the words we use to pray. Words are anchors for our prayers. They are the conductor's baton that orchestrates the music of our devotion. Or, to switch the metaphor again, they channel our worship or penitence or petition in particular directions so that our prayers don't become wide and shallow puddles. Lewis was willing to use prayers written by other people. The value of such ready-made forms

---

[15] Lewis, *Mere Christianity*, 134.
[16] Lewis, *Letters to Malcolm*, 23.

is threefold. First, assuming they are good prayers, they keep us rooted in sound doctrine; otherwise our religion becomes so individualized that it ceases to be the universal faith once delivered to the saints. Second, ready-made forms are often focused on the large, eternal issues that confront every soul. Thus, they keep the urgent, present needs from swallowing up the perennially important ones. Finally, ready-made prayers remind us that we are addressing the almighty Maker of heaven and earth. They bring an element of ceremony and solemnity into our prayer lives, lest we so emphasize God's nearness that we lose sight of his transcendence. We must constantly keep in mind the great mystery that in prayer we are speaking to the King of kings and the one to whom we cry, "Abba, Father!" Ceremonial, ready-made prayers help to keep the first half of that paradox alive.

At the same time, ready-made forms cannot substitute for our own words to God, any more than ready-made forms could be the staple of our conversations with our spouses or friends. Our individuality demands that we address God as ourselves and no one but ourselves. We must bring before him our concerns and situations, our needs and desires, our blessings and comforts.

Adorning the Lord's Prayer

Lewis may have found an important balance between the ready-made forms and his own words in his practice of "festooning." To festoon is to adorn a place with ribbons, garlands, or other decorations. Lewis's festoons were the private overtones he hung around certain petitions in the Lord's Prayer. They were Lewis's way of filling out and personalizing the prayer so that he made it his own.

For example, "*Thy* will be done" first expresses submission to sorrows and hardships, much as Jesus prayed in Gethsemane. At the same time, "Thy will *be done*" reminds us that God's will is often done by his creatures, including us. The festoon reminds us that we are to be active in doing God's will, not just patient in bearing up under it. "'Thy will be done—by me—now' brings one back to brass tacks."[17] Finally, while we all recognize the need to submit to trials and hardships, Lewis came to see the need for a preliminary act of submission to possible future *blessings*. But why should we need to say "Thy will be done" with regard to God's

---

[17] Ibid., 26.

gifts and blessings? Who among us has trouble accepting good things from God? Lewis knows us well. "It seems to me that we often, almost sulkily, reject the good that God offers us because, at that moment, we expected some other good."[18] We refuse to let God surprise us with joy. We cut ourselves off from God's blessing, because our dissatisfaction at *not* getting what we wanted or expected overshadows the possibility of the new joy in what God has given.

Lewis dramatizes this truth in *Perelandra*. Ransom is speaking to the Green Lady, the "Eve" of the planet Venus, and he is trying to help her to understand how it is possible for there to be something that we do not wish for or want. Because she is unfallen, she cannot fathom how she could be displeased with something that Maleldil (Christ) sent her. Ransom reminds her of her reaction when she first saw Ransom at a distance. "But even you," he said, "when you first saw me, I know now you were expecting and hoping that I was the King. When you found I was not, your face changed. Was that event not unwelcome? Did you not wish it to be otherwise?" The Lady thinks for a moment and then has an epiphany:

> "What you have made me see," answered the Lady, "is as plain as the sky, but I never saw it before. Yet it has happened every day. One goes into the forest to pick food and already the thought of one fruit rather than another has grown up in one's mind. Then, it may be, one finds a different fruit and not the fruit one thought of. One joy was expected and another is given. But this I had never noticed before—that at the very moment of the finding there is in the mind a kind of thrusting back, or a setting aside. The picture of the fruit you have not found is still, for a moment, before you. And if you wished—if it were possible to wish—you could keep it there. You could send your soul after the good you had expected, instead of turning it to the good you had got. You could refuse the real good; you could make the real fruit taste insipid by thinking of the other."[19]

This is why the preliminary act of submission is so important. The festoon that says, "Thy will be done, O God. Help me to receive the good things you want to give me today," is a necessary preemptive prayer that prepares our hearts for whatever God brings. It keeps us from wielding our

18 Ibid., 25.
19 Lewis, *Perelandra*, 59.

past joys or present hopes as a weapon against God's future blessings. It also shapes our hearts so that we can see the opportunities and goodness in the severe mercies.

The importance of this truth came home to me in the writing of this book. As a professor, I often struggle to find time for concerted writing during a semester. So in order to make progress on this book, I mentally set aside the early weeks of June. I also had a number of home projects scheduled for that time. And, of course, around my house June means Little League baseball with my boys. My plans for the month included (1) getting up, (2) going to work, (3) getting some writing done, (4) coming home and playing baseball with my boys, and (5) making progress on the house on the weekends. And then my June plans changed.

At the end of May, I broke my hand while diving for a catch in a softball game. As I drove home from urgent care with the brace on, I felt the waves of emotion. "How am I going to type a book with a broken hand? How am I going to swing a hammer or turn a screwdriver? How am I going to play catch with my sons when I can't use a glove?" The last one was the hardest. It brought me to tears in my car. I knew that, at one level, losing baseball for a summer is a small thing. But I live in Minnesota, and my sons and I look forward all year long to the few weeks of spring. We love to play base-ball together. And now, because of a broken hand, my boys and I would be deprived of a great joy in our lives.

Thankfully, as I drove home, I had Lewis sitting at my shoulder, help-ing me to fight the fight of faith. I found myself repeating over and over, "One good was expected; another is given. One good was expected; another is given." Now, I know that a broken hand is not a good in itself. The pain and loss are real, and I don't need to pretend otherwise. But "for those who love God all things work together for good" (Rom. 8:28). *All things.* "Give thanks always and for everything" (Eph. 5:20). Always and for everything, including the hard things, the severe mercies, the broken hands. And Lewis prepares us for these moments by encouraging us to festoon our prayers in ways that orient our hearts to respond to God with glad submission, whether he brings us blessings or pains.

Another of Lewis's festoons is worth mentioning. For him, "Lead me not into temptation" can be glossed as "In my ignorance I have asked for A, B, and C. But don't give me them if you foresee that they would in reality be to me either snares or sorrows." In doing so, we recognize the danger of "enormous prayers which heaven in vengeance grants."[20] We acknowledge that we are not God, that we do not know what is best for us, and we willingly place ourselves in his hands and leave it to his wisdom and goodness to grant us what is best for us.

While Lewis describes his festoons in relation to the Lord's Prayer, in principle one could festoon any biblical prayer. In fact, this is precisely how I often make use of Paul's prayers in my own devotional life. For example, I use Philippians 1:9–11 as a baseline prayer for myself and others. Paul wrote, "And it is my prayer that your love may abound more and more, with knowledge and all discernment, so that you may approve what is excellent, and so be pure and blameless for the day of Christ, filled with the fruit of righteousness that comes through Jesus Christ, to the glory and praise of God." When adorned, the prayer reads something like this:

> Father, may my love for you and my love for other people increase and grow and abound. May there be no limit to the increase of love in my heart. And make my love a wise and a discerning love. Keep me from mere sentimentality that substitutes good intentions for wise and considered actions. And with that wise and discerning and abounding love, help me to approve what is excellent. Not just what is acceptable or passing, but what is excellent and worthy of praise. Help me to know what is good, better, and best in any given situation that I face today, and help me to act accordingly. And as I act in this way, make it so that I maintain a purity and blamelessness that will stand at the final judgment. When you call me to account, may I come before you adorned in your righteousness—both in my status and in my conduct. May the result of your abounding love be a holy life that exalts Jesus and gives glory and praise to God.

The beauty of praying in this way is that it demands meditation on the Scripture; it forces us to make Scripture our own, to chew the words carefully so that we see their relevance to the trials and temptations we face each day. The Scriptures act as the riverbed for our prayers, the channel that carries our devotion to God in the proper direction. And our festoons make the current run swift and sure in the channels. And God gives the growth.

---

[20] Lewis, *Letters to Malcolm*, 28.

Dangers of Prayer

Lewis is very aware of the dangers of prayer. He knows that even our best acts can be subtly twisted in ugly directions. For instance, Screwtape knows that Wormwood's patient will undoubtedly pray for his mother. But Wormwood should attempt to make all such prayers "spiritual," concerned only with the state of her soul and not her physical needs.

Encouraging spiritual prayers may seem like an odd tactic from a devil, but the reasoning is shrewd. By praying only for the souls of others, our attention is often kept exclusively on what we regard as their sins, which often means those actions of theirs that we find most annoying. Thus, our frustration at them increases, even as we pray for them. More than that, because we are often ignorant of the true state of another's soul, we end up praying for an imaginary person who bears little resemblance to our spouse or parent or child or neighbor. As the object of our prayers diverges from the real person in our lives, the affection and compassion we express in our prayers for the imaginary neighbor never spills over into our treatment of the real one. The remedy for this danger is to include the tangible needs of those we pray for in our petitions on their behalf. Moreover, insofar as we pray for their souls, we must be vigilant to remember our own sins and failures even as we pray for others. There is, after all, a log in our eye and only a speck in theirs.

Lewis identifies another danger in our intercessory prayers. He notes that he often finds intercessory prayer for others easier than prayers for himself. Some of this may be rooted in the Screwtape strategy above. But Lewis identifies two other reasons for it. First, it's much easier to pray for others than to actually do things for them. Serving them in some practical way looks suspiciously like work. Second, asking God to help your friend with his besetting sin keeps the focus on *his* sin, not yours. To pray for our own besetting sins will again require work on our part. In both cases, prayer becomes a substitute for action, rather than the first (and crucially important) step in any of our actions. We pray so that we might act in the strength that God supplies. We pray, so that his works might uphold and enliven our works.

A final danger flows from the staggering promises in the Bible in places like Mark 11:24: "Therefore I tell you, whatever you ask in prayer, believe that you have received it, and it will be yours." This passage creates a number of challenges for the Christian. How do we reconcile the astonishing promise that if we pray with faith, we'll get exactly what we ask for, with the undeniable reality of unanswered prayer (including the prayer of Christ in Gethsemane)? This is the theological problem, and Lewis addresses it (without completely resolving it to his satisfaction) in *Letters to Malcolm* and "Petitionary Prayer: A Problem Without an Answer." Given the focus of this book, I'll leave somewhat to the side the theological question and focus on Lewis's approach to the practical problems such promises create for us.

The first counsel Lewis has is that we must not attempt to gin up this "faith" on our own. Lewis knows from experience that children are especially prone to this error. Faith is commanded, and so we seek to produce it in our own power, which often means combining a desperate desire with a strong imagination to produce a subjective feeling we then call "faith." Encouraging (or even allowing) children and new believers to approach prayer and faith in this way is the surest way to make them disillusioned with God. This is why such encouragement is a part of Screwtape's strategy with his patients. The devils encourage us to try and adopt a vaguely devotional mood and to call that faith. The goal is to turn us inward to ourselves, rather than outward to Christ.

> Keep them watching their own minds and trying to produce feelings there by the action of their own wills. When they meant to ask Him for charity, let them, instead, start trying to manufacture charitable feelings for themselves and not notice that this is what they are doing. When they meant to pray for courage, let them really be trying to feel brave. When they say they are praying for forgiveness, let them be trying to feel forgiven. Teach them to estimate the value of each prayer by their success in producing the desired feeling; and never let them suspect how much success or failure of that kind depends on whether they are well or ill, fresh or tired, at the moment.[21]

Lewis counters this devilish temptation in a letter to his goddaughter on the eve of her first communion:

---

[21] Lewis, *The Screwtape Letters*, 23. Lewis describes his own early attempts to do precisely this in his autobiography:

> I set myself a standard. No clause of my prayer was to be allowed to pass muster unless it was accompanied by what I called a "realization," by which I meant a certain vividness of the imagination and the affections. My nightly task was to produce by sheer will power a phenomenon which will power could never produce, which was so ill-defined that I could never say with absolute confidence whether it had occurred, and which, even when it did occur, was of very mediocre spiritual value. If only someone had read to me old Walter Hilton's warning that we must never in prayer strive to extort "by maistry" what God does not give! (Lewis, *Surprised by Joy*, 61–62)

Don't expect (I mean, don't count on and don't demand) that when you are confirmed, or when you make your first Communion, you will have all the feelings you would like to have. You may, of course: but also you may not. But don't worry if you don't get them. They aren't what matter. The things that are happening to you are quite real things whether you feel as you would wish or not, just as a meal will do a hungry person good even if he has a cold in the head which will rather spoil the taste. Our Lord will give us right feelings if He wishes—and then we must say Thank you. If He doesn't, then we must say to ourselves (and Him) that He knows best.[22]

Lewis's second answer to the problem of the prayer of faith is to remind us that, whatever Mark 11:24 means, it is not the place to send beginners. "If that passage contains a truth, it is a truth for very advanced pupils indeed."[23] Lewis distinguishes between three ways someone might approach God in prayer: as a suitor, as a servant, or as a friend.

A *suitor* makes requests but struggles to know whether he is truly *heard* by God. As a result, the suitor may be satisfied if his request is taken into account, even if it is not granted in the end.

We can bear to be refused but not to be ignored. In other words, our faith can survive many refusals if they are really refusals and not mere disregards. The apparent stone will be bread to us if we believe that a Father's hand put it into ours, in mercy or in justice or even in rebuke. It is hard and bitter, yet it can be chewed and swallowed.[24]

The struggle for the suitor is precisely to believe that, however circumstances may look, God does hear our prayers. Not one of them has been lost.

A step above the suitor is the *servant*. The servant has confidence in his master's reality and goodness. He knows that God hears him, but he doesn't know all that God is up to. He is not "in on his master's secrets," even if he is under his master's orders. Thus, to approach God as a servant is to be confident in God's existence, goodness, and wisdom and to stand ready to do his will, whatever that might be. The struggle for the servant is in carrying out that will.

Above the servant (in the highest place attainable by a man) is the

---

[22] Lewis to Sarah Neylan, April 3, 1949, in *Collected Letters*, 3:1587.
[23] Lewis, *Letters to Malcolm*, 60.
[24] Ibid., 52.

friend of God, the one who stands before the Lord, like Abraham and Moses, "face-to-face." The friend of God has been let in on the Master's secrets. He knows the plans behind the orders. He is God's fellow worker, and his requests are confident precisely because he sees the work as a whole and is simply asking for what is needed to complete the job. Here is where the promise of answered prayer in Mark 11:24 applies. "It is the prophet's, the apostle's, the missionary's, the healer's prayer that is made with this confidence and finds the confidence justified by the event."[25] When God grants us the special type of faith seen in Mark 11 or James 5, he makes us his colleagues, uniting us to himself to such a degree that something like the divine foreknowledge enters our minds so that in praying, we believe that we have already received what we asked for. Because of this, Jesus's words in Mark 11 are not really addressed to the condition in which most of us live. We live at the intersection of level 1 and level 2, sometimes suitors, sometimes servants. Should God in his wisdom elevate us to be his fellow workers and grant us the gift of faith, we should, by all means, seek to move mountains. But if he does not, we must be content to be servants, remembering with Milton that "they also serve who only stand and wait."[26]

Prayer Is the Meeting of Persons

To close this chapter, I want to underscore that Lewis insists he doesn't want to make his prayer life the standard for others. He would not presume to teach. "For me to offer the world instruction about prayer would be impudence" (though of course he says this in a fictional book devoted chiefly to the subject of prayer). But that is precisely how he wants his advice on prayer (and, we might add, on the Christian life in general) to be heard—"two people on the foothills comparing notes in private."[27]

At the same time, I think there is a center to Lewis's view of prayer, and (unsurprisingly) it fits with the larger picture of his approach to the Christian life. Fundamentally, *prayer is the meeting of persons.* It is

---

[25] Ibid., 60.
[26] John Milton, "When I Consider How My Light Is Spent."
[27] Lewis, *Letters to Malcolm*, 63. Lewis summarizes his own rules for prayer in a letter to a friend:

> I am certainly unfit to advise anyone else on the devotional life. My own rules are (1.) To make sure that, wherever else they may be placed, the main prayers should not be put "last thing at night." (2.) To avoid introspection in prayer—I mean not to watch one's own mind to see if it is in the right frame, but always to turn the attention outward to God. (3.) Never, never to try to generate an emotion by will power. (4.) To pray without words when I am able, but to fall back on words when tired or otherwise below par. (Lewis to F. Morgan Roberts, July 31, 1954, in *Collected Letters*, 3:500)

a personal contact between embryonic, incomplete persons (ourselves) and the utterly concrete Person. Prayer in the sense of petition, asking for things, is a small part of it; confession and penitence are its threshold, adoration its sanctuary, the presence and vision and enjoyment of God its bread and wine.[28]

When we pray, we take our place in the Great Dance. We are drawn into God's Trinitarian, three-personal life.

> An ordinary simple Christian kneels down to say his prayers. He is trying to get into touch with God. But if he is a Christian he knows that what is prompting him to pray is also God: God, so to speak, inside him [i.e., the Holy Spirit]. But he also knows that all his real knowledge of God comes through Christ, the Man who was God—that Christ is standing beside him, helping him to pray, praying for him. You see what is happening. God is the thing to which he is praying—the goal he is trying to reach. God is also the thing inside him which is pushing him on—the motive power. God is also the road or bridge along which he is being pushed to that goal. So that the whole threefold life of the three-personal Being is actually going on in that ordinary little bedroom where an ordinary man is saying his prayers. The man is being caught up into the higher kinds of life—what I called Zoe or spiritual life: he is being pulled into God, by God, while still remaining himself.[29]

Prayer is not only Trinitarian; it's Christological. As we saw earlier, when we pray the Lord's Prayer and we call God "our Father," we are dressing up like Christ.[30] We are putting on the Lord Jesus (Rom. 13:14) and approaching the throne of grace with confidence (Heb. 4:16), because we come in the name (indeed, in the clothing) of God's beloved Son, with whom he is well pleased.

This fact—that in prayer we are coming into contact with the living God—accounts for our reluctance to pray. Few of us want "the real nakedness of the soul in prayer."[31] In our confronting God, or rather our being confronted by him, he will certainly see us as we really are, and more than likely he will remind us of our duties. "We shrink from too naked a contact, because we are afraid of the divine demands upon us which it might make

---

[28] Lewis, "The Efficacy of Prayer," in *The World's Last Night*, 8.
[29] Lewis, *Mere Christianity*, 163.
[30] Ibid., 187.
[31] Lewis, *The Screwtape Letters*, 25.

too audible. As some old writer says, many a Christian prays faintly 'lest God might really hear him, which he, poor man, never intended.'"[32] So in praying, we open ourselves up to divine influence, and that might cost us something. Not anything large, mind you. We're more than willing to "sell all" if God demands it. What we try to avoid is not Christ's "sell all" but his "sell *this*." We have too much of the rich young ruler in us. To give all to God, we imagine, would be a joy. To give some, to give a trifle, to give these five dollars or this ten minutes or that afternoon—that is the impossible. Best to avoid contact then, at least until bedtime. By then, it will be too late for any overly burdensome demands.

This then is the Choice that confronts us whenever we are deciding whether to pray: Will we come out, unveil, and offer ourselves to God's view? Or like Adam and Eve, will we continue to hide (vainly) behind our fig leaves? "By unveiling, by confessing our sins and 'making known' our request, we assume the high rank of persons before Him."[33] In prayer, we become real persons in God's presence, and he reveals himself to us as *the* Person. Not only that, but this truly personal Person changes us through our prayers. When you pray, you believe that

> a real Person, Christ, here and now, in that very room where you are say-ing your prayers, is doing things to you. It is not a question of a good man who died two thousand years ago. It is a living Man, still as much a man as you, and still as much God as He was when He created the world, really coming and interfering with your very self; killing the old natural self in you and replacing it with the kind of self He has.[34]

This is the chief work of prayer—to fling aside the bright blur that our minds normally substitute for God and the phantasm that each of us nor-mally regards as self. In other words, the aim is to reawaken ourselves to the reality of our situation—that we always live *coram Deo*, before God's face. Doing so requires us, once again, to begin where we are. The room in which we sit and the self that sits in the room are both facades—masks—for impenetrable mysteries. The walls are made of wood and plaster, which are made of molecules, which are made of atoms, which are made of pro-tons and electrons, which are made of quarks and leptons, and on and on

32 Lewis, *Letters to Malcolm*, 114.
33 Ibid., 21.
34 Lewis, *Mere Christianity*, 191.

until we reach rock bottom, where the living God upholds the world by his Word and Breath. And beneath what I call my conscious self are all of my memories and experiences, my hopes and fears, my desires and appetites, jumbled and swirling together. My ordinary "self" is a facade. It is the thin film on the surface of an unsound and dangerous sea. Beneath that sea, there are both snarling resentments and radiant delights, nagging lusts and boundless aspirations, vicious sea dragons and noble mermen.[35]

In attending to ourselves and this stage on which we live, we seek to plant prayer right in the present reality. "Here is the actual meeting of God's activity and man's."[36] Embracing this situation, we may come to realize that the world as we perceive it and the self as we imagine it are far from rock-bottom realities. And in prayer, the real self, the self beneath the dramatic mask that we wear before others, attempts to speak, not to the other actors on stage, but to the Author, the Producer, the Audience of One. "The prayer preceding all prayers is 'May it be the real I who speaks. May it be the real Thou that I speak to.'" And after flinging aside the phantasms, after re-awakening to the reality of our situation, after coming (is it really possible?) into the presence of the living God, "the most blessed result of prayer would be to rise thinking 'But I never knew before. I never dreamed.'"[37]

---

[35] Lewis, "The Seeing Eye," in *Christian Reflections*, 169–70.
[36] Lewis, *Letters to Malcolm*, 79.
[37] Ibid., 81.

CHAPTER 8

A GRAND MYSTERY

Divine Providence and Human Freedom

In the previous chapter, I raised the problem of petitionary prayer: if God knows everything and has planned everything, why pray? Lewis does not consider this an isolated problem. If God's sovereignty renders prayer unnecessary, then God's sovereignty renders all human action unnecessary. If God knows everything and has planned everything, why evangelize? Why love your neighbor? Why pass the salt? In other words, the problem of petitionary prayer is simply one expression of the problem of divine sovereignty and human freedom. Thus, the present chapter will explore Lewis's thoughts on this larger subject. To do so, we'll look at how Lewis seeks to live in the tension between eternity and time, between God's will and ours, between God's providence and our choices.

Eternity and Time

In dealing with the question of God's sovereignty and man's free will, Lewis follows the view of the medieval philosopher Boethius. Boethius sought to solve the problem of predestination and free will by clarifying God's relation to time. God is timelessly eternal. That is, he is outside of time. Therefore, strictly speaking, he does not "foresee" anything, since the prefix "fore" implies a temporal movement between God's sight and the actual event. God does not, properly speaking, look down the corridors of time to see what we will do. Instead of foreseeing, God simply sees. Instead of foreknowing, God simply knows. And, by analogy with our own sight, seeing an event does not cause the event. I watch the squirrel run across the road, but I do not cause the squirrel to run across the road. Likewise, God sees my free decisions; he does not cause them. Thus, all of created reality is directly present to God in his eternal now, and yet we are perfectly free and responsible for all of our actions.[1]

Lewis knows that, as creatures in time, we will always struggle to grasp the eternal. Nevertheless, he believes that we are destined for timelessness. The eternal is the "deepest reality,"[2] and not merely for God. Because God sees our life as an endless present, our deepest reality is eternal as well. Reality for us is "fundamentally timeless," even if we experience it only "in the mode of succession."[3] God's perspective on things trumps, as it were, our experience of things.[4] And yet, Lewis says, we must never allow this "deeper reality" of eternity, with all its finality and fixedness, in any way to undermine the pressing reality of our freedom. "From within time . . . the choice of ways is before you."[5]

We catch a glimpse of Lewis's thought on this in *The Great Divorce* when the narrator sees the forms of giant figures standing motionless around a small silver chessboard. The chessboard is time, and the giant figures are our true selves, rooted in eternity, and watching our fundamental Choice play out on the temporal landscape of the chessboard. Our temporal selves

---

[1] "He does not remember you doing things yesterday; He simply sees you doing them, because, though you have lost yesterday, He has not. He does not 'foresee' you doing things tomorrow; He simply sees you doing them, because, though tomorrow is not yet there for you, it is for Him. You never supposed that your actions at this moment were any less free because God knows what you are doing. Well, He knows your tomorrow's actions in just the same way—because He is already in tomorrow and can simply watch you. In a sense, He does not know your action till you have done it: but then the moment at which you have done it is already 'Now' for Him" (Lewis, *Mere Christianity*, 170).

[2] "The task of dovetailing the spiritual and physical histories of the world into each other is accomplished in the total act of creation itself. Our prayers, and other free acts, are known to us only as we come to the moment of doing them. But they are eternally in the score of the great symphony. Not 'predetermined'; the syllable pre lets in the notion of eternity as simply an older time. For though we cannot experience our life as an endless present, we are eternal in God's eyes; that is, in our deepest reality. When I say we are 'in time' I don't mean that we are, impossibly, outside the endless present in which He beholds us as He beholds all else. I mean, our creaturely limitation is that our fundamentally timeless reality can be experienced by us only in the mode of succession" (Lewis, *Letters to Malcolm*, 110).

[3] Ibid.

[4] In one sense, I appreciate what Lewis does in stressing the priority of God's view of things. God is ultimate. At the same time, I worry that his view gives the impression that time is somehow lesser or illusory or unreal. Lewis is clearly aware of this danger; it's why MacDonald says that it's better not to try to translate the eternal into a temporal mode. The temporal mode inevitably misleads. Eternal reality, MacDonald says in *The Great Divorce*, 141, cannot be known by a definition (that is, by reason). Instead, we must try and catch a glimpse with an imaginative vision. And since we live in time, the whole point of the vision is to highlight the Choice that stands before us.

[5] Lewis, *The Great Divorce*, 140.

might be thought of as pantomimes or echoes of choices already made in eternity past. Or they might be thought of as anticipations of choices yet to be made at the end of all things. But according to George MacDonald, the Scottish guide in *The Great Divorce*, "ye'd do better to say neither."[6] The words "already" and "yet" are smuggling time into eternity, and this, Lewis says, we must not do.

Probing Lewis's Proposal

What can we say about this? We might start with a question: Can we make Lewis's theological move about more than God's sight and God's knowledge? Both of these suggest a kind of passivity on God's part; he is simply watching the world happen. But clearly God does more than observe; he designs and creates. As Lewis says elsewhere, he invents and utters. So, following Lewis, would it not be right to say that God does not "pre-determine"; he simply determines? He does not predestine; he simply destines? He does not foreordain; he simply ordains?

Lewis implies that he'd say yes to these questions, and this reintroduces the mystery of divine sovereignty and human freedom.

> The task of dovetailing the spiritual and physical histories of the world into each other is accomplished in the total act of creation itself. Our prayers, and other free acts, are known to us only as we come to the moment of doing them. But they are eternally in the score of the great symphony. Not "pre-determined"; the syllable pre lets in the notion of eternity as simply an older time.[7]

Lewis doesn't complete the thought, but he does suggest that our free acts are "eternally in the score of the great symphony" because they have been determined. And this determining happened in God's single "total act of creation." As Puddleglum says, "There are no accidents."[8] Likewise, Lewis writes, "Since nothing in His work is accidental, if He knew, He intended."[9]

The second thing worth noting is that, whatever the philosophical and metaphysical fruitfulness of Lewis's Boethian solution, it is a simple fact that God has shown no reluctance to speak of his eternal actions in temporal

---

[6] Ibid., 44.
[7] Lewis, *Letters to Malcolm*, 110.
[8] Lewis, *The Silver Chair*, 154.
[9] Lewis, *Miracles*, 258.

terms. When Lewis tells us to avoid smuggling in the notion of eternity as
an older time, we must remind him that it is the apostle Paul doing the
smuggling: "[God] chose us in him *before the foundation of the world*" (Eph.
1:4). Grace was given us in Christ "*before* the ages began" (2 Tim. 1:9). Paul
even emphasizes the temporal fact when he says that God chose Jacob over
Esau *before* the twins were born or had done anything good or bad (Rom.
9:11). Given God's timelessness, it might be that we should understand this
along the lines Lewis suggests: God graciously chose us (and Jacob) in his
eternal now. But, then, it was still his choice that determined it. And Paul
is clear that God's choice did not regard (did not take into account) the good
or bad deeds of Jacob or Esau.[10] Thus, Lewis's solution—remembering that
God is timeless and we are not—does not resolve the tension.

God's Will and Ours

We see a similar tension in Lewis's discussion of our will and God's will.
Let's begin with our free will. Lewis takes it for granted that at least some
of our acts are "self-determined." God created beings which have free will,
that is, beings "which can go either wrong or right."[11] "The freedom of a
creature must mean freedom to choose: and choice implies the existence
of things to choose between."[12] In insisting on the necessity of human
free will, Lewis is primarily rejecting the notion that we are robots. "Some
people think they can imagine a creature which was free but had no pos-

---

[10] In *The Four Loves* (123–24), Lewis argues that "hate" in Romans 9, like the "hate" in Jesus's command in
Matthew, means "prefer less." God preferred Jacob over Esau, just as we are to prefer God over our families.
The "hatred" is a relative hatred. In comparison to God, our love for our families is hatred. In comparison
to his love for Jacob, God hates Esau. Lewis goes on to insist that the hatred of Esau is purely a temporal
affair; it has nothing to do with eternal destinies, whether of Esau himself or of others.

  Whatever merits there are in Lewis's broader understanding of love and hate, his interpretation
of Romans 9 is truncated at best. Romans 9, following as it does the wonderful promises of ultimate
salvation and glorification in Romans 8, appears to be dealing, at least in part, with eternal salvation. It
is not merely the widespread rejection of Jesus by the Jews in general (what Paul calls "a partial hardening" in Rom. 11:25) that grieves the apostle. It is the fact that his kinsmen are accursed and cut off from
their Messiah, even as his "heart's desire and prayer to God . . . is that they may be saved" (Rom. 10:1).
While the destiny of the Jews as a people is certainly in view, it won't do to play this corporate election
and reprobation off against individual election and reprobation. After all, God's choice of Jacob over
Esau (and Isaac over Ishmael) was a choice within the children of Abraham. It is the eternal salvation
of individuals that concerns Paul, not merely the temporal fate of nations. Additionally, even if we
focused only on the temporal and historical dimensions of the passage, it is still the case that we have
God selecting one person over another, in matters of salvation and judgments, apart from any of their
deeds, whether good or bad. Jacob was no better than Esau; Esau no worse than Jacob. Pharaoh was
raised up and hardened for the glory of God; Moses was raised up and honored for the same purpose.
Of course, there is a profound asymmetry in God's mercy and God's hardening. The latter serves the
former, and not vice versa. The glory of mercy shines brightest against the backdrop of God's wrath.
But it is the sovereign freedom of God in hardening whom he will and pitying whom he will that makes
the ultimate difference.

[11] Lewis, *Mere Christianity*, 47.
[12] Lewis, *The Problem of Pain*, 20.

sibility of going wrong; I cannot. If a thing is free to be good it is also free to be bad. . . . A world of automata—of creatures that worked like machines—would hardly be worth creating."[13] God, in making us with free will, "has really and truly limited His power."[14] Lewis is even willing to talk about the "risk" God took in making such a world, and the "defeat" of omnipotence.[15]

On the other hand, Lewis insists quite rightly that the relationship between God's will and ours is utterly unique. God does not act upon us in the way that other creatures act upon us. His actions and ours do not exclude one another in the way that, say, my lifting a package excludes your lifting the package. "God did it" and "I did it" can both be said about the same act, without contradiction. Something can be both self-determined and God-determined. In insisting on this point, Lewis thinks that he is operating in some sort of middle ground. He comments on Philippians 2:12–13: "You will notice that Scripture just sails over the problem. 'Work out your own salvation in fear and trembling'—pure Pelagianism. But why? 'For it is God who worketh in you'—pure Augustinianism. It is presumably only our presuppositions that make this appear nonsensical."[16]

---

[13] Lewis, *Mere Christianity*, 47. Later in this same book (183), he writes: "The process of being turned from a creature into a son would not have been difficult or painful if the human race had not turned away from God centuries ago. They were able to do this because He gave them free will: He gave them free will because a world of mere automata could never love and therefore never know infinite happiness."

At one level, it seems that we have a failure of Lewis's imagination. Lewis can't imagine a world of perfectly free creatures that had no possibility of going wrong, and therefore, such creatures must be impossible. Imaginability implies possibility. But why should our imaginations (rather than, say, biblical testimony) be the measure? What's more, Lewis clearly can imagine (in some limited sense) a free being that has no possibility of going wrong. Isn't God himself just such a Being? Ah, but Lewis said "creature," not "being." Very well. What about the saints in glory? Are they less free because all possibility of going wrong has been removed? Are "the spirits of just men made perfect" no longer free? Must we step out of freedom in order to step into perfect goodness? And if Lewis admits both the freedom and unassailable perfection of glorified saints, does that not introduce precisely the third way that he rejects: beings that are neither robots nor ultimately self-determined, but instead true moral agents whose every thought, word, and action are determined, in some mysterious and unfathomable way, by God?

[14] Lewis, "The Trouble with 'X' . . . ," in *God in the Dock*, 153. In the same essay, Lewis writes, "God has made it a rule for Himself that He won't alter people's character by force. He can and will alter them—but only if the people will let Him" (ibid.).

[15] "Finally, it is objected that the ultimate loss of a single soul means the defeat of omnipotence. And so it does. In creating beings with free will, omnipotence from the outset submits to the possibility of such defeat" (Lewis, *The Problem of Pain*, 129).

[16] Lewis, *Letters to Malcolm*, 49. Lewis expresses the same thing in *Mere Christianity*, 149:

The first half is, "Work out your own salvation with fear and trembling"—which looks as if everything depended on us and our good actions: but the second half goes on, "For it is God who worketh in you"—which looks as if God did everything and we nothing. I am afraid that is the sort of thing we come up against in Christianity. I am puzzled, but I am not surprised. You see, we are now trying to understand, and to separate into water-tight compartments, what exactly God does and what man does when God and man are working together. And, of

But Lewis sets up a false equivalency here. Pure Pelagianism cannot accommodate both statements. Augustinianism has always been able to, however: "[Lord,] give what Thou commandest, and command what Thou wilt."[17] It was this statement by Augustine, itself almost a paraphrase of Philippians 2:12–13, that provoked Pelagius in the first place. Thus, if Lewis is embracing both sides of Philippians 2:12–13, he is Augustinian through and through. Moreover, it doesn't seem that we can reverse Paul's two statements; the word "for" at the beginning of the second statement (2:13) prohibits it. We work out our salvation *because* God is at work within. The reverse—God is at work within because we are already working it out—would be a significantly different statement. Lewis himself knows the importance of this order. In *The Silver Chair*, Aslan tells Jill, "You would not have called me, if I had not first been calling you."[18] The call of Aslan, the work of God, is "first." Whether we conceive of this temporally or in terms of logical priority, the point remains: God's actions precede and give rise to ours, not the other way around. Elsewhere the apostle captures the idea this way: "I worked harder than any of them, though it was not I, but the grace of God that is with me" (1 Cor. 15:10).

In *Letters to Malcolm*, Lewis broadens the picture to include not only the gracious acts of the saints but the acts of all creatures whatsoever. He calls this "the ontological continuity between Creator and creature" and notes that it "exists between God and a reprobate (or a devil) no less than between God and a saint."[19] Lewis is clear that this Creator-creature continuity is different from the "union of wills" that the saints, under grace, reach. Indeed, the ontological continuity between God and all his creatures is what accounts for the heinous sacrilege of sin.

> Every sin is the distortion of an energy breathed into us—an energy which, if not thus distorted, would have blossomed into one of those holy acts whereof "God did it" and "I did it" are both true descriptions. We poison the wine as He decants it into us; murder a melody He

---

course, we begin by thinking it is like two men working together, so that you could say, "He did this bit and I did that." But this way of thinking breaks down. God is not like that. He is inside you as well as outside: even if we could understand who did what, I do not think human language could properly express it.

17 Augustine, *Confessions* 39.40, in vol. 1 of *The Nicene and Post-Nicene Fathers*, series 1, ed. Philip Schaff (1886–1889; repr., Peabody, MA.: Hendrickson, 1994).
18 Lewis, *The Silver Chair*, 24.
19 Lewis, *Letters to Malcolm*, 69.

would play with us as the instrument. We caricature the self-portrait He would paint.[20]

Thus, again we see a tension in Lewis's view. On the one hand, the way he talks about the ontological continuity suggests that strictly causal thinking between God and man is somehow inappropriate. The continuity is too tight for the kind of separation required for a relation of cause and effect, as if God and man were simply two billiard balls, God being the (much larger) cue ball that bangs all of us around the table. On the other hand, whenever he talks about human free will, he appears to resort to causal thinking. He seems to suggest that if God governs our wills, then he causes our wills, and if he causes our wills, then we are robots, and robots are not worth creating.

Total Depravity

A similar tension or ambivalence is present in Lewis's view of the doctrine of total depravity, the Calvinistic teaching that "our rebellion against God is total, everything we do in this rebellion is sinful, our inability to submit to God or reform ourselves is total, and we are therefore totally deserving of eternal punishment."[21] In one place, he explicitly rejects the doctrine:

> This chapter will have been misunderstood if anyone describes it as a re-instatement of the doctrine of Total Depravity. I disbelieve that doctrine, partly on the logical ground that if our depravity were total we should not know ourselves to be depraved, and partly because experience shows us much goodness in human nature.[22]

As one writer on Lewis has said, this is not *total* depravity but *absolute* depravity.[23] Total depravity means that we human beings have been

---

20 Ibid.
21 John Piper, *Five Points: Toward a Deeper Experience of God's Grace* (Fearn, Ross-shire, Scotland: Christian Focus, 2013), 22. In this short booklet, Piper notes that

> the totality of that depravity is clearly not that man does as much evil as he could do. There is no doubt that man could perform more evil acts toward his fellow man than he does. But if he is restrained from performing more evil acts by motives that are not owing to his glad submission to God, then even his "virtue" is evil in the sight of God. Romans 14:23 says, "Whatever does not proceed from faith is sin". . . . This is a radical indictment of all natural "virtue" that does not flow from a heart humbly relying on God's grace. (Ibid. 17–18)

22 Lewis, *The Problem of Pain*, 61. It's worth highlighting that Lewis is very nuanced when it comes to defining the "goodness in human nature."
23 Douglas Wilson, "UnDragoned: C. S. Lewis on the Gift of Salvation," in *Romantic Rationalist: God, Life, and Imagination in the Work of C. S. Lewis*, ed. John Piper and David Mathis (Wheaton, IL: Crossway, 2014), 71. Wilson's chapter aims to show that Lewis was an asystematic adherent of historic Reformation theology.

marred in every aspect of our being. Mind and heart, reason and imagination, understanding and will—every part of us is tainted by sin, and our rebellion against God is total. But while the image of God has been marred, it has not been obliterated. Human beings are capable of much natural virtue in relation to other human beings, even if this natural virtue avails nothing with God since it does not rely on his strength or aim at his glory. What's more, there is a simple response to Lewis's logical objection to total depravity: the only reason we know ourselves to be depraved is that God has graciously revealed it to us. In fact, the Calvinism that Lewis rejects is also rejected by almost all of the Calvinists I've ever met.

But we can say more about Lewis and total depravity. Influenced as he was by Augustine, Lewis has a strong doctrine of sin as that which causes the soul to curve in on itself. Immediately after insisting that our sin is voluntary, he says that man has used that freedom to become "a horror to God and to himself."[24] We are "rebels who must lay down our arms."[25] Though we may cover it up, we still possess the self-will of childhood—"the bitter, prolonged rage at every thwarting, the burst of passionate tears, the black, Satanic wish to kill or die rather than to give in."[26] In fact, his doctrine of sin is so strong that Lewis knows people might call it "total depravity."[27] Furthermore, changing this self-will is beyond our control.

> I can to some extent control my acts: I have no direct control over my temperament. And if (as I said before) what we are matters even more than what we do—if, indeed, what we do matters chiefly as evidence of what we are—then it follows that the change which I most need to undergo is a change that my own direct, voluntary efforts cannot bring about. And this applies to my good actions too. How many of them were done for the right motive? How many for fear of public opinion, or a desire to show off? How many from a sort of obstinacy or sense of superiority which, in different circumstances, might equally have led to some very bad act? But I cannot, by direct moral effort, give myself new motives.[28]

As a Calvinist, I could hardly ask for a better description of the depth of human sin—we are unable to give ourselves new motives, and our motives are profoundly corrupt. And then we have the following two statements:

---

24 Lewis, *The Problem of Pain*, 63.
25 Ibid., 88.
26 Ibid., 89.
27 Lewis, *The Great Divorce*, 105.
28 Lewis, *Mere Christianity*, 192–93.

Now God, who has made us, knows what we are and that our happiness lies in Him. Yet we will not seek it in Him as long as He leaves us any other resort where it can even plausibly be looked for.[29]

If man could press one button on the radio of his experience and not hear the voice of God then he would always press that button and not the others.[30]

The first of those statements is from C. S. Lewis. The other is from Cornelius Van Til, a man no one has ever accused of being soft on total depravity.

Sovereign Grace

But the tension in Lewis's thought runs deeper, extending into his view of God's grace. If our situation is as desperate as Lewis says, if we cannot give ourselves new motives, then we must have intervention from outside. As we saw above, if we are to call on God, he must first call on us. "When you come to knowing God, the initiative lies on His side. If He does not show Himself, nothing you can do will enable you to find Him."[31] Of course, this divine initiative cannot cancel out human choice. Even Screwtape recognizes that God will not override the human will. "He cannot ravish. He can only woo. For His ignoble idea is to eat the cake and have it; the creatures are to be one with Him, but yet themselves; merely to cancel them, or assimilate them, will not serve."[32] But now we are simply back to affirming that the statements "God did it" and "I did it" are both true.

Lewis places this note of sovereign grace in his writings because he experienced it himself. In one of the last interviews of his life, Lewis was asked whether, in conversion, he made a decision for Christ. His response reflects the priority of sovereign grace:

I would not put it that way. What I wrote in *Surprised by Joy* was that "before God closed in on me, I was offered what now appears a moment of wholly free choice." But I feel my decision was not so important. I was the object rather than the subject in this affair. I was decided upon. I was glad afterwards at the way it came out, but at the moment what I heard was God saying, "Put down your gun and we'll talk."

[29] Lewis, *The Problem of Pain*, 94.
[30] Cornelius Van Til, *Common Grace and the Gospel*, 2nd ed., ed. K. Scott Oliphint (Phillipsburg, NJ: P&R, 2015), 203.
[31] Lewis, *Mere Christianity*, 164.
[32] Lewis, *The Screwtape Letters*, 48.

The interviewer interjects, "That sounds to me as if you came to a very definite point of decision." Lewis responds: "Well, I would say that the most deeply compelled action is also the freest action. By that I mean, no part of you is outside the action. It is a paradox. I expressed it in *Surprised by Joy* by saying that I chose, yet it really did not seem possible to do the opposite."[33]

He did not make a decision; he was "decided upon." His longer account in *Surprised by Joy* is worth quoting at length:

> The odd thing was that before God closed in on me, I was in fact offered what now appears a moment of wholly free choice. In a sense. I was going up Headington Hill on the top of a bus. Without words and (I think) almost without images, a fact about myself was somehow presented to me. I became aware that I was holding something at bay, or shutting something out. Or, if you like, that I was wearing some stiff clothing, like corsets, or even a suit of armor, as if I were a lobster. I felt myself being, there and then, given a free choice. I could open the door or keep it shut; I could unbuckle the armor or keep it on. Neither choice was presented as a duty; no threat or promise was attached to either, though I knew that to open the door or to take off the corset meant the incalculable. The choice appeared to be momentous but it was also strangely unemotional. I was moved by no desires or fears. In a sense I was not moved by anything. I chose to open, to unbuckle, to loosen the rein. I say, "I chose," yet it did not really seem possible to do the opposite. On the other hand, I was aware of no motives. You could argue that I was not a free agent, but I am more inclined to think that this came nearer to being a perfectly free act than most that I have ever done. Necessity may not be the opposite of freedom, and perhaps a man is most free when, instead of producing motives, he could only say, "I am what I do."[34]

Freedom (i.e., voluntary choices) and necessity are not opposites; they merge together. They do not cancel each other out, but instead run together. They are, as many theologians argue, compatible.

Perseverance and Preservation

We find the same mystery in Lewis's treatment of the question of perseverance and assurance. For example, in *Screwtape*, the patient "becomes

33 Lewis, "Cross-Examination," in *God in the Dock*, 261.
34 Lewis, *Surprised by Joy*, 224–25.

a Christian" sometime between the first and second letters. However, it's clear from the rest of the correspondence that the patient is still capable of being damned; the whole point of Screwtape's counsel and Wormwood's temptations is to reclaim the patient after a brief sojourn in the camp of the saints. This suggests that it is possible for the patient to "lose" his salvation. And in *Mere Christianity*, Lewis writes:

> The world does not consist of 100 [percent] Christians and 100 [percent] non-Christians. There are people (a great many of them) who are slowly ceasing to be Christians but who still call themselves by that name: some of them are clergymen. There are other people who are slowly becoming Christians though they do not yet call themselves so.[35]

For Lewis, the danger of apostasy is real.

At the same time, he recognizes that the Bible speaks of our salvation as an unchanging reality. "He who began a good work in you will bring it to completion at the day of Jesus Christ" (Phil. 1:6). "No one will snatch them out of my hand" (John 10:28). "[Nothing] will be able to separate us from the love of God in Christ Jesus" (Rom. 8:38–39). And so, when asked about how to reconcile these competing tendencies, Lewis encourages us to live in the mystery:

> The best I can do about these mysteries is to think that the N.T. gives us a sort of double vision. A. Into our salvation as eternal fact, as it (and all else) is in the timeless vision of God. B. Into the same thing as a process worked out in time. Both must be true in some sense but it is beyond our capacity to envisage both together. Can one get a faint idea of it by thinking of A. A musical score as it is written down with all the notes there at once. B. The same thing played as a process in time? For practical purposes, however, it seems to me we must usually live by the second vision "working out our own salvation in fear and trembling" (but it adds "for"—not "though"—but "for"—"it is God who worketh in us").
>
> And in this temporal process surely God saves different souls in different ways? To preach instantaneous conversion and eternal security as if they must be the experiences of all who are saved, seems to me very dangerous: the very way to drive some into presumption and others into despair. How very different were the callings of the disciples.[36]

35 Lewis, *Mere Christianity*, 208.
36 Lewis to Stuart Robertson, May 6, 1962, in *Collected Letters*, 3:1336–37. In saying this, Lewis is essentially channeling Chesterton: "His spiritual sight is stereoscopic, like his physical sight: he sees two

As we saw earlier, Lewis acknowledges the double vision created by God's will and our will. The eternal reality is the deeper of the two, but in our present condition, we must (usually) live by the second vision, recognizing that however we explain "falling away" from God's perspective, it is in fact possible for us make shipwreck of our faith. The choice of ways is always before *us*. Yet it seemed good to God for us to know about the eternal perspective and the reality of his power to keep us. Thus, we might say that we should live by the second vision (the temporal process), while resting and hoping in the first (the living hope that our salvation is secure). As always, Lewis is alert to twin dangers: we might proudly presume that because "once saved, always saved," we can live as we wish, or we might despair of ever finding salvation because our experience of the newness and freedom of the Christian life doesn't match the exalted language of New Testament.

The Mystery of God's Will and Ours

In living with this tension, Lewis seeks to avoid two significant errors. On the one hand, he everywhere resists the notion that our wills are somehow compelled by an outside force, as though we were forced to act "against our will." Our choices, if we are to be responsible for them, must be voluntary. Lose the voluntary nature of our choices and you lose human responsibility altogether. On the other hand, he is also very aware of the danger of making God passive in relation to human beings. Saying that God *knows* but does not *ordain* our actions runs the risk of compromising God's impassibility—the doctrine, related to divine immutability and affirmed throughout the history of the church, that God does not suffer change. "God, we believe, is impassible. All theology would reject the idea of a transaction in which a creature was the agent and God the patient."[37] To try to reverse this order is to make an assault on "the grammar of being."[38] At the same time, Lewis does propose "two way traffic at the junction" where the Creator meets the creature.[39]

---

different pictures at once and yet sees all the better for that. Thus he has always believed that there was such a thing as fate, but such a thing as free will also" (G. K. Chesterton, *Orthodoxy* [Chicago: Moody Publishers, 2009], 47).

[37] Lewis, *Letters to Malcolm*, 48.

[38] "For we are only creatures: our role must always be that of patient to agent, female to male, mirror to light, echo to voice. Our highest activity must be response, not initiative. To experience the love of God in a true, and not an illusory form, is therefore to experience it as our surrender to His demand, our conformity to His desire: to experience it in the opposite way is, as it were, a solecism against the grammar of being" (Lewis, *The Problem of Pain*, 44).

[39] Lewis, *Letters to Malcolm*, 50.

Thus, what I have described as a tension in Lewis is really a mystery in the proper theological sense of the word.[40] And since theology at its most basic consists in putting the mystery in the right place, my own sense is that Lewis is attempting to do just that. If there is an agent-patient relation between God and his creatures, God must be the agent, and we the patient. No true reversal of this relationship is possible. God is the Maker; we are the made. He is active; we are passive. He gives; we receive. And yet one of the things that he gives us is real moral agency. We are beings whose choices really matter, both to us and to others. Something momentous (indeed, nearly everything) really does hang upon our decisions.

But Lewis does not leave us simply with a bare mystery. He furnishes us with greater insight on how the mystery works (without, of course, removing it entirely). And he does so with the repeated use of the analogy I mentioned in an earlier chapter: God is an Author; the world is his story; we are his characters. For our present purposes, the analogy cuts right through the tension between God's will and ours. Saying "God did it" and "I did it" about the same action is no contradiction, since an author's actions do not cancel out the actions of his characters. "God can no more be in competition with a creature than Shakespeare can be in competition with Viola."[41]

Managerial God or Exhaustive Sovereignty?

What's more, the Author-story analogy enables us to avoid a misunderstanding of God's exhaustive sovereignty. For example, we often view God's governance of the world like that of a king over his subjects and then fight over how extensive his rule is. Those who emphasize human freedom

---

[40] In a letter to Mary Van Deusen, Lewis himself calls the whole question insoluble and urges Mary to leave it alone.

> All that Calvinist question—Free-Will & Predestination, is to my mind undiscussable, insoluble. Of course (say us) if a man repents God will accept him. Ah yes, (say they) but the fact of his repenting shows that God has already moved him to do so. This at any rate leaves us with the fact that in any concrete case the question never arrives as a practical one. But I suspect it is really a meaningless question. The difference between Freedom & Necessity is fairly clear on the bodily level: we know the difference between making our teeth chatter on purpose & just finding them chattering with cold. It begins to be less clear when we talk of human love (leaving out the erotic kind). "Do I like him because I choose or because I must?"—there are cases where this has an answer, but others where it seems to me to mean nothing. When we carry it up to relations between God & Man, has the distinction perhaps become nonsensical? After all, when we are most free, it is only with a freedom God has given us: and when our will is most influenced by Grace, it is still our will. And if what our will does is not "voluntary," and if "voluntary" does not mean "free," what are we talking about? I'd leave it all alone. (Lewis to Mary Van Deusen, October 20, 1952, in *Collected Letters*, 3:237)

[41] Lewis, *The Problem of Pain*, 42.

accuse those who emphasize divine sovereignty of making God into a micromanaging tyrant, while those who emphasize sovereignty accuse free-willers of making God an absentee landlord who is passive before his creatures. Lewis cuts through this debate by rejecting the entire image of the managerial God.

In *Letters to Malcolm*, he addresses the view that God works only by general laws, that we can distinguish between God's overall plan and the by-products of that plan which he does not intend. Lewis acknowledges that the distinction between a plan and its unintended consequence is true of us as creatures. But it has no meaning when applied to God. "I suggest that the distinction between plan and by-product must vanish entirely on the level of omniscience, omnipotence, and perfect goodness." Lewis mocks the notion that God is like a human ruler or a manager, as though, "if He ever considered me individually, He would begin by saying, 'Gabriel, bring me Mr. Lewis's file.'" The God of the Bible is bigger and grander than this. "I will not believe in the Managerial God and his general laws. If there is Providence at all, everything is providential and every providence is a special providence."[42]

At the same time, Lewis rejects the notion that God is a micromanaging busybody. Instead, Lewis says that God is more like a poet or composer of great genius, for whom every line and note is needed precisely in its place. Indeed, you can say (as Lewis does elsewhere) that the whole work was made for each note. If that is not exhaustive sovereignty, I don't know what is. Here is all my Calvinism: the whole of the divine symphony composed with such attentiveness and creativity that, taken as a whole, every part is in its place. And, of course, for Lewis, such theology is immensely practical.

> One of the purposes for which God instituted prayer may have been to bear witness that the course of events is not governed like a state but created like a work of art to which every being makes its contribution and (in prayer) a conscious contribution, and in which every being is both an end and a means. . . . The great work of art was made for the sake of all it does and is, down to the curve of every wave and the flight of every insect.[43]

In addition, the Author-story analogy dovetails perfectly with Lewis's view of eternity and time.

---

[42] Lewis, *Letters to Malcolm*, 55.
[43] Ibid., 55–56.

Suppose I am writing a novel. I write "Mary laid down her work; next moment came a knock at the door!" For Mary who has to live in the imaginary time of my story there is no interval between putting down the work and hearing the knock. But I, who am Mary's maker, do not live in that imaginary time at all. Between writing the first half of that sentence and the second, I might sit down for three hours and think steadily about Mary. I could think about Mary as if she were the only character in the book and for as long as I pleased, and the hours I spent in doing so would not appear in Mary's time (the time inside the story) at all. This is not a perfect illustration, of course. But it may give just a glimpse of what I believe to be the truth. God is not hurried along in the Time-stream of this universe any more than an author is hurried along in the imaginary time of his own novel. He has infinite attention to spare for each one of us.[44]

When the Author Writes Himself into the Story

The Author-story analogy also allows us to press further into the tension in Lewis's own view. As we noted in chapter 2, God is able to write himself into his own story. Thus, God relates to us both as Author and as fellow character. From his eternal vantage point as Author, God takes all of our decisions into account. He weaves them into his story, works them into his symphony, determines each one in its proper place. Our decisions cannot simply be reduced to God's decisions, as in pantheism; ours are really and truly *ours*. But neither can they (or we) be "enisled" (made into an independent island) from God. Such discontinuity would simply be annihilation. Our choices are ours, but as Lewis reminds us more than once, all things are more ours for being his.[45]

At the same time, God relates to us as a character in his story, wooing us and drawing us without doing any violence to our wills. In this sense, he watches and waits for us to make our choice. He offers us salvation, he pleads with us to accept it. But he does not overpower or override our will. As a fellow character (indeed, as the main character in this story), he gives us the full dignity of free moral agents. And, as we saw earlier, not only does he dignify human beings by treating us as free and responsible beings; he also becomes one of us. He elevates humanity by becoming a fellow human character. The miracles in the gospel "announce not merely that a King has

---

[44] Lewis, *Mere Christianity*, 167–68.
[45] Lewis, *Letters to Malcolm*, 69.

visited our town, but that it is *the* King, *our* King."[46] And now we can see how the distinction between God-as-Author and God-as-character enables us to fold back in the biblical image of God as King, which the managerial perspective calls into question. God the Author is telling a story. The main character in this story is a King, a divine King, who rules his realm with peace and justice. But like all good stories, God's story has conflict. A rebel lord seduces the King's subjects away from him and makes them his slaves, twisting them to his will. But the divine King will not leave his subjects to rot. The divine King, at great cost to himself, slays the dark lord and liberates his people. Or, if you prefer, kills the dragon to get the girl.

Living in the Mystery

Lewis lives in the mystery of God's exhaustive sovereignty and man's true freedom. He feels the tension, and he refuses to let one side of the tension override the other. As a result, he challenges Christians of all theological convictions. To those who would exalt human freedom at the expense of total sovereignty, Lewis essentially says: "God is the ground of our being. He is always both within us and over against us. There is no conflict between God doing an action and you doing it, any more than Shakespeare's authorship threatens the integrity of Hamlet. God is the Author who invented all, the Producer who controls all, and the Audience who observes and will judge all. Every providence is a special providence." And to those of us who love the exhaustive sovereignty of God, Lewis insists that we not forget the eternal significance of our choices. Everything may be determined in God's single act of creation. Every note may be established in God's single act of composition. But history is the actual performance of the symphony. Time is the lens through which we see the awesome gift of our freedom, and therefore the fundamental question that confronts every human being—the question on which everything hangs—is how we respond to the arrival of the King.

---

[46] Lewis, "Miracles," in *God in the Dock*, 32.

CHAPTER 9

PRIDE AND HUMILITY

Enjoying and Contemplating Ourselves

If I am being honest, one of my besetting sins is anxiety. I'm by nature a planner; I like to think about and anticipate the future. But since the future is often so uncertain, it's easy to worry about what's to come. The number of unknown possibilities can easily oppress someone like me. If I'm not careful, the *what if*'s of life can overwhelm me.

In the sixth Screwtape letter, Lewis exposes the true temptation of anxiety and provides us with a means to fight it. The devils love to fill our minds with maximum uncertainty. They want us to be fixated on the many different and contradictory pictures of the future that they parade before our minds. They encourage us to forget that it's impossible for all our fears to happen to us. Instead, they stoke our anxieties so that we try to fortify ourselves against all of them at once. This temptation is so effective because, as Christians, we know that God calls us to endure trials. "Through many tribulations we must enter the kingdom" (Acts 14:22). And so we try to prepare for all of the possible trials that may confront us in the coming days, weeks, months, and years.

But in preparing for the possible (and incompatible) future trials, we often neglect to bear up faithfully under the actual trial confronting us right now—the trial of not knowing the future. God does want us to be patient in tribulation. But for worriers like me, anxiety *is* the present tribulation. The anxiety itself—the not knowing—is our present cross, not all the things we don't (and can't) know. "It is about *this* that he is to say 'Thy will be done,' and for the daily task of bearing *this* that the daily bread will be provided."[1]

Lewis's wisdom, expressed in the mouth of Screwtape, is essentially an extension of Christ's words about worry, "Therefore do not be anxious about tomorrow, for tomorrow will be anxious for itself. Sufficient for the day is its own trouble" (Matt. 6:34). If you find yourself worried about whether you'll be able to face whatever happens to you tomorrow, remind yourself that the way to prepare for tomorrow's trials is to humbly and cheerfully confront today's. In other words, recognize the present anxiety as today's cross, and deny yourself, take it up, while entrusting your future to God. This is the spiritual law that will help us to overcome anxiety.

Looking At and Looking Along

The spiritual law at work in the situation above may be extended far beyond anxiety and worry. This law or principle is rooted in a distinction that is integral to all of Lewis's thought. He explores this distinction in an essay called "Meditation in a Toolshed."

> I was standing today in the dark toolshed. The sun was shining outside and through the crack at the top of the door there came a sunbeam. From where I stood that beam of light, with the specks of dust floating in it, was the most striking thing in the place. Everything else was almost pitch-black. I was seeing the beam, not seeing things by it.
>
> Then I moved, so that the beam fell on my eyes. Instantly the whole previous picture vanished. I saw no toolshed, and (above all) no beam. Instead I saw, framed in the irregular cranny at the top of the door, green leaves moving on the branches of a tree outside and beyond that, 90 odd million miles away, the sun. Looking along the beam, and looking at the beam are very different experiences.[2]

There are two different ways of thinking about our experience of the world. "Looking at" the beam is the attempt to get outside an experience in

---

[1] Lewis, *The Screwtape Letters*, 34. Later Screwtape underscores that our duties are always given to us in the present: "He would therefore have them continually concerned either with eternity (which means being concerned with Him) or with the Present—either meditating on their eternal union with, or separation from, Himself, or else obeying the present voice of conscience, bearing the present cross, receiving the present grace, giving thanks for the present pleasure" (ibid., 88).
[2] Lewis, "Meditation in a Toolshed," in *God in the Dock*, 230.

order to analyze it "objectively," whereas "looking along" the beam is the same experience "from the inside." A man in love with a woman is "looking along" the beam of love; a scientist studying the man's experience in terms of hormones and chemical reactions is "looking at" the experience of love from the outside. A young girl cries over her broken doll; she is experiencing the loss from the inside. A psychologist would describe the same event in terms of nascent maternal instincts projected onto plastic. Lewis's purpose in the essay is to challenge the modern tendency to treat "looking at" as inherently more valid and true than "looking along." "The people who 'look at' things have had it all their own way; the people who look along things have simply been brow-beaten." And the browbeating, Lewis says, must end. Both experiences are needed: "One must look both *along* and *at* everything."[3]

Now, as I said, this distinction is, in many ways, integral to all of Lewis's thought. Elsewhere he describes it as the difference between enjoying something and contemplating it. Enjoyment is the experience from the inside, contemplation the view from without. Lewis adopts the distinction from philosopher Samuel Alexander.

> I read in Alexander's Space Time and Deity his theory of "Enjoyment" and "Contemplation." These are technical terms in Alexander's philosophy; "Enjoyment" has nothing to do with pleasure, nor "Contemplation" with the contemplative life. When you see a table you "enjoy" the act of seeing and "contemplate" the table. Later, if you took up Optics and thought about Seeing itself, you would be contemplating the seeing and enjoying the thought. In bereavement you contemplate the beloved and the beloved's death and, in Alexander's sense, "enjoy" the loneliness and grief; but a psychologist, if he were considering you as a case of melancholia, would be contemplating your grief and enjoying psychology. We do not "think a thought" in the same sense in which we "think that Herodotus is unreliable." When we think a thought, "thought" is a cognate accusative (like "blow" in "strike a blow"). We enjoy the thought (that Herodotus is unreliable) and, in so doing, contemplate the unreliability of Herodotus. I accepted this distinction at once and have ever since regarded it as an indispensable tool of thought.[4]

Here we see how we are always engaged in both enjoyment and contemplation. That is, we are always enjoying some *act*, and contemplating or

---

[3] Ibid., 232.
[4] Lewis, *Surprised by Joy*, 217–18.

attending to some *object*. We can never escape from them. As Lewis says in "Meditation in a Toolshed," "You can step outside one experience only by stepping inside another."[5] Nevertheless, while we are always enjoying and contemplating, we can never do both of them simultaneously *in the same sense* or *about the same object*. As in the case of anxiety, this latter truth has significant ramifications for our spiritual lives. For example, the distinction is relevant for our attempts at self-examination.

Self-Examination

Lewis writes:

> The enjoyment and the contemplation of our inner activities are incompatible. You cannot hope and also think about hoping at the same moment; for in hope we look to hope's object and we interrupt this by (so to speak) turning round to look at the hope itself. Of course the two activities can and do alternate with great rapidity; but they are distinct and incompatible.[6]

Self-examination is like "stepping out of life into the Alongside and looking at [myself] living as if [I] were not alive."[7] Every Christian has experienced something like it. You're in a church service, and in the midst of the singing, you are caught up in your heart and mind to God. You are adoring him. That is, you are enjoying the act of worship, as you contemplate the living God (he is the object of your attention). But then something happens. Your inner voice interrupts the enjoyment, and immediately you, as it were, step outside yourself and contemplate the act of worship itself. "What exactly is going on here?" the inner voice asks. "Oh, do shut up," you reply. "You just ruined it." "The surest way of spoiling a pleasure," says Lewis, "[is] to start examining your satisfaction."[8]

Of course, examining our satisfaction doesn't have to spoil our pleasure. The move from "I love you, God" to "Look, I'm loving God right now" may dampen the love. But it may also increase it. It may produce pride ("What a spiritual person I must be to worship God in this way"). Or it may produce gratitude ("What a wonderful gift this time of worship is"). We may

---

[5] Lewis, "Meditation in a Toolshed," in *God in the Dock*, 232.
[6] Lewis, *Surprised by Joy*, 218–19.
[7] Lewis, *Perelandra*, 52.
[8] Lewis, *Surprised by Joy*, 218–19.

slide from adoration (the contemplation of God himself) into gratitude (the contemplation of his gift of worship). But gratitude can just as easily lead us back to adoration. We look along the beam while we look at God, and then we take a moment (it need only be brief) to step outside to look at the beam itself. Then, with a sincere "thank you," we follow the beam back up and contemplate God again, renewed and enlarged by the gratitude for his gift.

But contemplating our inner activities can aid us in the Christian life in another way. Sometimes our pleasures need to be spoiled. "The surest means of disarming an anger or a lust was to turn your attention from the girl or the insult and start examining the passion itself."[9] This is how we fought anxiety earlier: we turned our attention away from the future possibilities that created the worry and instead turned our attention to the worry itself. Stepping outside the experience allows us to gain perspective, to diffuse the passion of the moment so that we can, as they say, "get a grip."

The Great Sin of Pride

Which brings us back to Screwtape, and his attempts to use this distinction to lead us away from God.

> In all activities of mind which favour our [demonic] cause, encourage the patient to be unselfconscious and to concentrate on the object, but in all activities favourable to the Enemy bend his mind back on itself. Let an insult or a woman's body so fix his attention outward that he does not reflect "I am now entering into the state called Anger—or the state called Lust." Contrariwise let the reflection "My feelings are now growing more devout, or more charitable" so fix his attention inward that he no longer looks beyond himself to see our Enemy or his own neighbours.[10]

We've seen how self-examination—contemplating our inner activities—enables us to kill our sin. But as Screwtape notes, it can also kill our virtues. When we begin to grow devout or charitable, we are ever in danger of noticing our progress and taking pride in it. And pride, as Lewis insists, is the great sin, the worst of sins, the utmost evil. It is the essential vice, the fountain whence all other sins spring. "Pride is spiritual cancer: it eats up the very possibility of love, or contentment, or even common sense."[11]

---

9 Ibid., 219.
10 Lewis, *The Screwtape Letters*, 35.
11 Lewis, *Mere Christianity*, 125.

> Pride is *essentially* competitive. . . . Pride gets no pleasure out of having
> something, only out of having more of it than the next man. We say
> that people are proud of being rich, or clever, or good-looking, but they
> are not. They are proud of being richer, or cleverer, or better-looking
> than others.[12]

Thus, pride "always means enmity—it *is* enmity." "If I am a proud man,
then, as long as there is one man in the whole world more powerful, or
richer, or cleverer than I, he is my rival and my enemy."[13] It is pride, not
lust, that often leads a pretty girl to collect admirers; she loves the thrill of
the power it gives her. For pride loves power; it loves to be able to push others around like toy soldiers or lead them around like puppies. That is why
pride "has been the chief cause of misery in every nation and every family
since the world began."[14]

But pride doesn't just set us against other men; it sets us against God. It
is the "complete anti-God state of mind." Thus, pride keeps us from knowing God. "A proud man is always looking down on things and people: and,
of course, as long as you are looking down, you cannot see something that
is above you."[15]

What's more, pride is so subtle that it can work itself into the most
virtuous of our actions. Amazingly, it can even attach itself to our humility. Screwtape encourages this precisely in terms of enjoyment and
contemplation.

> Your patient has become humble; have you drawn his attention to the
> fact? All virtues are less formidable to us once the man is aware that he
> has them, but this is specially true of humility. Catch him at the moment
> when he is really poor in spirit and smuggle into his mind the gratifying
> reflection, "By jove! I'm being humble," and almost immediately pride—
> pride at his own humility—will appear. If he awakes to the danger and
> tries to smother this new form of pride, make him proud of his attempt—
> and so on, through as many stages as you please.[16]

This is the diabolical way that contemplation kills our virtues. It fixes
our attention on humility rather than on God, who is humbling us. In hu-

[12] Ibid., 122.
[13] Ibid., 123.
[14] Ibid., 123–24.
[15] Ibid., 124.
[16] Lewis, *The Screwtape Letters*, 81–82.

mility, we recognize ourselves to be the foremost of sinners and then turn right around and take pride in being the chief.

Confusions about Pride and Humility

But pride in our humility is not the only danger; we can also fall prey to two confusions—one about pride and one about humility. The first confusion is to regard any pleasure in being praised or admired as a form of pride. But this is quite clearly not true. To enter heaven, we must become like children. And few things are more childlike than an innocent and undisguised pleasure in being praised by someone you've wanted (rightly) to please. This type of pleasure—the pleasure of the inferior before his superior— shows itself in a dog who loves to please his master, a child eager for his father's approval, a pupil hoping for high marks from his teacher.

Of course, this humble pleasure in being praised can quickly go wrong. It may turn into "the deadly poison of self-admiration."[17] But this trouble comes only when we move from thinking, "I have pleased the one I wanted to please" to "What a fine person I must be to have done it." The delight migrates from our Father's praise to ourselves, and we become vain. Worse still, if unchecked, our vanity continues its dark path until we no longer care for the opinions of others at all. "Why should I care for the applause of that rabble as if their opinion were worth anything? . . . They're nothing to me."[18]

But there is another path that the pleasure in being praised might take. We might see it as an anticipation of the final reckoning, "when the redeemed soul, beyond all hope and nearly beyond belief, learns at last that she has pleased Him whom she was created to please." On that day, there will be no room for vanity or self-approval; neither will there be room for modesty. "Perfect humility dispenses with modesty. If God is satisfied with the work, the work may be satisfied with itself; 'it is not for her to bandy compliments with her Sovereign.'"[19] The little fleeting glimpses of this pleasure that we receive in this life are only the briefest of anticipations of the day when we hear (can it be?) the Creator of all things say, "Well done, good and faithful servant. . . . Enter into the joy of your master" (Matt. 25:23)—a joy which apparently (wonder of wonders) includes us as a real ingredient in the divine happiness.

---

[17] Lewis, "The Weight of Glory," in *The Weight of Glory and Other Addresses*, 37.
[18] Lewis, *Mere Christianity*, 126.
[19] Lewis, "The Weight of Glory," in *The Weight of Glory and Other Addresses*, 38.

But I mentioned that there were two confusions. The other is a confusion about humility. People often think that a humble person is a greasy, smarmy sort of person who is always talking about how low he is. On this view, humble people are always running down their own talents and efforts. Often they are incapable of receiving a compliment. Try to tell them you sincerely appreciate something they've done, and you'll watch their faces contort as they try to dismiss your praise as quickly as possible. Who among us hasn't been on the giving (or receiving) end of compliments when this peculiarly Christian awkwardness descends?

The devils, of course, encourage this confusion. They want us to think that humility means having a low opinion of our talents and character (especially our *real* talents and character). They want to introduce an element of dishonesty into our opinions.

> By this method thousands of humans have been brought to think that humility means pretty women trying to believe they are ugly and clever men trying to believe they are fools. And since what they are trying to believe may, in some cases, be manifest nonsense, they cannot succeed in believing it and we have the chance of keeping their minds endlessly revolving on themselves in an effort to achieve the impossible.[20]

True Humility

Lewis refuses to let this faux humility, or semi-humility, stand for the real thing. If forced to choose between thinking very highly of ourselves and thinking that we are very small and dirty objects, we ought to choose the latter. But it is better not to think of ourselves at all. For this is what humility truly is: blessed self-forgetfulness. Three features mark Lewis's view of true, self-forgetful humility.

First, we are humble when we are able to admire something other than ourselves with cheerful innocence and without guile. "To love and admire anything outside yourself is to take one step away from utter spiritual ruin." We might admire a sunset or a symphony or even a dime novel. In this sense, anything that takes us outside the prison of our own self-centeredness is fuel for humility. But true humility, true self-forgetfulness, cannot sustain itself on admiration of created things. Such admiration will inevitably turn back inward into pride. We need stronger medicine. "We

---

[20] Lewis, *The Screwtape Letters*, 83.

shall not be well so long as we love and admire anything more than we love and admire God."[21]

Second, self-forgetfulness is able to enjoy life and love others sincerely.

> If you meet a really humble man . . . probably all you will think about him is that he seemed a cheerful, intelligent chap who took a real interest in what *you* said to *him*. If you do dislike him it will be because you feel a little envious of anyone who seems to enjoy life so easily. He will not be thinking about humility: he will not be thinking about himself at all.[22]

The humble man laughs easily, even at his own expense, like the Jackdaw in *The Magician's Nephew*, who didn't just make the first joke but instead *became* the first joke. For it is only "the devil . . . the prowde spirit . . . [that] cannot endure to be mocked."[23] This is why Screwtape chafes at the notion that the patient's new love interest, who happens to be a sincere Christian, is the sort of person who would find him funny. It's also why, in telling Wormwood to stoke pride in the patient's humility, Screwtape urges him not to overdo it, lest "you awake his sense of humour and proportion, in which case he will merely laugh at you and go to bed."[24]

Finally, the self-forgetful person loses his sense of ownership in his own works. This is the true aim of humility. God "wants to bring [us] to a state of mind in which [we] could design the best cathedral in the world, and know it to be the best, and rejoice in the fact, without being any more (or less) or otherwise glad at having done it than [we] would be if it had been done by another."[25] He wants to free us from self-admiration and conceit and bias in our own favor, so that we are able to rejoice in our own talents as cheerfully and honestly as we can in our neighbor's (or in a sunrise, an elephant, or a waterfall).

Self-Forgetfulness in *The Great Divorce*

Lewis displays the beauty of self-forgetfulness throughout his writings.[26] But all three of these elements show up clearly in a conversation between a ghost and a spirit in *The Great Divorce*. In Lewis's imaginary supposal about

---

21 Lewis, *Mere Christianity*, 127.
22 Ibid., 128.
23 Lewis, *The Screwtape Letters*, xlv.
24 Ibid., 82.
25 Ibid., 83.
26 I devote chap. 11 of *Live Like a Narnian: Christian Discipleship in Lewis's Chronicles* (Minneapolis: Eyes & Pen, 2013) to exploring self-forgetfulness and humility in *The Horse and His Boy*.

the afterlife, the spirits or saints in heaven are the "solid people," whereas the damned souls who have come from hell to the doorstep of heaven are ghosts. The typical pattern is that a ghost meets one of the solid people (usually someone he knew on earth), and the spirit tries to persuade the ghost to turn from a particular sin and stay in the high countries.

In this particular conversation, both the ghost and the spirit were semi-famous artists on earth. The ghost looks around at the solid and beautiful lands of the Valley of the Shadow of Life and is astonished. "I should like to paint this," he says. The spirit tells him that it's no good trying to paint at the present moment; seeing comes first. Painting is necessary on earth because through it we enable others to see glimpses of heaven in earthly landscapes. But there's no need for that in heaven, since the solid people already see heaven much better than the ghosts do. "At present your business is to see. Come and see. He is endless. Come and feed." The ghost goes along reluctantly, and he and the spirit have a conversation about the purpose of painting. The ghost argues that real artists see the country only for the purpose of painting. The spirit reminds him that that's not true: "That was not how you began. Light itself was your first love: you loved paint only as a means of telling about light."[27] This is the first aspect of humility: learning to admire something outside of you for its own sake (and not for the sake of your own self-advancement). And it's the opposite of the hellish attitude: "Every poet and musician and artist, but for Grace, is drawn away from love of the thing he tells, to love of the telling till, down in Deep Hell, they cannot be interested in God at all but only in what they say about Him."[28]

The second element—the easy enjoyment of life, expressed especially in laughter, even at one's own expense—shows up a few times in the conversation. The spirit breaks into laughter as he corrects the ghost's view of painting. More importantly, later in the conversation, the two are discussing the artistic lust for a good reputation. The ghost initially said that he was not concerned with his own fame or reputation. But as the two journey toward the mountains, the ghost looks forward to meeting famous and interesting artists in heaven, like Cézanne and Claude Monet. The spirit reminds him that in heaven, everyone is interesting and famous: "The Glory flows into everyone, and back from everyone: like light and mirrors. . . . They are all known, remembered, recognized by the only Mind that can

27 Lewis, *The Great Divorce*, 84.
28 Ibid., 85.

give a perfect judgement." Here, of course, is the theme "Well done, good and faithful servant." When the ghost, who doesn't much like the notion that there are no distinguished people in heaven, consoles himself with the words, "One must be content with one's reputation among posterity," the solid spirit, "shaking and shining with laughter," informs him that both of them have already been completely forgotten on earth. The fact that they are both "dead out of fashion" in Europe and America is a source of amusement for the spirit.[29]

Finally, in the midst of the conversation, the solid spirit holds out the promise of a cure for any remaining self-regard in the ghost's heart. The cure is drinking from a fountain, high in the mountains, that behaves like Lethe, the river of forgetfulness in Dante's *Divine Comedy*. "When you have drunk of it you forget forever all proprietorship in your own works. You enjoy them just as if they were someone else's: without pride and without modesty."[30] This is precisely the note struck earlier by Screwtape. "He wants each man, in the long run, to be able to recognise all creatures (even himself) as glorious and excellent things." And, in keeping with the overall theme of this book, the solid spirit in *The Great Divorce* describes this process as "growing into a Person." What's more, when we've grown into true persons, we'll see some things about God better than others. And one of the things we'll want to do is to tell others about them. And thus what we had to give up in order to find God (painting or writing or preaching or whatever) will be restored to us in glory. For God "always gives back . . . with His right hand what He has taken away with His left."[31]

To become humble and self-forgetful is to become truly human so that we might truly know God. God wants to give us himself. To do so, he must first kill our animal self-love. He must persuade us to take the fancy dress off, to get "rid of the false self, with all its 'Look at me' and 'Aren't I a good boy?' and all its posing and posturing."[32] When we do so, we discover "the infinite relief of having for once got rid of all the silly nonsense about [our] own dignity which has made [us] restless and unhappy all [our lives]."[33] But as great as this relief is, it's not even the end of the goodness. God is indeed endless, and he doesn't simply want to kill our animal self-love; more than that, he wants to restore to us a new kind of self-love—a charity and

---

[29] Ibid., 85–86.
[30] Ibid.
[31] Lewis, *The Screwtape Letters*, 84.
[32] Lewis, *Mere Christianity*, 128.
[33] Ibid., 127.

gratitude for all selves, including our own; when we have really learned to love our neighbors as ourselves, we will be allowed to love ourselves as our neighbors.

When we've become truly human, we will still enjoy and contemplate; we'll love and admire things outside ourselves. We'll even be able to love ourselves, as it were, from the outside. But we'll do so with no fear of pride and no threat to virtue. In the presence of God, we'll dispense with modesty and vanity; we won't fixate on our virtue and the good things that we've done.

> One has a glimpse of a country where they do not talk of [morality and virtue], except perhaps as a joke. Every one there is filled full with what we should call goodness as a mirror is filled with light. But they do not call it goodness. They do not call it anything. They are not thinking of it. They are too busy looking at the source from which it comes.[34]

Beholding the glory, we'll be transformed into the same image, from one degree of glory to another.

---

[34] Ibid., 149–50.

CHAPTER 10

CHRISTIAN HEDONICS

Beams of Glory and the Quest for Joy

"God is a hedonist at heart."[1] Screwtape's words sound shocking to our ears. God, a hedonist, a lover of pleasure? Could that be true?

The world would have us believe that God is the great forbidder, the cosmic killjoy. It is the devils who try to lead us into pleasures, in order to ensnare our souls. God calls us away from pleasure to self-denial and fasting.

But Screwtape (and Lewis) know better. The fasts and vigils and renunciation are only a facade; they are not the deepest reality. God *is* a hedonist. He made the pleasures, invented every last one of them. There is no such thing as a fundamentally diabolical pleasure. Hell has not been able to produce one. All demons can do is to twist legitimate pleasures by tempting us to enjoy them at times, or in ways, or in degrees that God has forbidden. When we speak of "bad pleasures," we mean "pleasures snatched by unlawful acts." "It is the stealing of the apple that is bad, not the sweetness,"[2] Lewis notes, channeling Augustine. In fact, the devils hate the sweetness of the apple; if they could remove pleasure from the process of sin, they would. Since they cannot completely eliminate pleasures and still draw us

[1] Lewis, *The Screwtape* Letters, 130.
[2] Lewis, *Letters to Malcolm*, 89.

into sin, they settle for making pleasures as unnatural as they can. They twist pleasures into a form that is least reminiscent of God himself, and therefore least pleasurable. As Screwtape says, "An ever increasing craving for an ever diminishing pleasure is the formula."[3]

Such is the diabolical strategy inherent in worldliness. The world tries to pawn off vanity, bustle, irony, and expensive tedium as pleasures; in reality, these are parodies and corruptions of pleasure as God designed it. Over time, the confusion of worldly, twisted pleasures with God's design for pleasures builds up a crust around the soul that prevents us from knowing God at all. Such small twisted pleasures are a great threat to the Christian life. Rather than commit acts of high defiance, we drift, almost passively and imperceptibly, away from God. As the crust around our souls builds up, we shy away from our spiritual duties. We grow reluctant to actually engage with God. Our sins become big enough to hinder prayer, but not large enough (so we think) to demand repentance. And so we drift and drift and drift.

The result is that the pleasures that pull us away from a vibrant trust in God become less and less pleasurable and yet harder and harder to resist. Worldliness hardens into habit. We practically beg for distractions, and between endless entertainment and constant social media, we never find them lacking. And so our best years are stolen from us, not by high defiance and exquisite sins, but

> in a dreary flickering of the mind over it knows not what and knows not why, in the gratification of curiosities so feeble that the man is only half aware of them, in drumming of fingers and kicking of heels, in whis-tling tunes that he does not like, or in the long, dim labyrinth of reveries that have not even lust or ambition to give them a relish, but which, once chance association has started them, the creature is too weak and fuddled to shake off.[4]

This is the safe and gradual road to hell—"the gentle slope, soft under-foot, without sudden turnings, without milestones, without signposts."[5] And judging by the present state of the world, this road is still broad and well traveled.

---

[3] Lewis, *The Screwtape Letters*, 53.
[4] Ibid., 73.
[5] Ibid.

The real threat of this gradual drift to hell is why we need to be re-minded that God is a hedonist at heart. He has scattered pleasures and mer-riment abroad. "He has filled His world full of pleasures. There are things for humans to do all day long without His minding in the least—sleep-ing, washing, eating, drinking, making love, playing, praying, working."[6] These are gifts from his right hand, intended for our enjoyment and our good. Even more, they are weapons in the fight of faith. Pleasure, like pain, is unmistakably real. Both give us "a touchstone of reality."[7]

Thus, real, positive pleasures are a protection and deliverance from worldliness. Worldly pleasures create a crust of vague, half-conscious guilt and triviality around our souls. Genuine pleasures, enjoyed without guile and without regard for the approval of others, puncture that crust. A walk in the countryside, playing a sport for the love of the game, a good book (or even a third-rate book enjoyed with innocence and self-forgetfulness)—all of these inoculate us against the twisted mockeries that dark powers offer up in their place.[8] They have the ability to shock us awake when the dreary music of the world has lulled us into a stupor.

Hedonics

If God is in fact a hedonist, it follows that Christians ought to be in some sense hedonists. This does not mean that we turn pleasure into the only good. Rather, it means, first of all, that we recognize God as the inventor and origin of all genuine pleasures. More than that, it means we ought to pay attention to pleasure. We ought to examine and study it. This science or philosophy of pleasure Lewis calls "Hedonics," and he regards it as a worthy endeavor. According to Lewis, the first step in Hedonics is to knock down what he calls "the Jailer." The jailer is the inner impulse that urges us to reject simple and seemingly trivial joys when they are offered us. The jailer is a "sham realist" who debunks pleasures as illusions and mirages. He ruins our joys by provoking anxiety or shaming us by calling us "childish."

---

[6] Ibid., 131.

[7] Ibid., 76.

[8] "I would make it a rule to eradicate from my patient any strong personal taste which is not actually a sin, even if it is something quite trivial such as a fondness for county cricket or collecting stamps or drinking cocoa. Such things, I grant you, have nothing of virtue in them; but there is a sort of innocence and humility and self-forgetfulness about them which I distrust. The man who truly and disinterestedly enjoys any one thing in the world, for its own sake, and without caring two-pence what other people say about it, is by that very fact forearmed against some of our subtlest modes of attack. You should always try to make the patient abandon the people or food or books he really likes in favour of the 'best' people, the 'right' food, the 'important' books" (ibid., 78–79).

Silencing this inner jailer is the first step in really understanding and en-joying our pleasures.[9]

Once we have done so, Lewis encourages us to accept the quiet and un-predicted invitations to joy that surprise as we pass through our otherwise normal lives. We should allow the simple pleasures to invade us and attend to "the murmur of life" and to discover there "all that quivering and wonder and (in a sense) infinity" that it carries.[10] To strengthen our enjoyment of pleasures, Lewis also calls us to contemplate them, to turn our attention to the quality and character of the particular pleasures themselves. Hedonics then has, as one of its goals, the cataloging and distinguishing of various kinds of pleasures.

For example, in *The Four Loves*, Lewis distinguishes between pleasures of appreciation and pleasures of need. A need-pleasure is the pleasure of a drink of water after a hot day in the sun, or a hearty meal after a long day's work, or (and this is an example Lewis himself gives) the feeling of joy when a gas station is found at just the right moment on a long road trip. The distinctive element of this pleasure is that it is preceded by desire and dies in the fulfillment of it. The thirst, once quenched, no longer demands or desires water. The lavatory no longer calls forth a "Hallelujah Chorus" once our business has been done.

Pleasures of appreciation, on the other hand, are not necessarily pre-ceded by desire or hunger or thirst. Pleasant smells, beautiful sights, de-lightful tastes—these are things we enjoy in their own right and not because of some need. They claim our appreciation by right. A man who enjoys a sweet smell "does not merely enjoy, he feels that this fragrance somehow *deserves* to be enjoyed."[11] Such pleasures *demand* that we respond; failure to do so would reveal some sort of defect in us. "The objects which afford pleasures of appreciation give us the feeling—whether irrational or not—that we somehow owe it to them to savour, to attend to and praise them."[12]

These simple pleasures of appreciation are "the starting point for our whole experience of beauty."[13] The sensuous pleasures of smell or sight or taste give way—we cannot draw a hard and fast line—to the higher aes-thetic pleasure of the landscape "as a whole." From there, the landscape broadens upward into some larger, more universal notion of beauty itself.

[9] Lewis, "Hedonics," in *Present Concerns*, 54–55.
[10] Ibid., 55.
[11] Lewis, *The Four Loves*, 13, italics mine.
[12] Ibid., 14.
[13] Ibid., 15.

These sorts of pleasures call us out of ourselves, make us "disinterested" lovers (or at least, appreciators) of the objects, meaning that our present enjoyment of an early morning lakeside scene is secondary to the sheer existence of the water and the trees and the fog themselves. As Lewis says, "We do not merely like the things; we pronounce them, in a momentarily God-like sense, 'very good.'"[14] We would rejoice in the wonder of the lake's existence even if we ourselves never got to visit it.

Making the distinction between need-pleasures and appreciative-pleasures is an exercise in Hedonics. The distinction is necessary because the category "pleasure" is too abstract to be of much use to us. We experience all pleasures as concrete; every joy is a particular joy, with a particular flavor or quality. One of Lewis's aims in his writings is to bring these different qualities home to us. For example, in his essay "Hedonics," he attempts to describe the particular pleasure of "seeing things the wrong way round . . . of seeing as an outside what is to others an inside."[15] He calls this the mirror pleasure, and the instance he provides is the pleasure one takes in other people's domesticities. You drive by homes in a place that is unlike your own home. You feel the strangeness and foreignness of these places; you are an outsider there. And yet (and this is where the pleasure comes for Lewis), you know that others feel perfectly at home there. They have the experience of intense familiarity in a place that feels to you like another planet. This, Lewis says, gave him an almost incalculable degree of happiness. (He refrains from describing the depth of his pleasure because he thinks we will assume him to be exaggerating.) Lewis spends the bulk of this essay attempting to make this pleasure real and imaginable to us.[16]

Or again, in another essay, he describes the particular joy he had as a boy when he went to the theater and imagined the difference between "the stage" and "behind the scenes." For him, the idea of this transition between the stage world and the backstage world was incredibly alluring. "To come from dressing rooms and bare walls and utilitarian corridors—and to come suddenly—into Aladdin's cave or the Darlings' nursery or whatever it was—to become what you weren't and be where you weren't—this seemed most enviable."[17]

As a boy, Lewis wished he could sit in the stage boxes, where he might,

---

[14] Ibid., 16.
[15] Lewis, "Hedonics," in *Present Concerns*, 52.
[16] Ibid., 50–55.
[17] Lewis, "Behind the Scenes," in *God in the Dock*, 246.

if he strained his neck, be able to see the stage and backstage at the same time. When he was older, he took great pleasure in standing on a wooden plank and looking out through a piece of canvas that, to the audience, appeared to be a palace with a balcony. In the essay, "Behind the Scenes," Lewis is attempting to explore the difference between the world as it appears to us (the stage), and the world "as it really is" (behind the scenes). He wishes to use this distinction to talk about scientific language and our access to reality. But his particular use of the distinction is not my point here. I'm simply drawing attention to Lewis's attempt to capture the quality and particularity of different pleasures. If God gives us pleasures from his right hand, then it seems we have a duty to know and study the gift.

Hedonics in *Perelandra*

In fact, we might say that this is one of Lewis's main goals in *Perelandra*, where he regularly tries to make paradise real to us by describing the different types of pleasure that Ransom experiences there. Here is a sampling:

- *When drinking the ocean:* "Though he had not been aware of thirst till now, his drink gave him a quite astonishing pleasure. It was almost like meeting pleasure itself for the first time."[18]
- *When smelling the flowers:* "The smells in the forest were beyond all that he had ever conceived. To say that they made him feel hungry and thirsty would be misleading; almost, they created a new kind of hunger and thirst, a longing that seemed to flow over from the body into the soul and which was a heaven to feel."[19]
- *When eating his first Perelandrian gourd:* "It was like the discovery of a totally new genus of pleasures, something unheard of among men, out of all reckoning, beyond all covenant. For one draft of this on Earth wars would be fought and nations betrayed. It could not be classified. He could never tell us, when he came back to the world of men, whether it was sharp or sweet, savory or voluptuous, creamy or piercing. 'Not like that' was all he could ever say to such inquiries."[20]
- *When splashed with the bubble tree:* "Immediately his head, face, and shoulders were drenched with what seemed (in that warm world) an ice-cold shower bath, and his nostrils filled with a sharp, shrill, exquisite scent that somehow brought to his mind the verse in Pope, 'die of a rose

---

[18] Lewis, *Perelandra*, 32.
[19] Ibid., 37.
[20] Ibid.

in aromatic pain.' Such was the refreshment that he seemed to himself
to have been, till now, but half awake. When he opened his eyes—which
had closed involuntarily at the shock of moisture—all the colors about
him seemed richer and the dimness of that world seemed clarified."[21]

- *When eating the Perelandrian banana:* "The flesh was dryish and bread-
  like, something of the same kind as a banana. It turned out to be good
  to eat. It did not give the orgiastic and almost alarming pleasure of the
  gourds, but rather the specific pleasure of plain food—the delight of
  munching and being nourished, a 'Sober certainty of waking bliss.' A
  man, or at least a man like Ransom, felt he ought to say grace over it, and
  so he presently did. The gourds would have required rather an oratorio
  or a mystical meditation. But the meal had its unexpected highlights."[22]

Perelandra is a paradise of pleasures. But not the same pleasures. The
ecstasy of the gourd differs from the sharpness of the bubble tree, which
differs yet again from the plain pleasure of the Perelandrian banana. The
aim of cataloging distinct pleasures is first to enjoy them as gifts, and then,
as we saw earlier, to wield them in the fight of faith, puncturing the worldly
crust that threatens to numb our souls.

Self-Restraint and Encore

But, of course, it's not enough to encourage people to enjoy real, particular
pleasures. If our Hedonics is to be Christian, then it must be obedient to
God, and this means that there must be some element of self-restraint in
our earthly enjoyments. Again, *Perelandra* gives us a window into Lewis's
thinking on the subject. After each of the intense pleasures above, Ransom
immediately desires to repeat the pleasure. Even though the first gourd
satisfies him, he desires to have another. Even though the bubble trees re-
fresh him, he considers running through an entire cluster of them in order
to get the magical refreshment tenfold. However, in each case, his impulse
to repeat the pleasure is checked by an internal sense that to demand the
same pleasure immediately after experiencing it would somehow be vulgar
and wrong. It would be "like asking to hear the same symphony twice in
one day." (No doubt the vulgarity of this demand is not as obvious to us
living in the age of iPods and Spotify playlists.) This demand for an encore,
this "itch to have things over again," spoils the pleasure it wants to repeat.

---

[21] Ibid., 42.
[22] Ibid., 44.

As Ransom considers why self-restraint is so important, he wonders whether the itch for encore is the root of all evils. Remembering that the Bible assigns that title to the love of money, Ransom realizes that money is precisely the thing that allows us to say "encore" in a voice that cannot be disobeyed.

The rejection of encore is fundamental to Lewis's view of self-denial. He is clear that pleasures, whether of Perelandrian fruit or of earthly delights, are not bad in themselves. Christian self-denial, unlike other religious forms of self-denial, celebrates the good even when it is denied. "Marriage is good, though not for me; wine is good, though I must not drink it; feasts are good, though today we fast."[23] This is the paradoxical, two-edged character of Christianity, and it flows from the fact that God has made a good world, and yet this world has fallen. Thus, the Christian demand that we order our loves, that we love things in proportion to their worth (no more and no less). The lust for encore is an expression of our fallenness, an attempt to treat a single good as if it were the only good. Instead of embracing the Solomonic truth that there is a time for everything, a season for every activity under the sun, we refuse other, different goods and pleasures in favor of the one that has enthralled us in the moment. We gorge ourselves on one good and reject the other goods that God intended for us. Rather than allow God to give us a symphony, we insist on playing the same note over and over and over again.

Encore and Memory

But Lewis's rejection of encore, his insistence on self-restraint, serves another purpose as well. By refusing to say "encore," we create the possibility of the distinct pleasure of memory. When Ransom visits the planet Mars, he discovers that the unfallen inhabitants make love for only a few years out of their lives. While love making is as pleasurable to them as it is to us, they do not insist on gratifying this desire with the same reckless abandon as fallen humans. Ransom is puzzled by this and asks his Malacandrian friend Hyoi, "But the pleasure [of love-making] he must be content only to remember?"[24] Hyoi corrects his view of pleasure and memory:

> A pleasure is full grown only when it is remembered. You are speaking, *Hmān*, as if the pleasure were one thing and the memory another. It is all

---

23 Lewis, "Some Thoughts," in *God in the Dock*, 149.
24 Lewis, *Out of the Silent Planet*, 74.

one thing. . . . What you call remembering is the last part of the pleasure, as the *crah* is the last part of a poem. When you and I met, the meeting was over very shortly, it was nothing. Now it is growing something as we remember it, but still we know very little about it. What it will be when I remember it as I lie down to die, what it makes in me all my days till then—that is the real meeting. The other is only the beginning of it. You say you have poets in your world. Do they not teach you this?[25]

The real pleasure of meeting is the pleasure as it grows within us over time as it makes something inside of us, as it makes us into something more. To demand the continual experience of the pleasure is to cut ourselves off from the subsequent pleasure that God intended. This principle—that memory is the capstone of pleasure—is for Lewis one instance of Christ's teaching that a thing will not really live unless it dies, and it has many applications. "On every level of our life—in our religious experience, in our gastronomic, erotic, aesthetic, and social experience—we are always harking back to some occasion which seemed to us to reach perfection, setting that up as a norm, and depreciating all other occasions by comparison."[26] Many Christians look back with longing on the bright days after their conversion or after some great spiritual moment. They lament that those fervent desires have in some measure died away. No doubt sometimes the death of those initial pantings is due to sin. But not always. Lewis suggests that God intends those intense passions to pass away. They were the explosion that started the engine of the Christian life. But man does not live on explosions alone.

Undulation and Self-Denial

In addition, God has built us so that we can't keep these explosions going. Our bodies will not suffer the intensity of thrills for long. Lewis calls this the law of undulation (a fancy word for a wave-like rhythm). Humans, as Screwtape tells Wormwood, "are amphibians—half spirit and half animal. . . . As spirits they belong to the eternal world, but as animals they inhabit time. This means that while their spirit can be directed to an eternal object, their bodies, passions, and imaginations are in continual change." The result is undulation, "the repeated return to a level from which they

---

25 Ibid., 76.
26 Lewis, *Letters to Malcolm*, 26.

repeatedly fall back, a series of troughs and peaks." Periods of emotional and bodily richness are inevitably followed by periods of numbness and poverty.[27] Undulation is the natural, bodily way that God regulates our desires. Self-denial is the supernatural way that we join God in ordering our loves. As fallen humans, we're sorely tempted to ignore undulation and seek to get maximum and repeated joy out of the same pleasures. Self-denial is our resistance to this temptation, not because we wish to hinder our joy, but because we believe that God wishes to give us additional joys.

> It is simply no good trying to keep any thrill: that is the very worst thing you can do. Let the thrill go—let it die away—go on through that period of death into the quieter interest and happiness that follow—and you will find you are living in a world of new thrills all the time. But if you decide to make thrills your regular diet and try to prolong them artificially, they will all get weaker and weaker, and fewer and fewer, and you will be a bored, disillusioned old man for the rest of your life.[28]

Instead of being tormented by the lost golden moments of our past, Lewis encourages us to accept them as memories. When we do, we find that they are entirely wholesome, nourishing, and enchanting. "Properly bedded down in a past which we do not miserably try to conjure back, they will send up exquisite growths. Leave the bulbs alone, and the new flowers will come up. Grub them up and hope, by fondling and sniffing, to get last year's blooms, and you will get nothing."[29] The past joy must die if it is to live.

Completing Delight through Praise

So Christian Hedonics will attend to the diversity of pleasures, will refuse the siren song of encore, and in so doing will open the way for the distinct pleasures of memory. As Lewis's friend Owen Barfield once wrote, each great experience "is a whisper which Memory will warehouse as a shout."[30] Barfield wrote this in a poem, and Ransom's friend Hyoi saw it as the responsibility of the poets to teach us the proper relation between pleasure and memory. According to Hyoi, all the pleasures in our lives are remembered and boiled inside us so that we can make them into poems and songs.

[27] Lewis, *The Screwtape Letters*, 46.
[28] Lewis, *Mere Christianity*, 111.
[29] Lewis, *Letters to Malcolm*, 27.
[30] Lewis, "Talking about Bicycles," in *Present Concerns*, 71.

It's not enough for us to remember the bare facts. We must capture and condense these pleasures into words and poems, stories and songs. And thus we see how Lewis's view of memory and pleasure dovetails with another of his insights about praise. Not only is a pleasure not full grown until it is remembered, but also our delight is incomplete until it is expressed.

Lewis discovered the necessity of expressing our joy as he wrestled with God's demand for praise in the Psalms. Lewis was troubled that God seemed to crave our worship, as an old woman craves compliments. Yet he knew that God has no needs: "If I were hungry, I would not tell *you*" (Ps. 50:12). Thinking about God's demand for praise, Lewis realized the obvious fact that

> all enjoyment spontaneously overflows into praise. . . . The world rings with praise—lovers praising their mistresses, readers their favorite poet, walkers praising the countryside, players praising their favorite game— praise of weather, wines, dishes, actors, motors, horses, colleges, countries, historical personages, children, flowers, mountains, rare stamps, rare beetle, even sometimes politicians or scholars.[31]

Not only do people praise what they value; they also urge us to join them in praising it. Lewis realizes that, in objecting to the praise of God, he was denying us the very thing we always do and can't help doing with everything else we value. And he was doing so in regard to the most valuable Being in the universe. And this leads him to his final realization about the relationship between joy and praise: "I think we delight to praise what we enjoy because the praise not merely expresses but completes the enjoyment; it is its appointed consummation."[32]

For Lewis, there is an art to pleasure. There is a music of joy, a poetry of delight. And like poetry, everything has its place. Pleasure passing into memory. Memory forming itself into poetry. Poetry erupting into praise. "The most splendid line becomes fully splendid only by means of all the lines after it."[33] Again this is Solomonic. There is a time to enjoy, and a time to remember. A time to be pleased, and a time to praise. These are the rhythms of pleasure, and they are essential to the Christian life. And if we attend to them, if we both indulge ourselves and deny ourselves, we

---

[31] Lewis, *Reflections on the Psalms*, 94.
[32] Ibid., 95.
[33] Lewis, *Out of the Silent Planet*, 74.

discover that there is a Joy that runs through them all. Our enjoyment is completed and enhanced by our remembering. Our pleasure is enlarged and consummated by our praise.

Joy

But whatever we may say about the distinct varieties of pleasure, they are not to be confused with what Lewis calls Joy (with a capital *J*). The pleasures and delights surveyed earlier may be the occasion for the arrival of Joy, but they must never be identified with it. Joy, for Lewis, is a very particular and massively important phenomenon. In his writings, he calls it by various names: Joy, *Sehnsucht*, Romanticism. But each of these is misleading (though for simplicity's sake I will use the capitalized *Joy* for the remainder of this chapter). More important is his description of the experience. Joy, as distinct from pleasure, is an experience of intense longing with two distinct qualities.

The first is the paradox that it is a pleasing pain, an absence that is more satisfying than any presence, an unsatisfied desire that is more desirable than any satisfaction, a hunger that is better than any fullness, a poverty better than all wealth. Most of our desires long for fruition; with Joy, we want to desire and keep on desiring; we long for this unending and pleasing pain. More than mere aesthetic pleasure, Joy must have "the stab, the pain, the inconsolable longing."[34]

Second, in experiencing this desire, we long for we-know-not-what. The desire may be triggered by many different things: imaginative literature, faraway hills, a suggestive title of a book, a smell, a particular strain of music, even the memory of a cookie tin made to resemble a toy garden. Yet these things are not the objects of our desire but merely the occasions of it. And we know this because Joy is not satisfied even when we possess these things.

In his writings, Lewis describes this desire in various ways. In *The Pilgrim's Regress*, he shows it to us as John's longing for the faraway island. In *Surprised by Joy*, it is the bright shadow that flowed out of George MacDonald's *Phantastes*, transforming all the common things and baptizing Lewis's imagination. In *Perelandra*, it is a homesickness, a cord of longing that is sharp, sweet, wild, and holy, all in one.

In *The Problem of Pain*, Lewis describes it as the signature of each soul

---

[34] Lewis, *Surprised by Joy*, 72.

(thus stressing that it comes to each of us in its own way or on its own occasions), "the incommunicable and unappeasable want, the thing we desired before we met our wives or made our friends or chose our work, and which we shall still desire on our deathbeds, when the mind no longer knows wife or friend or work."[35] We have never possessed the object of this great desire; we have only experienced the wanting.

> All the things that have ever deeply possessed your soul have been but hints of it—tantalising glimpses, promises never quite fulfilled, echoes that died away just as they caught your ear. But if it should really become manifest—if there ever came an echo that did not die away but swelled into the sound itself—you would know it. Beyond all possibility of doubt you would say "Here at last is the thing I was made for."[36]

Lewis tells us that his experience of Joy led him on many false roads and rabbit trails. He sought to find the object of this great desire; he looked to sex, to beauty, to music, to literature, to philosophy. Yet his failure to find anything in his earthly experience to answer this desire did not lead him to despair. It led him to God. The quest for Joy became for him a lived ontological proof of God's existence. We might call this the argument from desire: "If I find in myself a desire which no experience in this world can satisfy, the most probable explanation is that I was made for another world."[37]

The argument from desire pervades Lewis's apologetic works. He employs it whenever he seeks to weave the spell of Joy by ripping open the inconsolable secret in his audience.[38] But as this is not a book on Lewis's apologetics, we must press through to see the relevance of the quest for Joy for the Christian life. Before he became a Christian, Lewis's

---

[35] Lewis, *The Problem of Pain*, 150.

[36] Ibid., 150–51.

[37] Lewis's fuller statement is as follows:

The Christian says, "Creatures are not born with desires unless satisfaction for those desires exists. A baby feels hunger: well, there is such a thing as food. A duckling wants to swim: well, there is such a thing as water. Men feel sexual desire: well, there is such a thing as sex. If I find in myself a desire which no experience in this world can satisfy, the most probable explanation is that I was made for another world. If none of my earthly pleasures satisfy it, that does not prove that the universe is a fraud. Probably earthly pleasures were never meant to satisfy it, but only to arouse it, to suggest the real thing. If that is so, I must take care, on the one hand, never to despise, or be unthankful for, these earthly blessings, and on the other, never to mistake them for the something else of which they are only a kind of copy, or echo, or mirage. I must keep alive in myself the desire for my true country, which I shall not find till after death; I must never let it get snowed under or turned aside; I must make it the main object of life to press on to that other country and to help others to do the same." (Lewis, *Mere Christianity*, 136–37)

[38] For the Narnian version of the argument from desire, see chap. 9 in Joe Rigney, *Live Like a Narnian: Christian Discipleship in Lewis's Chronicles* (Minneapolis: Eyes & Pen, 2013).

experience of Joy was a desire for he-knew-not-what; he simply wanted to find the place where all the Joy came from. Once he became a Christian, the quest for Joy became far less important to Lewis. This was not because the stabs of Joy diminished or decreased. The sharpness was still there. But Lewis now realized that the stabs of Joy were merely pointers to something other and outer. They were not the destination but merely signposts along the way. Now that he knew where this journey led, the signposts lost their allure, even as they continued to encourage him on the narrow road.

Joy and Pleasure

We could leave the subject aside here; in fact, this is precisely where Lewis leaves us at the end of his autobiography. But as this is a book on the Christian life, I believe a final step to tie these threads together is in order. Pleasures are distinct from Joy. But they are not unrelated to Joy. When God grants them, they may become occasions of Joy. In a passage that has shaped me as much as any other in Lewis, he unfolds how simple pleasures may become occasions for adoration of God. Since I've written another book detailing how the things of earth help us to enjoy God himself, I'll content myself with the briefest summary here.

Begin with the simple, unchanging, absolutely unique glory of God. God is completely and absolutely himself, and his glory is completely and absolutely itself. Nevertheless, we give different names to this glory as it touches our various faculties. When God's glory touches our wills, we speak of goodness. When it touches our minds, we call it truth. And when the glory strikes our senses, we call it pleasure. "Pleasures are shafts of the glory as it strikes our sensibility." As a result, any pleasure, no matter how simple, can become a "channel of adoration."

> We can't—or I can't—hear the song of a bird simply as a sound. Its meaning or message ("That's a bird") comes with it inevitably—just as one can't see a familiar word in print as a merely visual pattern. The reading is as involuntary as the seeing. When the wind roars I don't just hear the roar; I "hear the wind." In the same way it is possible to "read" as well as to "have" a pleasure. Or not even "as well as." The distinction ought to become, and sometimes is, impossible; to receive it and to recognise its divine source are a single experience. This heavenly fruit is instantly redolent of the orchard where it grew. This sweet air whispers of the

country from whence it blows. It is a message. We know we are being touched by a finger of that right hand at which there are pleasures for evermore. There need be no question of thanks or praise as a separate event, something done afterwards. To experience the tiny theophany is itself to adore.[39]

What keeps us from experiencing these tiny theophanies?[40] Lewis gives us four answers: (1) Inattention—we ignore the presence of God everywhere. We fail to see that every bush is a burning bush. (2) The wrong kind of attention—we subjectify the experience and see only the internal workings of our own minds or bodies. The pleasure comes and we kill it by turning around and directing our attention inward. (3) Greed—we demand the exact experience again. We shout "Encore!" forgetting that all of space and time are not enough for God to utter himself even once. (4) Conceit—we take pride in our ability to find God in the little things, forgetting that those who are looking down their noses at others are never able to see the One who is above them.[41]

For Lewis, the quest for Joy launched by his early experiences of enchantment led him down many false trails and almost left him disenchanted. He almost concluded that the promise of Joy that his early experiences offered was an optical illusion, a mirage. But in finding God in Christ, Lewis was re-enchanted.[42] He came to realize that the universe was not a fraud. Earthly pleasures were never meant to satisfy the ache in our souls, but "only to arouse it, to suggest the real thing." Thus, he came to see that we must avoid the twin errors of ingratitude and idolatry. We must not despise the earthly blessings that awaken Joy. But neither must we mistake them for the "Something Else" of which they are only a kind of copy, or echo, or mirage.

Instead we must be alert and awake to pleasures, while also embracing the necessity of self-denial in governing our earthly joys. When God gives us earthly pleasures, we must say "thank you" for the gifts. "How good of

---

39 Lewis, *Letters to Malcolm*, 89–90.
40 It is important to stress that, in Lewis's view, these tiny theophanies yield only "adoration in infinitesimals." On the scale of importance, they are at the bottom. The simplest act of mere obedience is far more important than attending to the tiny theophanies. However, being at the bottom of the scale doesn't render them completely null and void; "the higher does not stand without the lower." Or again, "We . . . shall not be able to adore God on the highest occasions if we have learned no habit of doing so on the lowest" (ibid., 91).
41 Ibid., 89.
42 Lewis uses the language of enchantment, disenchantment, and re-enchantment in an essay called "Talking about Bicycles," in *Present Concerns*, 67–72.

God to give me this." And then we must labor with God's help to adore him, to run our minds back up the sunbeam to the sun, saying, "What must be the quality of that Being whose far off and momentary coruscations are like this!"[43] Christian Hedonics—the science and study of pleasure—leads us to Christian Hedonism—the pursuit of our deepest pleasure and highest satisfaction in God through Christ.

---

[43] Lewis, *Letters to Malcolm*, 90.

CHAPTER II

REASON AND IMAGINATION

Truth, Meaning, and
the Life of Faith

In the last chapter, we saw that Christian hedonism, containing as it does Christian Hedonics, is "a very arduous discipline."[1] The pursuit of Joy is a difficult and dangerous quest. Like Aslan, it's not safe, but it's good. The labor is worth it. We also saw that one of the purposes of studying our pleasures—of enjoying them and then contemplating them—is that each pleasure is an echo or image of God, their inventor. They show us something of what he is like. They give us what Lewis calls "bearings on the Bright Blur." In the same way that we learn something about the sun from a walk in the woods that we could never learn from a book on astronomy, so also "pure and spontaneous pleasures are 'patches of Godlight' in the woods of our experience."[2] Faith and reason may tell us *that* God is good, but we need more than this; we need to taste and see how this is so.

Getting our bearings on the Bright Blur is essential for the Christian life. It is an affair of reason and imagination, actively taking in the world that God has made as a way of creating categories for us to know God. We've seen the distinction between reason and imagination already in our discussion of scientific and poetic language. The present chapter will flesh out

---

[1] Lewis, *Letters to Malcolm*, 90–91.
[2] Ibid., 90.

this distinction in greater detail and show how reason and imagination can help, or hinder, the life of faith.

Lakeside Scene

Let's begin with a scene. A cabin in northwestern Wisconsin. June. The day is moist and rainy (though it's really only a light sprinkle). The cabin overlooks a small lake. Fog, which has hovered in the air all day, gives the far side of the lake a hazy and greyish appearance. Birds flutter by and alight on the trees by the water's edge. A chipmunk climbs up on the deck and then scampers down again, while a squirrel makes its way carefully through the branches overhead. A cool breeze ruffles the surface of the water as well as the leaves in the trees, giving the whole scene a nearly constant but gentle movement. Though the scene is dominated by greys and greens, it makes a quite pleasant landscape.

For Lewis, reason is the faculty of the mind that analyzes, distinguishes, and abstracts. Reason uses logic to make deductions, to draw conclusions, to take things apart so we can look at the pieces individually. Reason looks at our lakeside scene and breaks it down into its components—the smell of the water, the sensation of the moisture, the movement of the branches. It makes further distinctions, recognizing the green of the grass versus the green of the leaves, the grey of the water versus the grey of the sky, the bounding of the chipmunk verses the smoother hops of the squirrel. Reason isolates, disassembles, and deconstructs. When we reason, we produce arguments—a succession of linked concepts that we offer to others as evidence that we have thought about something.

But reason isn't the only faculty at work at the lakeside. Imagination is also active. Where reason isolates and analyzes the distinct components of our lakeside scene, imagination "loves to embrace its object completely, to take it in at a single glance, and see it as something harmonious, symmetrical, and self-explanatory." Imagination also "loves to lose itself in a labyrinth, to surrender to the inextricable."[3] Thus, it is imagination that takes in the lakeside scene and calls it "beautiful." When asked, "What makes it beautiful?" imagination can only point. It's not one thing, not merely the colors or sensations or smells. It is the whole, taken in with all of its realness and quiddity, that renders it beautiful and calls forth our response.

---

[3] Lewis, "Is Theology Poetry?," in *The Weight of Glory and Other Addresses*, 119.

Of course, imagination is not merely directed at real landscapes; it can also attend to things that aren't real. Imagination may involve "a reshuffling of universals taken from the real world." "When we imagine Britomart [a character in Edmund Spenser's *The Faerie Queene*] we take our idea of 'a girl,' which is part of our general knowledge, and our idea of 'medieval knight,' which is another part of our general knowledge, and put them together."[4] If reason produces arguments as we think through a subject, then imagination produces images as we imagine a scene, say the city of Carthage, or Lucy at Tumnus's house, or Ransom on the floating islands of Perelandra. The images we produce "come and go rapidly and assist what I regard as the real imagining only if I take them all as provisional makeshifts, each to be dropped as soon as it has served its (instantaneous) turn."[5] But imagination itself is the capturing of a quality of a thing, taking it in, as it were, in a single glance. It is imagination that grasps the Minnesota-ness of Minnesota or the homeliness of childhood memories. When applied to works of literature, our imagination attends to what Lewis calls *ipseitas:* "the peculiar unity of effect produced by a special balancing and patterning of thought."[6]

Lewis associates reason with the intellect and thought, imagination with the heart and the emotions. Reason focuses on the abstract and universal; imagination, on the concrete and particular. Reason distances itself from the object in order to analyze it. Imagination submits to the whole of the object in order to imbibe its quality. The danger with reason is that, in engaging in analysis and abstraction, we kill the object analyzed. "We murder to dissect," as Wordsworth put it in "The Tables Turned." The danger with imagination is that, because it targets our emotions, we will be swept away by them, that untethered from reason, we will believe, embrace, and love what is false and wrong.

Lewis once wrote a sonnet that contrasts reason and imagination:

Set on the soul's acropolis the reason stands
A virgin, arm'd, commercing with celestial light,
And he who sins against her has defiled his own

---

4 Lewis, *Image and Imagination*, 49.
5 Lewis, "The Language of Religion," in *Christian Reflections*, 138–39.
6 Lewis, "The Empty Universe," in *Present Concerns*, 86. See also "On Stories," in *On Stories and Other Essays on Literature*, 3–32. Schakel writes that reason is "the capacity for analysis, abstraction, logical deductions," whereas imagination is "the image-making, fictionalizing, integrating power" (Peter Schakel, *Reason and Imagination in C. S. Lewis: A Study of Till We Have Faces* [Grand Rapids: Eerdmans, 1984], x).

Virginity: no cleansing makes his garment white;
So clear is reason. But how dark, imagining,
Warm, dark, obscure and infinite, daughter of Night:
Dark is her brow, the beauty of her eyes with sleep
Is loaded and her pains are long, and her delight.
Tempt not Athene. Wound not in her fertile pains
Demeter, nor rebel against her mother-right.
Oh who will reconcile in me both maid and mother,
Who make in me a concord of the depth and height?
Who make imagination's dim exploring touch
Ever report the same as intellectual sight?
Then could I truly say, and not deceive,
Then wholly say, that I BELIEVE.[7]

Reason here is linked with Athena, the virgin goddess of wisdom who sprang from the mind of Zeus. She is defensive, armed, and unrelenting in her pursuit of error (no cleansing can wipe away one's sins against Athena). Her fundamental virtue is clarity; reason enables us to see, to distinguish, to parse and define.

Imagination, on the other hand, is connected to the motherly Demeter. At every point she contrasts with the virginal reason. She is warm (not cool), dark (not bright), obscure (not clear), and infinite (not definite or finite). Reason commerces with celestial light, but imagination is the "daughter of Night" and is associated with sleep, dreams, visions, and mysteries. If reason is as clear as the sky, imagination is as thick as the earth.

When Lewis wrote this poem, he felt the tension between reason and imagination. They pulled him in seemingly opposite directions. They did not speak with one voice, and their discord was one of the central struggles of his early life. In his autobiography he describes the war between his intellectual and imaginative life. "The two hemispheres of my mind were in the sharpest contrast. On the one side a many-islanded sea of poetry and myth; on the other a glib and shallow 'rationalism.' Nearly all that I loved I believed to be imaginary; nearly all that I believed to be real I thought grim and meaningless."[8]

It would eventually be Christianity that reconciled these two hemi-

---

[7] Lewis, *Collected Poems*, 95.
[8] Lewis, *Surprised by Joy*, 170.

spheres. In fact, *Surprised by Joy* is Lewis's telling of their initial reconciliation in prose form; *The Pilgrim's Regress*, with its journey between the bleak rationalism of the north and the mystic romanticism of the south, is essentially the same story in an allegory. The reconciliation of reason and imagination, the lifelong journey from what Lewis felt was an either–or to a glorious both–and is, I think, one of the main reasons Lewis is such a joy to read. It's the combination of penetrating clarity and evocative imagery. "One has an image." With Lewis, one always has an image. The images tumble downstairs, one after another, like children on Christmas morning. But these images don't float untethered in a sea of subjectivity. The images are anchored to propositions; the art is embedded in the argument, the argument embedded in the art.

Whole books have been written on reason and imagination in Lewis's thought. For now, we must look at one additional place where Lewis distinguishes the work of reason from that of imagination:

> But it must not be supposed that I am in any sense putting forward the imagination as the organ of truth. We are not talking of truth, but of meaning: meaning which is the antecedent condition both of truth and falsehood, whose antithesis is not error but nonsense. I am a rationalist. For me, reason is the natural organ of truth; but imagination is the organ of meaning. Imagination, producing new metaphors or revivifying old, is not the cause of truth, but its condition.[9]

Reason is the organ of truth. Imagination is the organ of meaning. And imagination is the precondition for evaluating the truth of a claim. In other words, before we can know whether something is true or false, we must know what it *means*. And it is imagination that supplies this meaning. To see how it does so, and how the two together help to give us bearings on the Bright Blur, we must reflect further on how nature reveals God.

Creation Reveals God

The Bible tells us that creation reveals God.

> The heavens declare the glory of God,
>   and the sky above proclaims his handiwork. (Ps. 19:1)

---

[9] Lewis, "Bluspels and Flalansferes," in *Selected Literary Essays*, 354.

> For his invisible attributes, namely, his eternal power and divine nature,
> have been clearly perceived, ever since the creation of the world, in the
> things that have been made. (Rom. 1:20)

Made things make invisible attributes visible. This, of course, includes our
lakeside scene. The freshness of the air, the songs of the birds, the coolness
of the breeze.

> In the rustling grass, I hear him pass.
> He speaks to me everywhere.[10]

Given the clarity of the biblical testimony on such matters, we might be
surprised to hear Lewis say, "Nature never taught me that there exists a God
of glory and of infinite majesty."[11] Now, I love Lewis dearly, but whenever
he gets into an argument with Saint Paul, you'll find me standing with the
apostle. But before we dismiss Lewis on this point, let us try to understand
what he means. He is discussing what he calls "nature-lovers," romantic
poets like Wordsworth and Coleridge who tried to derive their philosophy
from their impressions of nature. They attempted to lay themselves bare
to the sheer quality of every countryside, "to absorb it into themselves, to
be colored through and through by it."[12]

The problem with this sort of philosophy is that nature "will teach
you exactly the lessons you had already decided to learn."[13] We mistake
the qualities of nature—overwhelming gaiety, insupportable grandeur,
somber desolation; the richness, grace, and harmony of some scenes, as
well as the "grimness, bleakness, terror, monotony, or 'visionary dreari-
ness' of others"[14]—for moral imperatives or religious truth. Instead,
Lewis argues, what we really get from nature is "an iconography, a language of images."[15] In other words, our lakeside cannot tell us what to
believe, that is, what is true and false. To discover that, we need reason,
philosophy, and theology.[16] But what our lakeside can do is furnish us
with a language of images with which to clothe or incarnate our beliefs.

---

10 Maltbie D. Babcock, "This Is My Father's World," 1901.
11 Lewis, *The Four Loves*, 20.
12 Ibid., 18.
13 Ibid., 19.
14 Ibid., 18.
15 Ibid., 19.
16 "What we learn from experience depends on the kind of philosophy we bring to experience" (Lewis,
Miracles, 2).

It may not give us truth, but it can give us meaning.[17] This is precisely what Lewis suggests.

> Nature never taught me that there exists a God of glory and of infinite majesty. I had to learn that in other ways. But nature gave the word *glory* a meaning for me. I still do not know where else I could have found one. I do not see how the "fear" of God could have ever meant to me anything but the lowest prudential efforts to be safe, if I had never seen certain ominous ravines and unapproachable crags. And if nature had never awakened certain longings in me, huge areas of what I can now mean by the "love" of God would never, so far as I can see, have existed.[18]

Nature, then, cannot tell us whether the statement "God is powerful and glorious" is true. It will not "verify any theological or metaphysical proposition." But "she will help to show what [the statement] means."[19] Because we have experienced nature—because we have seen a tornado tear across the sky or have stood atop a mountain at sunset—we know what the words "powerful" and "glorious" *mean*. Through nature, we have experiential knowledge that creates categories in our minds for knowing and loving God. This is because "everything God has made has some likeness to Himself."[20] Space, matter, vegetable life, animal life, the fertility of insects, the affection of mammals, the rationality of man—all of these provide little windows on what God is like.

Because of this, nature can "initiate" us into the spiritual life. Our imaginative experience, while not a stepping stone in itself, can *become* one when we begin to recognize the pattern or likeness between the lower world of nature and the higher world of God, between creation and the God who reveals himself in it.

Now, I think Lewis overstates his point about nature not teaching us; Paul implies that we can derive conclusions about God and his attributes from the things that have been made. Thus, we might say to Lewis, "Take it up with Saint Paul." But Lewis does aid us in discerning *how* creation helps us to know God. When we're taking in the scene at the lake, we are

---

[17] Significantly, Lewis uses the term "iconography" or language of images to describe what we receive from literature as well. Good readers, he says, "mouth over their favourite lines and stanzas in solitude. Scenes and characters from books provide them with a sort of iconography by which they interpret or sum up their own experience" (Lewis, *An Experiment in Criticism*, 3). Thus, not only nature but culture too furnishes us with images with which to incarnate our belief and interpret our experience.
[18] Lewis, *The Four Loves*, 20.
[19] Ibid.
[20] Lewis, *Mere Christianity*, 158.

receiving an image of glory. Nature is giving us qualities and moods, the "spirit" of the place. But the path from these qualities and moods to an increasing knowledge of God is not direct. It's easy to become lost in a labyrinth of nature worship or paganism or folly if we try the direct route. Instead, we must take a detour—"leave the hills and woods and go back to our studies, to church, to our Bibles, to our knees."[21] This is what keeps our love of nature from turning into a nature religion. The Scriptures, our obedience to God, our prayers, the life of the Christian church—these tell us *what* to believe; they give faith its substance. But nature fills out and incarnates this substance. It clothes our belief. It gives it meaning. Scripture gives us the bones of our faith; nature puts meat on those bones. And, of course, God gives the body life.

Reason, Imagination, and Faith

So reason and imagination work together to help us know, taste, and see the goodness of God in the world he made. But as this is a book on Lewis on the Christian life, we should examine the relationship between reason, imagination, and faith. In the most basic sense, faith simply means "accepting or regarding as true the doctrines of Christianity." When we believe in something, we embrace it as a true representation of reality. To believe in Christianity is to accept it because, so far as you can tell, the weight of evidence is in its favor. In this sense, "faith is based on reason."[22]

Lewis believed that this is the only ground upon which we ought to accept Christianity. To accept Christianity because we think it is useful or dynamic or practical or relevant is to prostitute our faith. It is devilish propaganda to decide whether to embrace some claim based on whether it is academic or practical, courageous or cowardly, progressive or conservative. When deciding whether to believe a doctrine or philosophy, the deciding criterion must be whether it is *true* or *false*. This is why Lewis places such an emphasis on Christian apologetics. He wants to show the reasonableness of the Christian faith and the unreasonableness of the alternatives. As we saw in an earlier chapter, Lewis believed that reality is given. Reality simply *is*. The world we inhabit is objective and real. It confronts us at every point with an absolute firmness and solidity, and in doing so, presses obligations upon us.

---

[21] Lewis, *The Four Loves*, 21.
[22] Lewis, *Mere Christianity*, 138.

These obligations take various forms. For example, our universal tendency to use logical arguments in persuasion testifies to the fact that reason transcends human minds and brains. Or, again, the fact that human beings universally argue about fair play testifies to our universal experience of a law of human nature that stands over us (and that we all violate). Or, to return to something from the last chapter, our experience of desires that nothing in this world can satisfy testifies to the existence of another world in which such satisfaction is possible. In each of these cases, Lewis reasons from our common experience of reality to certain doctrines of the Christian faith: that there is an ultimate truth, an ultimate goodness, and an ultimate beauty. It is on these grounds that he embraced Christianity himself, and it is these arguments that he commends to others.

So, then, faith in its most basic sense is based on reason. What role does imagination play? Imagination is often the main avenue for temptation. In Lewis's mind, often "the battle is between faith and reason on one side and emotion and imagination on the other."[23] Imagination provokes our emotions, and our emotions carry out a blitz on our belief. We believe Christianity to be true based on good evidence, but then bad news, or danger, or peer pressure creates a mood that makes Christianity appear less probable. Or we want to do some action that God forbids, and we find that it would be very convenient for Christianity to be false, and so our desire to sin carries out a blitz. In these cases, we have not discovered new evidence against Christianity; our desires and fears, fed by imagination, lure us away. Of course, often in such circumstances we find reasons to doubt the truth of Christianity, but in these cases, the reasons exist to justify our wants. But it is the wants, sparked by imagination, that are steering the ship.

Temptation in *Perelandra*

In his Space Trilogy, Lewis shows us how the imagination can be used to tempt us to sin. These three stories follow the adventures of Dr. Elwin Ransom, a Cambridge philologist, who is caught up in an interplanetary conflict involving God, angels (called *eldila*), and human beings. In the stories, Mars and Venus (or Malacandra and Perelandra in the language of Deep Heaven) are unfallen and inhabited by rational creatures. Ransom journeys

---

[23] Ibid., 139.

to Mars in the first book, and to Perelandra in the second. He is brought to
Perelandra at the bidding of Maleldil (the name of Christ in the stories) for
some unknown purpose. When Ransom arrives, he meets the Green Lady,
the Eve of this unfallen world. Over the course of the first chapters, Ransom's nemesis from the first book, a scientist named Weston, arrives and
soon demonstrates that he is possessed by the Devil, the bent *eldil* who is
responsible for Earth's silence and exile from Deep Heaven. It quickly becomes clear that the Devil's purpose on Perelandra is the same as it was on
Earth with Adam and Eve. He intends to persuade the Green Lady to violate
the command of Maleldil, for there is a Perelandrian equivalent to the tree
of the knowledge of good and evil.

Perelandra is a planet filled with seas and floating islands. However,
there is a Fixed Land as well, and Maleldil's command to the king and
queen of Perelandra is that, while they may visit the Fixed Land, they may
not stay there overnight. For multiple chapters, Weston (now called the
Unman, since he is wholly possessed by the Devil) again and again tries to
convince the Green Lady to stay overnight on this Fixed Land. The Unman's
temptation of the Green Lady unfolds through many stages, all of them
designed first to corrupt her imagination in order to eventually corrupt her
will. He begins by introducing her to the idea of stories and poetry. "The
world is made up not only of what is but of what might be. Maleldil knows
both and wants us to know both."[24] Stories are good, and we tell them for
mirth and wonder and wisdom. The Unman suggests that Maleldil's command might serve the purpose of story: he has given the command so that
the Green Lady would "have a Might Be to think about."

In addition to introducing the idea of stories and fiction, the Unman
also seeks to detach the Green Lady from her husband's opinion. She is sep-
arated from her husband for the entirety of the temptation, and the Unman
encourages her to think for herself and not rely on the king to make her
"older" (the Perelandrian term for wiser and more mature). He encourages
her to become a "full woman," like the women of Earth, who "are of great
spirit," and "always reach out their hands for the new and unexpected good,
and see that it is good long before the men understand it."[25] This is the first
stage of the temptation: introducing the notion of stories, of independence
from the king, and of the greatness of earthly women.

---

[24] Lewis, *Perelandra*, 89.
[25] Ibid., 91.

From this foundation, the Unman then encourages the Green Lady to make a story about living on the Fixed Land. In other words, he tries to encourage actual disobedience by first encouraging her to imagine a world of disobedience so that she can become older, wiser, and more beautiful, like the women of Earth. When Ransom disrupts the temptation, the Unman paints him as a coward "who always shrinks back from the wave that is coming." In a diabolical twisting of the truth, the Unman describes Ransom as "bad," as "one who rejects the fruit he is given for the sake of the fruit he expected or the fruit he found last time."[26] The Green Lady thus views Ransom as a child who needs to be taught rather than a source of Maleldil's wisdom.

The Unman then moves to stressing the unique and arbitrary nature of the command to not live on the Fixed Land. The goodness of Maleldil's other commands—to love, to sleep, to fill the world with children—is obvious. Our own reason tells us that such things are good. Additionally, they are the same in all worlds. However, the command against living on the Fixed Land is not like this; Maleldil gave no such command on Earth or Malacandra. Nor is its goodness as obvious as the obligation to love one's spouse and children. The Unman suggests that the reason for this difference is that this command is only a "seeming." God really intends for her to disobey. According to the Unman, "Maleldil longs . . . to see His creature become fully itself, to stand up in its own reason and its own courage even against Him."[27] He wants the Green Lady to walk in her own way, to attain a kind of separation from Maleldil, to make herself older on her own rather than always stay as a child or beast before Maleldil. Becoming older in this way is hard; it will require great courage "to go on—on out of this smallness in which you now live—through the dark wave of His forbidding, into the real life, Deep Life, with all its joy and splendor and hardness."[28] Thus, the second stage of temptation fixates on a story of disobedience and accents the need to be courageous and brave enough to venture out on one's own and disobey the arbitrary command of God.

The next stage of the temptation is where the imagination comes even more strongly into play. The Unman begins to tell the Green Lady story after story after story about great women who suffered much at the hands of their fathers, husbands, children, and society. Over time, Ransom

---

26 Ibid., 98.
27 Ibid., 101.
28 Ibid., 103.

recognizes the common thread in the stories: "Each one of these women had stood forth alone and braved a terrible risk for her child, her lover, or her people. Each had been misunderstood, reviled and persecuted: but each also magnificently vindicated by the event."[29] The cumulative effect of the stories is to create two images, one in the foreground and the other in the background. The dominant image is of the goddess, "the tall, slender form, unbowed though the world's weight rested upon its shoulders, stepping forth fearless and friendless into the dark to do for others what those others forbade it to do yet needed to have done."[30] The background image, which emerges more by way of unspoken contrast, is that of men—a countless multitude of childish, arrogant, timid, and lazy creatures "prepared to try nothing, to risk nothing, to make no exertion, and capable of being raised into full life only by the unthanked and rebellious virtue of their females."[31]

The result of these images, forged by dozens of stories, is to captivate the Green Lady. Ransom is horrified to see her face as she listens to the Unman with rapt attention and a new expression: a touch "of invited grandeur, of enjoyed pathos—the assumption, however slight, of a role." She has begun to imagine herself as a great tragic queen, and her thoughts are consumed with the question of whether there is some "great deed to be done by me for the King and for the children of our children."[32] "The idea of the Great Deed, of the Great Risk, of a kind of martyrdom, were presented to her every day, varied in a thousand forms."[33] This great deed must be done by her alone; she cannot ask the king's permission (he would certainly disapprove; men are like that).

Ransom knows that her persistence in fondling the idea of disobedience comes from mixed motives, and that the dominant motives are noble. To become a risk-bearer, a tragic pioneer, is, for the Green Lady, rooted in her love for the king and their unborn children and even Maleldil himself. What had chiefly enchanted her was the picture of the nobility of self-sacrifice and self-dedication. At the same time, another motive was growing in her imagination—"the faintest touch of theatricality, the first hint of a self-admiring inclination to seize a grand role in the drama of her

---

[29] Ibid., 108.
[30] Ibid.
[31] Ibid.
[32] Ibid., 112.
[33] Ibid.

world." The Unman's goal is to enflame this "veiled egoism in the conception of noble revolt."[34]

The Unman's final step in capturing the Lady's imagination is to reveal her own reflection in a mirror. He wants her to see her own splendor, not mainly so that she can know her own physical beauty but so that she can become enthralled with the greatness of her soul. This is the perilous image that the Unman has been seeking to cultivate. He wants her to learn to love herself, to become a true woman, "to walk alongside oneself as if one were a second person and to delight in one's own beauty."[35] After she sees her reflection, the expression on her face turns noble; "greatness, tragedy, high sentiment" clearly occupy her thoughts.

At this point, though her will is yet uncorrupted, though no evil intention has formed in her mind, her imagination has nevertheless been poisoned, and as we saw earlier, the effect is to carry out a blitz on reason.

> It became harder to recall her mind to the *data*—a command from Maleldil, a complete uncertainty about the results of breaking it, and a present happiness so great that hardly any change could be for the better. The turgid swell of indistinctly splendid images which the Unman aroused, and the transcendent importance of the central image, carried all this away.[36]

The enemy's aim was to create a tragic and dramatic conception of the self. "He was making her mind a theater in which that phantom self should hold the stage. He had already written the play."[37]

Good and Bad Stories

The outcome of this particular temptation will have to wait for the next chapter. Our focus for the moment is on the role of imagination in seducing us to sin. Bad stories shape us. They weaken our ability to make the right choice. They loosen our grip on what we know to be true. Before the Devil can corrupt our will, he must first corrupt our imagination. He must create a fantasy reality in which disobedience appears noble and good, or in which God appears restrictive and stingy. He must write a false play and invite us to perform in it.

---

34 Ibid., 113.
35 Ibid., 117.
36 Ibid., 114.
37 Ibid., 118.

Elsewhere Lewis notes how many foolish ideas we pick up from the novels and plays we read or watch (in our own day, he'd no doubt talk about the movies and shows we watch). How many people believe that "falling in love" is irresistible because of the way the books and shows they devour have shaped their imaginations? How many people have lost their chastity partly because the stories and images they take in have made monogamy seem odd and boring while promiscuity, fornication, and adultery appear normal and exciting? "Just as if you have a rut in your path all the rainwater will run into that rut, and if you wear blue spectacles everything you see will turn blue,"[38] so also, if you fill your mind with sentimental songs and sexually suggestive images, your resistance to certain types of temptations will be almost nonexistent, like trying to dam up a river with a fistful of gravel. The channel you've cut by the stories you've inhaled is too deep.

Imagination and the Christian Life

Of course, the inverse is true as well. As we saw earlier, it's possible for our imaginations to be weapons in the fight of faith. Though this topic in Lewis is worth a book itself, I'll content myself with two ways we can resist the corruption of our imaginations.

First, we should imbibe good stories. Stories, like nature, furnish us with a collection of images that help us to understand ourselves and our world. Good readers, Lewis says, "mouth over their favourite lines and stanzas in solitude. Scenes and characters from books provide them with a sort of iconography by which they interpret or sum up their own experience."[39] Thus, it is essential that the scenes and characters that shape us are, to use a simple word, "good." Good stories—by which I mean faithful stories well told—train us in what it means to be human. They teach us to recognize and respond appropriately to the value of reality.[40]

Recall something we saw about pleasures of appreciation in the last chapter. There we noted that pleasures of appreciation seem to demand a certain kind of response. We feel that certain things *deserve* to be enjoyed,

---

[38] Lewis, *Mere Christianity*, 112.
[39] Lewis, *An Experiment in Criticism*, 3.
[40] It's worth noting that "good" stories may (and likely will) have great evil within them (just as God's story has evil within it). The key is how good and evil are treated within the story. For further reflections on evaluating stories, see chap. 7 in Joe Rigney, *The Things of Earth: Treasuring God by Enjoying His Gifts* (Wheaton, IL: Crossway, 2014), 137–52.

that they can somehow merit our approval. Pleasures of appreciation open for us windows into what Lewis calls "the doctrine of objective value."

> Until quite modern times all teachers and even all men believed the universe to be such that certain emotional reactions on our part could be either congruous or incongruous to it—believed, in fact, that objects did not merely receive, but could *merit*, our approval or disapproval, our reverence or our contempt.[41]

The doctrine of objective value is at the heart of what Lewis calls the *Tao*, or the God-given order of the universe, the combination of the givenness of the world and the human way of life that conforms to it. In various places, he calls it natural law, or traditional morality, or first principles, or the law of human nature, and argues that some aspect of the *Tao* is present in all major ancient philosophies and religions (Christian, Platonic, Oriental, Stoic, etc.).

> It is the doctrine of objective value, the belief that certain attitudes are really true, and others really false, to the kind of thing the universe is and the kind of things we are. Those who know the *Tao* can hold that to call children delightful or old men venerable is not simply to record a psychological fact about our own parental or filial emotions at the moment, but to recognize a quality which *demands* a certain response from us whether we make it or not.[42]

In drawing attention to this objective order in the universe, Lewis aims to rescue us from the abyss of subjectivism. Our words about things (such as "What a beautiful day at the lake") don't simply register *our* emotional reactions; instead they identify features of reality that impose duties upon us. The *Tao* demands that there be a fitness, a propriety, a harmony between the objective order in the universe and our rational and emotional responses to it. Responses that harmonize with this order are "right," and responses that don't harmonize are "wrong."

> "Can you be righteous," asks Traherne, "unless you be just in rendering to things their due esteem? All things were made to be yours and you were made to prize them according to their value. . . . " St Augustine defines

41 Lewis, *The Abolition of Man*, 14–15.
42 Ibid., 18–19.

virtue as *ordo amoris*, the ordinate condition of the affections in which every object is accorded that kind of degree of love which is appropriate to it. Aristotle says that the aim of education is to make the pupil like and dislike what he ought.[43]

Rendering things their due esteem. Prizing things according to their value. Possessing ordinate love. Liking and disliking what we ought. And since we don't naturally like and dislike what we ought, we need help. "The little human animal will not at first have the right responses. It must be trained to feel pleasure, liking, disgust, and hatred at those things which really are pleasant, likeable, disgusting, and hateful."[44] Therefore, the task of education is to train the pupil in the responses that are themselves appropriate.

Lewis believes that we ought to initiate the young into these right responses, even before they are able to rationally understand or explain what they are feeling. We do this so that when the child grows up and encounters truth, goodness, and beauty, he will welcome them with open arms, because he has been prepared for and indeed resembles them already. Thus, good stories, faithful stories, are food for the soul, nourishing us and strengthening us so that we can cling to what we know to be true, no matter our circumstances.

Remember the Signs

Beyond simply reading good stories, we must strengthen our convictions about the truth. We know that our moods will change; the blitz will come. So we have to teach our moods "where they get off."[45] We do so by holding the doctrines of Christianity before our minds every day. Daily prayers, daily reading of the Scriptures, gathering together with other believers—these are essential for the Christian life. "We have to be continually reminded of what we believe. Neither this belief nor any other will automatically remain alive in the mind. It must be fed."[46]

Lewis shows the importance of these daily devotions in *The Silver Chair*. Jill and Eustace are sent on a vital mission by Aslan: find the lost prince. Aslan also gives them four signs by which he will guide them on

---

[43] Ibid., 16.
[44] Ibid.
[45] Lewis, *Mere Christianity*, 140.
[46] Ibid., 141.

their quest: (1) greet Eustace's old friend when they arrive; (2) travel north to the ruined city of ancient giants; (3) do what the writing on the stone in that city tells them to do; (4) recognize the prince by the fact that he will be the first to ask them to do something "in the name of Aslan."[47]

Aslan insists that Jill repeat the signs until she has them memorized perfectly. And, echoing Deuteronomy 6:7, he stresses the importance of reciting the signs:

> But, first, remember, remember, remember the signs. Say them to yourself when you wake in the morning and when you lie down at night, and when you wake in the middle of the night. And whatever strange things may happen to you, let nothing turn your mind from following the signs. And secondly, I give you a warning. Here on the mountain I have spoken to you clearly: I will not often do so down in Narnia. Here on the mountain, the air is clear and your mind is clear; as you drop down into Narnia, the air will thicken. Take great care that it does not confuse your mind. And the signs which you have learned here will not look at all as you expect them to look, when you meet them there. That is why it is so important to know them by heart and pay no attention to appearances. Remember the signs and believe the signs. Nothing else matters. And now, daughter of Eve, farewell.[48]

Whatever strange things may happen, whatever blitzes your imagination carries out, whatever fog of falsehood falls on your mind, don't lose sight of the signs. Repeat them, remember them, call them to mind, know them by heart. "Nothing else matters."

Jill, Eustace, and their guide, Puddleglum, face many hardships on their journey. They grow cold and tired, sick of the wind and rain and hard ground. They long for comfort and warmth. And in the midst of this hardship—what Screwtape would call "a trough"—the Lady of the Green Kirtle appears and promises them warmth and welcome in the castle of the "gentle giants" of Harfang. Puddleglum tries to remind them that the signs say nothing about staying with gentle giants, but Jill and Eustace are fixated on "the hot meals and warm rooms" of Harfang.

However, the prospect of "steaming baths, soft beds, and bright hearths" has an ominous effect on the children.

---

[47] Lewis, *The Silver Chair*, 25.
[48] Ibid., 27.

> Whatever the Lady had intended by telling them about Harfang, the actual effect on the children was a bad one. They could think about nothing but beds and baths and hot meals and how lovely it would be to get indoors. They never talked about Aslan, or even about the lost prince, now. And Jill gave up her habit of repeating the signs over to herself every night and morning. She said to herself, at first, that she was too tired, but she soon forgot all about it. And though you might have expected that the idea of having a good time at Harfang would have made them more cheerful, it really made them more sorry for themselves and more grumpy and snappy with each other and with Puddleglum.[49]

Eventually Jill forgets the signs altogether, and in their eagerness to arrive at Harfang, they miss the giant city and the instructions written on the stone (and almost lose their lives). The entire story underscores everything we've seen in Lewis about reason, imagination, and temptation. Aslan gave them a mission and signs to accomplish it, just as God has given Christians a mission and the Scriptures as the means of accomplishing it. In our best moments, we embrace the mission and clearly see the signs that God has given us. But we don't always live in the clear mountain air of Aslan's country. Inevitably we have to come down from the mountain, and the journey gets hard. The low times, the trough periods, are prime opportunities for certain types of temptation.[50] Or, alternatively, we grow distracted by the things of this world, just as Jill earlier forgot the signs "during the feasting and story-telling" in the hall at Cair Paravel.[51]

In this case, the Lady's temptation appeals to their imagination: she offers the hope of warm beds and full bellies, just around the corner. And in the midst of the children's hardship, their desire, fueled by this image of comfort, carries out a blitz. Not only does it take them off the task; it also makes them more grumpy and snappy with each other. Having lost sight of the their Aslan-given mission, they also lose sight of basic kindness and decency toward one another. Because they are not rightly oriented to him, they cannot be rightly related to each other.

Thus, we see that repeating the signs is necessary to complete the mission. Bringing the truths of Scripture before our mind and believing them is essential to defending against the blitzes of temptation. More than that,

---

49 Ibid., 92–93.
50 Lewis, *The Screwtape Letters*, 51. Screwtape notes that temptations to sexual sin are particularly effective in trough periods.
51 Lewis, *The Silver Chair*, 49.

repeating the signs reminds us that we are on a mission. If we fail to remember the signs, we forget what our purpose is. Like Jill and Eustace, we begin to think that the point of this journey is our comfort and ease, rather than the task God has given us.

Jill and Eustace muff the first three signs; they quarrel with one another and are seduced by promises of short-term relief. As a result, they don't know the signs by heart, and they can't recognize them when they appear. But I would be remiss if I didn't note that, despite their failures, Aslan guides them anyway. Sin and failure do not thwart his plans. As Ransom says, "Is Maleldil a beast that we can stop His path, or a leaf that we can twist His shape? Whatever you do, He will make good of it."[52] We may not receive the good that God prepared for us if we obeyed, but all things will work together for good.

---

[52] Lewis, *Perelandra*, 104.

CHAPTER 12

HEALTHY INTROSPECTION

The Precarious Path to
Self-Knowledge

In the introduction, I noted that Lewis's effectiveness as an author is in large measure owing to his mastery of the heart. He understands our motives and evasions, our rationalizations and excuses. He knows how to expose the secret springs of our actions, because he has had his own exposed.

Part of Lewis's brilliance is helping us to navigate the Choice *after* the Choice. Here's what I mean. In facing temptation, we have two options: resist or give in. This is the simplest Choice, the one we've focused on for much of this book. But once we've made it, the temptations don't end. Our decision, for good or ill, births new choices, new dangers, new temptations. For example, let us say that we're tempted to do something dishonest, but God gives us grace and we resist. We do the hard but good thing. Having done good, we are now faced with a new choice: how will we respond to our own good actions? As we saw in our discussion of humility, the thing we must not do is pretend that our good deeds are in fact bad. No doubt they are tainted with our remaining sin; our motives, however pure in this life, are yet mixed. But gold is still gold despite the dross that surrounds it. If God calls it good, let no man gainsay it. "If God is satisfied with the work, the work may be satisfied with itself; 'it is not for her to bandy compliments

with her Sovereign.'"[1] At the same time, we ought not give too much attention to our virtues. Again, as we saw earlier, the surest way to ruin a virtue
is to notice it. Better to do it than to think about it; better to enjoy it than
to contemplate it. Self-forgetfulness, not congratulatory self-approval, is
the order of the day.

But let's say that we have noticed it. What then? If we've done good deeds
and seen them to be so, we ought to thank God for them. This is especially
true of what we might call our "native niceness." You or I may not be "one
of those wretched creatures who are always being tripped up by sex, or dip-
somania, or nervousness, or bad temper." God may have blessed us with a
healthy and stable constitution. The danger is that we begin to think that this
niceness is our own doing. But what do we have that we did not receive? Much
of our character is owing to sound nerves, intelligence, health, and a good up-
bringing. And none of these are things we have achieved of ourselves.[2] They
are gifts from God. This is why we must be careful not to judge by external
appearances, especially in our own case. So if we resist temptation and do the
right thing, the best course of action is to thank God and move on.

Vague Guilt

But sometimes we find it difficult to move on. We may have resisted the
temptation before us, but we still feel a vague sense of guilt. In fact, for
some of us, this vague sense of guilt may hover over our lives nearly all
the time. It haunts our best moments and smothers us in our worst. What
should we do when faced with this sort of guilt? We cannot dismiss it as
pathological; there may be real sin underneath. But, Lewis warns us, we
must be careful about how we go looking for it. "Some Christians would
tell us to go on rummaging and scratching till we find something specific."
Lewis is skeptical of this approach precisely because it is impossible to verify. If we hunt long enough, we may find (or think we've found) something
concrete. But what if, instead of discovering a real sin, our rummaging has
simply created "scruples." What if, in our efforts to justify or explain our
vague feeling of guilt, we persuade ourselves that something innocent is in
fact wrong? Hunting for sin in our hearts has a tendency to turn innocent
joys into sins, thereby distracting us from our real duties.[3]

---

[1] Lewis, "The Weight of Glory," in *The Weight of Glory and Other Addresses*, 38.
[2] Lewis, *Mere Christianity*, 207–16.
[3] Lewis, *Letters to Malcolm*, 33.

But if we aren't to keep rummaging until we either find a real sin or create a false one, what should we do? First, we are not to believe the vague feeling, for "how can one believe a fog?" Instead, we should labor to believe the promise of 1 John 3:20: "Whenever our heart condemns us, God is greater than our heart." Lewis returns to this verse again and again in his correspondence with struggling Christians. And *believing* this to be true is far more important than *feeling* it to be true. "Remember what St. John says[:] 'If our *heart* condemn us, God is stronger than our heart.' The *feeling* of being, or not being, forgiven & loved, is not what matters." Then, once we've believed the promise, we "must come down to brass tacks. If there is a particular sin on your conscience, repent & confess it. If there isn't, tell the despondent devil not to be silly."[4] Lewis recommends that we treat this vague feeling of guilt like an irrational noise, a buzzing in our ears; we should not try to debate with it (they love to draw you into an interminable argument). Instead, our response to the vague guilt should be, "Details, please!" If none are forthcoming, then "we must say to it, like Herbert, 'Peace, prattler'—and get on."[5]

We must be clear what Lewis means by "getting on." He does not mean that we ought to try and gin up the proper feelings. "Our emotional reactions to our behavior," he says, "are of limited ethical significance."[6] This is because, as we saw in the last chapter, our reason and imagination are often out of sync. Our feelings about our spiritual state often depend far more on our bodily health, our diet, how much sleep we've had, and so forth. This is why Screwtape tells Wormwood to "teach them to estimate the value of each prayer by their success in producing the desired feeling; and never let them suspect how much success or failure of that kind depends on whether they are well or ill, fresh or tired, at the moment."[7] The attempt to force oneself to feel the "right" thing was one of Lewis's early errors as a young Christian. When he prayed, he sought to will himself into what he called "realizations": "a certain vividness of the imagination and the affections" in relation to the subject of his prayers. "My nightly task was to produce by sheer will power a phenomenon which will power could never produce, which was so ill-defined that I could never say with absolute confidence whether it had occurred, and which, even when it did occur, was of very

---

[4] Lewis to Mary Willis Shelburne, July 21, 1958, in *Collected Letters*, 3:962.
[5] Lewis, *Letters to Malcolm*, 34.
[6] Ibid., 99.
[7] Lewis, *The Screwtape Letters*, 23.

mediocre spiritual value."[8] Lewis's experience of this error led him to caution Christians against it throughout his life.

No, "getting on" means focusing on the present responsibility, the next duty. We must not be like the unfinished picture that wants to jump off the easel to look at itself. Instead, we ought to put our hand to the plow and do the next thing.

Confessing Our Real Sins

But the dangers don't merely come when we've successfully resisted temptation. If anything, failing to resist temptation creates more problems down the road. For instance, there are times when we do something wicked and don't feel a whit of conviction or guilt. We are expert excuse makers and blame shifters. Other people may sin because they are wicked; when we "sin" (note the quotation marks), it is because we have "reasons." This, of course, is why true self-knowledge is so important. We need to know ourselves and our sins so that we can confess them. Thus, many wise Christians commend self-examination as a means of growing in this self-knowledge. But self-examination is not always a help. Screwtape knows that it is possible to bring someone to "a condition in which he can practice self-examination for an hour without discovering any of those facts about himself which are perfectly clear to anyone who has ever lived in the same house with him or worked in the same office."[9] This difficulty is why Lewis spends so much effort in trying to get around our defenses and show us who we really are. Like Nathan the prophet, he tells us stories about other people, wicked people, in order to turn and say, "You are the man" (2 Sam. 12:7—though perhaps without the prophetic flair I always detect in the biblical story).

A good example of what I mean is found in Lewis's essay "Miserable Offenders."[10] He begins with some reflections on the language of the Book of Common Prayer. In it we read that "the burden of our sins is intolerable" and that we are "miserable offenders." This does not mean that we all *feel* miserable; our feelings are often out of joint with the truth. Rather, it means that "if we could see things from a sufficient height above we should all realize that we are in fact proper objects of pity."[11]

---

8 Lewis, *Surprised by Joy*, 61.
9 Lewis, *The Screwtape Letters*, 16.
10 In Lewis, *God in the Dock*. The same basic method, with many of the same illustrations, appears in "The Trouble with 'X' . . . ," in *God in the Dock*, 151–55.
11 Lewis, "Miserable Offenders," in *God in the Dock*, 121.

So also with the intolerable burden. We may not feel this burden to be intolerable or unbearable, but the load is there nonetheless. Lewis thus examines whether we have any reason for thinking that this language is true. How could there be such a weight on our backs and yet we be so ignorant of it? And this is where he shows how Nathan-like he is. Rather than go for the direct hit, he takes the roundabout way. He asks us to consider whether we have a friend or a relation who has a serious flaw that for years has made our lives more difficult: "someone whose fatal laziness or jealousy or intolerable temper, or the fact that he never tells the truth, or the fact that he will always backbite and bear tales, or whatever the fatal flaw may be, which, whether it breaks him or not, will certainly break you."[12] Lewis assumes that most people will know someone like that. The experience, if not universal, will be close to it. He goes on to describe the ways we have tried to bear the burden of this other person's fatal flaw—how we have thought that a change of environment would make it better, only to be disappointed; how this continual disappointment has turned into an utter resignation, so that we scoff when others try to suggest a new way of bringing change to the situation.

And then Lewis begins the turn. He broadens the perspective. He invites God into the picture. God knows about this person's fatal flaw, better even than we do. In fact, God is up against all the fatal flaws of all the people we know. God and us, we're in the same boat. We both "can see that under the influence of nagging jealousy, or possessive selfishness, their character is day by day ceasing to be human."[13]

Then Lewis takes the final step. He has been showing us the world as in a mirror; now he turns the mirror around on us.

> When God looks into your office, or parish, or school, or hospital, or factory, or home, He sees all these people like that, and of course, sees one more, the one whom you do not see. For we may be quite certain that, just as in other people, there is something on which our best endeavours have again and again been shipwrecked, so in us there is something quite equally fatal, on which their endeavours have again and again been shipwrecked.[14]

Lewis has us cornered. We have already agreed with him about others; we know how stubborn and ignorant they can be. And we also know

---

12 Ibid., 122.
13 Ibid., 123.
14 Ibid.

that the person with the smelly breath rarely knows that it smells. Thus, our resistance to the suggestion that we too have fatal flaws would be precisely what we would expect. So Lewis has sprung his trap; you and I are the man. But then, like Nathan, Lewis shows us the way out. He tells us to confess our sins, perhaps to even write them down. And he insists that we do so honestly and forthrightly, avoiding the twin dangers of sensational exaggeration, on the one hand, and of slurring things over, on the other. He knows how easy it is for us to turn our face away from our evil at precisely the moment when we need a steady gaze. We are experts at making mountains out of molehills, or worse, molehills out of mountains.

> It is essential to use the plain, simple, old-fashioned words that you would use about anyone else. I mean words like theft, or fornication, or hatred, instead of "I did not mean to be dishonest," or "I was only a boy then," or "I lost my temper." I think that this steady facing of what one does know and bringing it before God, without excuses, and seriously asking for Forgiveness and Grace, and resolving as far as in one lies to do better, is the only way in which we can ever begin to know the fatal thing which is always there, and preventing us from becoming perfectly just to our wife or husband, or being a better employer or employee. If this process is gone through, I do not doubt that most of us will come to understand and to share these old words like "contrite," "miserable" and "intolerable."[15]

This kind of exercise is important. It is the opposite of morbid introspection. In fact, it keeps us from the more deadly morbidity—fixating on our neighbor's vices. "Those who do not think about their own sins make up for it by thinking incessantly about the sins of others." And in the long run, the serious attempt to repent and to know one's own sins is "a lightening and relieving process."[16] The diminishing pain of the pulled tooth is better than the festering ache of the rotted one.

Self-Examination

But what about the biblical call for self-examination? We can't simply brush aside the need for introspection. "Examine yourselves," says the apostle (2 Cor. 13:5). But there is a right way and a wrong way to administer such tests. Lewis associates the wrong way with certain streams of Puritanism.

---

[15] Ibid., 124.
[16] Ibid.

For [the Puritan], one essential symptom of the regenerate life is a permanent, and permanently horrified, perception of one's natural and (it seems) unalterable corruption. The true Christian's nostril is to be continually attentive to the inner cesspool. I knew that the experience was a regular feature of the old conversion stories. As in [John Bunyan's] *Grace Abounding*: "But my inward and original corruption . . . that I had the guilt of to amazement . . . I was more loathsom in mine own eyes than was a toad . . . sin and corruption, I said, would as naturally bubble out of my heart, as water would bubble out of a fountain." Another author, quoted in Haller's *Rise of Puritanism*, says that when he looked into his heart, it was "as if I had in the heat of summer lookt down into the Filth of a Dungeon, where I discerned Millions of crawling living things in the midst of that Sink and liquid Corruption."[17]

Continually attentive to the inner cesspool. Permanently horrified by the sink and squalor of the sinful soul. On this view, the true Christian lives always with his nostrils hovering above the rotten fens of his wickedness. His eyes are ever on the filth and corruption, the slimy twists and wretched vomit, of his own heart. He is constantly taking spiritual emetics (vomit-inducing drugs), trying to purge himself of his apparently unalterable corruption. Again, Lewis believes that this is the wrong way to go about it.[18] But it is important to see why he thinks it is wrong. It is not the wrong way because the picture is untrue. Lewis knows as well as anyone the slimy things lurking in his heart. His own experience of mortification was "like fighting the hydra (you remember, when you cut off one head another grew). There seems to be no end to it. Depth under depth of self-love and self admiration."[19]

The crucial difference is between a permanent attentiveness and an imaginative glimpse. According to Lewis, we ought to catch glimpses of the cesspool, but we should not engage in a daily, lifelong scrutiny of the bog. The glimpse is enough to teach us sense, to remind us that we are, at best, only

---

[17] Lewis, *Letters to Malcolm*, 98.

[18] In a letter to a struggling saint, Lewis writes:

> The habit of taking isolated texts from the Bible and treating the effect which they have on one in a particular mood at a particular moment as direct messages from God, is v. misleading. It fills some people (who are in one state) with morbid terror, and fills others (who are in a different state) with presumption. This, I say, *can* be learned from B. but I don't think that is what *you* wd. get from him at present. No very introspective book—no book in which a man is wholly preoccupied with his own spiritual state—would be very safe reading for you just now. Convalescents need a careful diet! You need something that will direct your attention away from yourself to God and your neighbours. (Lewis to Mr. Green, June 18, 1962, in *Collected Letters*, 3:1353)

[19] Lewis to Arthur Greeves, January 30, 1930, in *Collected Letters*, 1:878.

ever half-done. But to Lewis, pitching our tent next to the cesspool runs counter to the tenor of the New Testament. Paul sets an example for us of "forgetting what lies behind and straining forward to what lies ahead" (Phil. 3:13–14). What's more, what would be the purpose of camping at the brink of the cesspool after one has turned from one's sins? To ensure, I assume, that our repentance is real. But when the soldiers asked John the Baptist what they should do now that they had turned, he did not tell them to meditate on the cesspool in private. He told them to bear fruit in keeping with repentance (Matt. 3:8; Luke 3:7–14). And what better fruit than that of the Spirit—love, joy, peace, patience, kindness, goodness, faithfulness, gentleness, and self-control?

To return to what we saw earlier, Lewis is wary of any attempt to lay down a program of permanent emotions. They can be permanent only by being fake. What's more, man cannot live on emetics alone. (And if he tried, would he not develop a tolerance, perhaps even a pride in his hovel overlooking the sink?) We are to eat, not just vomit.

Again, Lewis doesn't deny the value of the glimpse of the cesspool. Nor does he want us just to leave our sin alone. We must "learn to detect the same real inexcusable corruption under more and more of its complex guises."[20] But the value of the glimpse in producing lasting godliness seems to diminish as the glimpse turns into a stare. Excessive introspection—that morbid and fidgety curiosity about oneself—is not the primary path to godliness. Better to pray with the psalmist:

> Search me, O God, and know my heart!
> 　Try me and know my thoughts!
> And see if there be any grievous way in me,
> 　and lead me in the way everlasting! (Ps. 139:23–24)

Self-examination, in truth, is examination by God. This does not make us passive, any more than our self-control is passive because it is a fruit of the Spirit. God is in the business of restoring control of you to you. So also with self-examination. Introspection is safe only when it is a divinely guided endeavor.

This divine guidance would look something like this: We surrender ourselves to God; we give Christ the keys to every room in our hearts. No dark closet held back. No basement corner off limits. The whole house be-

---

20 Lewis, *The Problem of Pain*, 52.

longs to him (and he is free to demolish, if he deems it best). We lay our-selves open before him and ask "for just so much self-knowledge at the moment as [we] can bear and use at the moment."[21] There may be deeper sins, down in the black caves, that we don't yet see. But perhaps we don't see them because God knows we're not ready to face them yet. We must learn to crawl before we can walk. Before Saint George could fight the Great Dragon, he had to defeat the simple Monster of Error. Let a man complete boot camp before sending him off to the war.

And then, having surrendered and having asked for our little daily dose of self-knowledge, we believe (and, for some, this is one of the greatest acts of faith they ever do) that he is fully capable of drawing our sin and our sinfulness into the light, into our conscious attention where it can be confessed and killed. In the meantime, as we've seen again and again, if we are daily surrendering ourselves to God in this way, we ought to forget about ourselves and do our work.[22]

Lewis is somehow able to combine real self-knowledge with real self-forgetfulness. His writing is characteristically sunny and capacious. Few things distinguish him as much as his joviality, his glad-heartedness, his brightness. At the same time, few writers can rival him in their knowledge of the slipperiness of the human heart. He slices our motivations (and his) with a master touch. He avoids the twin dangers of sunny superficiality and morbid introspection.[23] Instead, he attempts to live before the face of God with a deep and open sincerity, trusting God to do what only he can do. This self-surrender, this opening of oneself to God's inspection and exami-nation, Lewis calls "imaginative honesty," and he shows us what it looks like in chapter 11 of *Perelandra*. And, conveniently enough, exploring this God-inspection in *Perelandra* also allows us to complete the short narrative from the last chapter about the temptation of the Green Lady.

Ransom's Imaginative Honesty

Recall that in *Perelandra*, Ransom is brought to the planet Venus and is caught up in the temptation of the unfallen Eve of that planet. His opponent,

---

[21] Lewis, *Letters to Malcolm*, 34.
[22] "Even of his sins the Enemy does not want him to think too much: once they are repented, the sooner the man turns his attention outward, the better the Enemy is pleased" (Lewis, *The Screwtape Letters*, 85).
[23] I'm grateful to Doug Wilson who highlighted this juxtaposition. Wilson's term for this unusual com-bination is "jovial introspection" (https://dougwils.com/s7-engaging-the-culture/jovial-introspection .html, accessed April 28, 2017).

Weston, has been possessed by a dark power, a demon, and has become the Unman. For days the Unman has sought to persuade the Green Lady to disobey God. He plies her imagination and attempts to erect a perilous image of the greatness of her soul. Though she has not yet sinned, she is tottering on the edge of believing that she must perform a great and terrible deed (i.e., disobey Maleldil) for the "good" of her husband and future children.

Throughout the temptation, Ransom has attempted to strengthen the Lady's resistance to the Unman's lies, to draw her attention back to the simplicity of obedience. But he knows that she is faltering. After a particularly harrowing day, Ransom lies awake dreading the next day's session of temptation. "This can't go on," he thinks, all while feeling powerless to stop it. He begins to question divine justice: why did hell get to work a miracle in sending Weston, while heaven is silent and absent? In the midst of his questions, Ransom suddenly finds himself in the Presence of a mysterious Someone or something.

Ransom had encountered this Presence earlier in the book. Whenever the Presence descended, "the darkness was packed quite full" and Ransom felt "an unbearable pressure," which pressed "upon his trunk so that he could hardly use his lungs: it seemed to close in on his skull like a crown of intolerable weight so that for a space he could hardly think."[24]

> At first it was almost intolerable; as he put it to us, in telling the story, "There seemed no room." But later on, he discovered that it was intolerable only at certain moments—at just those moments in fact (symbolized by his impulse to smoke and to put his hands in his pockets) when a man asserts his independence and feels that now at last he's on his own. When you felt like that, then the very air seemed too crowded to breathe; a complete fullness seemed to be excluding you from a place which, nevertheless, you were unable to leave. But when you gave in to the thing, gave yourself up to it, there was no burden to be borne. It became not a load but a medium, a sort of splendor as of eatable, drinkable, breathable gold, which fed and carried you and not only poured into you but out from you as well. Taken the wrong way, it suffocated; taken the right way, it made terrestrial life seem, by comparison, a vacuum.[25]

As he lies awake musing on divine justice, Ransom is initially com-

---

forted by this Presence; Maleldil has not abandoned Perelandra. But then Ransom's voluble self—"the chattering part of the mind which continues, until it is corrected, to chatter on even in the holiest places"—begins to pour questions and objections into the darkness. "The Enemy is really here. . . . Where is Maleldil's representative?" Immediately, there's an answer "out of the silence and the darkness." Ransom is Maleldil's man on the ground, as much of a miracle as the Unman's diabolical presence. The chattering continues, now filled with excuses. "What can I do? . . . It's no good, I tell you." He tries to escape by pleading the sovereignty of God. What will be, will be. Even though Ransom has failed, he did his best, and now Maleldil must see to the outcome.[26]

But then "relentlessly, unmistakably, the Darkness [notice how it's now capitalized] pressed down upon him." More chattering, protesting, and spinning, followed by blessed relief when he realizes that no definite task lies before him. No use worrying; just generally resolve to do one's best if circumstances require. But then, a crazy thought arises (does it come from within Ransom or from without?)—what if this spiritual struggle includes physical combat? What if Maleldil expects Ransom to fight the Unman with fists and blows? The Silence and Darkness (again with the capital letters) presses in again, while the voluble self rallies. Ransom's inner chatterer protests wildly at every turn, but the Silence continues to corner him, leaving him no place of escape. In the end, slowly but surely, the Voice unravels his excuses, punctures his falsehoods, leaving the voluble self as "a whimpering child begging to be let off, to be allowed to go home."[27]

As the voluble self peters out, the Darkness "became more and more like a face, a face not without sadness, that looks upon you while you are telling lies, and never interrupts, but gradually you know that it knows, and falter, and contradict yourself, and lapse into silence."[28] And then the Darkness speaks. Or, rather, as Ransom's resistance weakens, the Silence becomes clear and audible. The Darkness becomes a Voice, and Ransom's task becomes clear. More importantly, Ransom resolves to do it.

So this is the movement: a comforting Presence becomes a silent and oppressive Darkness in the face of our chattering, voluble, resistant selves, but then becomes a face with a clear and distinct Voice as we surrender and lay ourselves down.

---

[26] Ibid., 120.
[27] Ibid., 122.
[28] Ibid., 123.

Standing in the Presence

What then is the point? All of us have been Ransom, with our attempted evasions, rationalizations, and excuses before God. How often we find ourselves shirking our duties and justifying our shirking with makeshift justifications. We hem and haw; we rally to our own defense. You know what I mean. We've had an argument with our husband, wife, or close friend. We replay the tape in our minds, casting our own words and motives in the best light, while condemning the other's as intentional malice. In our selectively edited version of events, we are the heroes, the other the villain. We are the justified, the other the guilty. All benefit of the doubt must be granted to us; none falls to our opponent.

But then, the Presence descends. Or, rather, we become aware of the Presence that has been standing before us the whole time. Or even better, we awake to the reality that we've been standing before it—or is it him?—in a vast hall, like a courtroom. We realize with a start what we've been doing: stewing in bitterness, nursing a grievance, wallowing in self-pity. But the presence of the Presence doesn't end our sojourn in the muck of our self. The chattering self awakes and goes to work. We throw up an argument only to have it flung back in our face. We offer excuses, which are swiftly snapped like a violin string. Every question is answered "quick . . . as a tennis player's riposte."[29] The Darkness or the Silence calls to mind truths and information we would just as soon forget. The Presence refuses to let the facts be suppressed. "The truth, the whole truth, and nothing but the truth," and God will give more help than we could possibly want.

No excuses will stand, and yet we continue to offer them anyway. We hastily construct our defense. We make concessions to the Presence: "I suppose you might be right. Perhaps she didn't mean it quite like that. I'm willing to grant that I may have been a little harsh a moment ago." We offer ourselves congratulations for being so humble and magnanimous as to grant the legitimacy of the other person's point of view. And all the while, the Presence stands there, or hovers, or looms, or all of these. Sometimes the Presence seems to speak, drawing attention to the glaring weaknesses in our defense, highlighting the manifest double standards at play in our version of events, unveiling our excuses for the travesty that they are. At other times, the Presence just hovers in silence, with a look that says, "You know you are only wasting time."

---

[29] Ibid., 120.

And so we see the necessity of imaginative honesty. We must learn to stand before God with a good conscience, to so live in God's presence that the moment we try to get away with anything or justify our sin, that silent, looming presence begins to suffocate us until we make things right.

Through Many Hands

If this were all we learned from Ransom's encounter with the Presence, it would already be an embarrassment of riches. But Lewis has woven other key truths for the Christian life into this chapter. The first involves the unfathomable consequences of the incarnation. While Ransom is trying to resist the suggestion that he should stop the Unman by force, he draws comparisons between Perelandra and Earth, between the temptation of the Lady and the temptation of Eve. He protests:

> If the Lady were to be kept in obedience only by the forcible removal of the Tempter, what was the use of that? . . . Did Maleldil suggest that our own world might have been saved if the elephant had accidentally trodden on the serpent a moment before Eve was about to yield? . . . The thing was patently absurd.[30]

The Darkness responds:

> What had happened on Earth, when Maleldil was born a man at Bethlehem, had altered the universe forever. The new world of Perelandra was not a mere repetition of the old world Tellus. Maleldil never repeated Himself. As the Lady had said, the same wave never came twice. When Eve fell, God was not Man. He had not yet made men members of His body: since then He had, and through them henceforward He would save and suffer. One of the purposes for which He had done all this was to save Perelandra not through Himself but through Himself in Ransom.[31]

The incarnation changed everything. The Word became flesh, human flesh; therefore, God now saves and suffers through human flesh. God has taken to himself a body; now he intends to save others through the breaking of that body. As the apostle Paul says, "Now I rejoice in my sufferings for your sake, and in my flesh I am filling up what is lacking in Christ's

---

[30] Ibid., 123.
[31] Ibid.

afflictions for the sake of his body, that is, the church" (Col. 1:24). Or, as Ransom discovers in this chapter, "If the issue lay in Maleldil's hands, Ransom and the Lady were those hands." So also with us. We are the hands of Maleldil. "God seems to do nothing of himself which he could do through others."[32] As one of the solid spirits exhorts a ghost in *The Great Divorce*, "You can begin as if nothing had ever gone wrong. White as snow. It's all true, you know. He is in me, for you, with that power."[33]

This is the great privilege we have as the body of Christ. We are his ambassadors, his representatives, his limbs. In our conversations and our counsel, in our presence and our prayers, in our words and our deeds, we are the vessels of his glory. The living water flows from one Fountain, but we are the streams. The light shines from one Sun, but we are the scattered beams. As Ransom learns later in the novel, everything comes from the hand of God; all is truly gift. But the gifts of God are thick and sweeter because of his delegation. "Through many hands, enriched with many different kinds of love and labor, the gift comes to me."[34]

The Choice

Which brings me to the other truth that has played like a melody throughout *Perelandra*: the centrality of the Choice. The Presence that presses on Ransom is constantly bringing him back to the Choice before him. "Patiently and inexorably it brought him back to the here and the now, and to the growing certainty of what was here and now demanded."[35] Ransom discovers what we explored in the opening chapter of this book—God is here, God is now, God demands all.

And as Ransom reflects on the consequences of his obedience and the success or failure of his fight, the overwhelming weight and uniqueness of the Choice lands on him.

> [Ransom] had long known that great issues hung on his choice; but as he now realized the true width of the frightful freedom that was being put into his hands . . . he felt like a man brought out under naked heaven, on the edge of a precipice, into the teeth of a wind that came howling from the Pole.[36]

---

32 Ibid., 121.
33 Lewis, *The Great Divorce*, 39.
34 Lewis, *Perelandra*, 180.
35 Ibid., 124.
36 Ibid.

This is the way God made the world.

> Either something or nothing must depend on individual choices. And if
> something, who could set bounds to it? A stone may determine the course
> of a river. He was that stone at this horrible moment which had become
> the center of the whole universe. The *eldila* of all worlds, the sinless or-
> ganisms of everlasting light, were silent in Deep Heaven to see what Elwin
> Ransom of Cambridge would do.[37]

Everything hangs on what Ransom will do. And yet, at the same moment that he feels the weight of human choice, he also experiences the
clearest proof of God's exhaustive and total sovereignty. In the end, Ransom discovers that predestination and freedom are apparently identical.
Inflexible destiny and unassailable freedom resolve into each other. The
tension that we feel between them is purely terrestrial, owing to the fall.
Beyond the moon, in those places where Maleldil's creatures still tread the
Great Dance without sin, the distinction between God's ordination and
our decision, like the distinction between things accidental and things
designed, has no meaning.

Ransom learns this both intellectually and experientially. Intellectually, he sees the hand of Maleldil in the Voice's words about his name. Ransom is being called to fight, to suffer, perhaps even to be killed in order that
Perelandra might be delivered. As the gravity of this calling settles in on
him, the Voice speaks. "It is not for nothing that you are named Ransom."[38]
Ransom the philologist knows that the linguistic origins of his name have
nothing to do with the act of ransoming; Ransom is simply a shortening of
"Ranelf's son." But he also knows that the Voice is not making a mere play
on words. In a flash, he realizes that what would appear to some to be an
accidental pun was in fact *designed*. It was part of a pattern so large that our
little frame of earthly experience cannot contain it.

> Before his Mother had borne him, before his ancestors had been called
> Ransoms, before ransom had been the name for a payment that deliv-
> ers, before the world was made, all these things had so stood together in
> eternity that the very significance of the pattern at this point lay in their
> coming together in just this fashion.[39]

---

[37] Ibid., 121.
[38] Ibid., 124.
[39] Ibid., 125.

Inside the story, there may be value in distinguishing things that are accidental from things that are designed and essential. But from the widest perspective, from the point of view of the divine Author, there is no distinction. Ultimately there are no accidents; all is planned.

Experientially, Ransom discovers the unity of predestination and freedom when the impossible act that stands before him (killing the Unman to deliver Perelandra) somehow becomes a certain fact of history, even before it happens. "The future act stood there, fixed and unalterable as if he had already performed it."[40] Like Lewis in his own conversion, Ransom makes his Choice, and discovers that his Choice had already made him.

Conclusion

What is the Choice? At one moment, Ransom feels that he is like Peter in the Bible, considering whether he will deny the Lord or not. If he does, if he refuses his calling in that moment, Perelandra will fall, as Earth did. But then the Voice reminds him that Ransom is not the only one with that name. "My name also is Ransom." And in a moment, Ransom realizes the full significance of the Voice's words. If Perelandra falls, it too, like Earth, will be redeemed. If Ransom refuses to live up to his name, Another will step into his place. And this time it will not be a second crucifixion—nothing is ever repeated—but "some act of even more appalling love, some glory of yet deeper humility."[41] The pattern of God's descent and sacrifice would carry on, even if the precise form of redemption is beyond conceiving. And so Ransom realizes that, in that terrible moment, he is not standing before the Lord like Peter in the courtyard after Christ's arrest. Rather, he is sitting before the Lord, like Pilate. "It lay with him to save or to spill."[42]

Now, of course this Choice is fictional; it only works in science fiction, since only in this novel is there the possibility of another planet's fall and redemption. But Ransom's Choice can be framed another way. What is Ransom's Choice? To stand for Maleldil. This is what Ransom learns from his encounter with the Presence. "In that sense, he stood for Maleldil: but no more than Eve would have stood for Him by simply not eating the apple, or that any man stands for Him in doing any good action,"[43] or that any of us stand for him in our daily acts of obedience.

---

40 Ibid., 127.
41 Ibid., 126.
42 Ibid.
43 Ibid., 127.

This is the reality, the Choice that confronts us all. In the end, no single choice is more important than any other. "The fierce light which [Ransom] had seen resting on this moment of decision rested in reality *on all*."[44] That includes the simple choices you've already made today—to get out of bed, to keep trusting in Jesus, to fall on your knees, to read this book, to love your neighbor. All of these choices matter because all of them are at the center of the Great Dance. As the heroes sing in the last chapter of *Perelandra*, "Each grain is at the center. The Dust is at the center. The Worlds are at the center. The beasts are at the center. The ancient peoples are there. The race that sinned is there. Tor and Tinidril are there. The gods are there also."[45] And I'll add, "You are there also."

> Where Maleldil is, there is the center. . . . Because we are with him, each of us is at the center. . . . In His city, all things are made for each. . . . Each thing, from the single grain of Dust to the strongest *eldil*, is the end and final cause of all creation and the mirror in which the beam of His brightness comes to rest and so returns to Him. Blessed be he![46]

---

44 Ibid., italics mine.
45 Ibid., 185.
46 Ibid., 186.

CHAPTER 13

THE NATURAL LOVES

Affection, Friendship, and Eros

In *The Screwtape Letters*, Wormwood's patient has three primary relationships: with his mother, with his friends, and with his girlfriend. Each of these relationships corresponds to one of the natural loves: affection, or familial love; friendship; and Eros, or romantic love. The relationships built on these loves make up a great part of our lives, including both our happiness and our virtue. They are the context in which God grows us into true persons as we learn to love God and neighbor in the proper ways. Throughout his writings, Lewis devoted significant effort to understanding the natural loves. The present chapter will take each love in turn, exploring what it is and how it goes wrong. In the next, we will then revisit each of the loves to show how divine love reorients and restores them to their appropriate place in the Christian life.

Gift-Love and Need-Love

In his book *The Four Loves*, Lewis begins by making two crucial distinctions about love. First, he distinguishes between gift-love and need-love. *Gift-love* is rooted in the love of God himself in his triune life: "The Father gives all He is and has to the Son. The Son gives Himself back to the Father, and gives Himself to the world, and for the world to the Father, and thus gives the world (in Himself) back to the Father too."[1] On the human level,

---

[1] Lewis, *The Four Loves*, 1–2.

this is the love that sacrifices for the good of others, whether or not we gain any direct benefit. On the other hand, *need-love*, such as the impulse that sends a lonely child running to his mother's arms, is "the son of Poverty." We feel need-love when we become aware of our helplessness, emptiness, and loneliness. It is the recognition of our true nature as creatures who need others physically, emotionally, and intellectually. Lewis is careful to note that need-love is not mere selfishness (though it may become selfish). Given our nature, it is right for us to feel that we need other people (and ultimately God) in all kinds of ways.

Lewis makes this first distinction in order to introduce a second one: the distinction between two kinds of nearness to God. On the one hand, there is the kind of nearness to God that we explored in chapters 2 and 11. This is the *nearness of likeness*. "God has impressed some sort of likeness to Himself . . . in all that He has made."[2] Space, time, earth, sea, plants, animals, man, and angels—all of these are in some ways like God. Yet, the created world can be arranged in a sort of hierarchy or order, with things at the top—like men and angels—being nearer to God by likeness than things at the bottom; the rationality of a man makes him more like God than a shrub or beast is. On the other hand, there is a nearness to God that comes from actually approaching him and enjoying him. This *nearness of approach* is an increasing nearness of union with God in will. It is a willed imitation of God, a conformity of our actions and desires to his actions and desires, expressed in particular by Christ in his incarnate life. Lewis points out that these two types of nearness need not coincide. A fallen archangel may be nearer to God by likeness than a poor fisherman—the bent angel is an invisible and powerful spirit of great intelligence. But the poor fisherman may be nearer to God in terms of approach since, unlike the Devil, he seeks to love God with his heart, mind, and strength, however feeble he may be.

These two distinctions—between need-love and gift-love, and between nearness of likeness and nearness of approach—will shape how Lewis treats the natural loves and their corruptions. But he introduces the distinctions in order to make an absolutely crucial point: "Love ceases to be a demon only when he ceases to be a god." Or stated the other way around, love begins to be a demon the moment he begins to be a god. "Every human love, at its height, has a tendency to claim for itself a divine authority."[3] It

---

[2] Ibid., 4.
[3] Ibid., 6.

demands a total commitment; any action, however perverse in itself, may be justified "for love's sake." Erotic love, familial love, even love of friend and country can demand an absolute allegiance that in essence becomes a pretension to deity; these loves can tend to become gods and thereby become idolatrous, demonic, and destructive.

For Lewis, this means that the real threat to the Christian life comes from the natural loves in their highest and best forms. It is when they are most like God (in terms of nearness by likeness) that they are their most dangerous. Our boundless gift-loves, filled with energy and vitality and desire for the good of the beloved, are godlike in their splendor. But it is just because they are so godlike that we may come to "mistake Like for Same." In such moments, we may render to a creature what is due only to God, with disastrous effects.

> We may give our human loves the unconditional allegiance which we owe only to God. Then they become gods: then they become demons. Then they will destroy us, and also destroy themselves. For natural loves that are allowed to become gods do not remain loves. They are still called so, but can become in fact complicated forms of hatred.[4]

In light of this fundamental principle, we are now ready to examine the natural loves and their corruptions. We'll begin with affection.

Affection

Affection is family love and, by extension, love for anyone with whom we are familiar, whether kin to us or not. Our first experience of it is in the home—parent to child and child to parent. On the child's side, this love is a need-love; a child desires and wants his father's approval and his mother's affection. On the parental side, the love is a paradoxical mix of need-love and gift-love. "It is a Need-love but what it needs is to give. It is a Gift-love but it needs to be needed."[5]

From the relation of parent and child, affection broadens out. It is the humblest and least discriminating of the natural loves. We choose our friends and lovers, but affection embraces whoever happens to be near to us—starting with our families, of course, but including the old man next door, the ugly cat, the awkward boy down the street. Our affection for them

---

4 Ibid., 8.
5 Ibid., 32.

is at least partially due to their proximity to us. An outsider might reject them, but to us, they are "old so-and-so." Affection reveals itself when we feel the need to defend others because they are in some sense "ours." "No one can talk that way about my brother." Even a bully may defend one of his regular victims who is mocked by someone from another school.

Affection is humble and modest. It puts on no airs and makes no boasts. When Lewis describes it, he uses images of comfort, warmth, softness, and privacy: "soft slippers, old clothes, old jokes, the thump of a sleepy dog's tail on the kitchen floor."[6] And because affection takes in whoever happens to be there, it often has the affect of enlarging our "tastes." When affection binds us to those for whom we have no other affinity, "we are getting beyond our own idiosyncrasies, . . . learning to appreciate goodness or intelligence in themselves, not merely goodness or intelligence flavoured and served to suit our own palate."[7] Affection takes us outside the narrow and confined strictures of our own personalities and helps us "first to notice, then to endure, then to smile at, then to enjoy, and finally to appreciate, the people who 'happen to be there.'"[8] Once we've experienced this in our own homes and neighborhoods, we may, if we choose, extend it into every area of our lives. Every person we meet may become "dear" to us. "Made for us? Thank God, no. They are themselves, odder than you could have believed and worth far more than we guessed."[9]

Because of this humility and broad-mindedness, affection does bear a striking resemblance to charity, or Christian love. But they must not be equated. Like all natural loves, affection may be a preparatory imitation of Christian love, "training . . . the spiritual muscles which Grace may later put to a higher service."[10] In this way, "natural liking or affection for people makes it easier to be 'charitable' towards them."[11] But, like all natural loves, affection may also become God's rival.

Corrupted Affection: The Tyranny of Possessiveness

The ways in which familial love can go wrong are legion. The first and most fundamental is that affection may become unduly possessive. We love our

---

6 Ibid., 34.
7 Ibid., 36.
8 Ibid., 37.
9 Ibid.
10 Ibid., 24.
11 Lewis, *Mere Christianity*, 130.

family members because they are, in some sense, "ours." But they are ours only "in some sense." Yet "some sense" can easily expand until it becomes "every sense." Screwtape encourages Wormwood to cultivate the patient's sense of ownership in his life. The devils introduce a confusion in our use of the word *my*.

> We teach them not to notice the different senses of the possessive pro-noun—the finely graded differences that run from "my boots" through "my dog," "my servant," "my wife," "my father," "my master" and "my country," to "my God." They can be taught to reduce all these senses to that of "my boots," the "my" of ownership.[12]

One of the most recurring characters in Lewis's writing is the tyranni-cal mother. In *The Four Loves*, she is called Mrs. Fidget. In *The Great Divorce*, she is called Pam, the ghost who is Michael's mother. In *Screwtape*, she is described as "the sort of woman who lives for others—you can always tell the others by their hunted expression."[13] Such people (and certainly not only mothers) "'live for others' but always in a discontented, grumbling way—always wondering why the others do not notice it more and always making a martyr of [themselves]."[14]

Mrs. Fidget oppressed her family with affection when she was alive. She wearied her husband, embittered her sons, and so "protected" her daughter that she robbed her of almost all joy. Even the dog felt her tyranny. She lived for her family—doing all the washing (though she did it badly and they begged her not to), cooking them hot lunches (despite her family's desire for cold ones), made them clothes (which they felt obligated to wear, no matter how ugly), and cared for their health (especially the "delicate" daughter who was caressed and babied to within an inch of her life). All of this help was a tyranny to her family, who were forced to do "things for her to help her to do things for them which they didn't want done."[15]

Mrs. Fidget's maternal instinct, like Pam's in *The Great Divorce*, was "uncontrolled and fierce and monomaniac." Without God's hand on the rein, this natural love had set up on its own and made itself into a false god. And as we saw before, one of Lewis's fundamental principles is that loves which set themselves up as gods eventually become demons. "Left to

---

12 Lewis, *The Screwtape Letters*, 126.
13 Ibid., 157.
14 Lewis, *Mere Christianity*, 196.
15 Lewis, *The Four Loves*, 50.

its natural bent affection becomes in the end greedy, naggingly solicitous, jealousy exacting, timorous."[16]

In addition, when we set up a natural love as an idol, we can no longer see ourselves rightly. Pam believes that she lived for Michael, that she sacrificed for him, that she "gave up [her] whole life." This she calls "love." But it was actually a very complicated form of hatred.

We see this in her demand for Michael. "I want my boy, and I mean to have him. He is mine, do you understand? Mine, mine, mine, for ever and ever."[17] This possessiveness is the demonic form of affection. Such idolatry, justified in the name of mother-love, appears to be an excess of maternal affection. But, according to Lewis, it is nothing of the sort.

> Excess of love, did ye say? There was no excess, there was defect. She loved her son too little, not too much. If she had loved him more there'd be no difficulty. I do not know how her affair will end. But it may well be that at this moment she's demanding to have him down with her in Hell. That kind is sometimes perfectly ready to plunge the soul they say they love in endless misery if only they can still in some fashion possess it.[18]

This is hatred indeed, wearing the face, but lacking the substance, of love. It prefers to possess the beloved in everlasting misery, rather than release them into joy.

Where does this tyrannical, possessive love come from? It is, according to Lewis, the twisted form of the need to be needed that marks the parental side of affection. It is a corrupt gift-love that *needs* to give, and therefore *demands* to give, whether the beloved wishes to receive or not. Mrs. Fidget knows that sitting up for her children spoils their evening and fills them with frustration and misery. But she does it because she is desperate not to feel that she is unnecessary. The needless washing, the needless cooking, the needless sowing, the needless waiting up—all of these are a protection against feeling unneeded. She works her fingers to the bone and works her family to the dust, all to avoid hearing what to her are the most horrible of all words: "They need me no longer."

But there is a darker motivation as well. If all that animated Mrs. Fidget were the fear of being unneeded, we could sympathize with her.

---

[16] Lewis, "The Sermon and the Lunch," in *God in the Dock*, 285.
[17] Lewis, *The Great Divorce*, 103.
[18] Ibid., 114–15.

We have felt that fear ourselves. Her labors and toil, however frustrating to us, take on a different cast when we realize they are a complicated way of her protecting herself. But Mrs. Fidget has been too long in her twisted self-protection; uglier motives have appeared, what Lewis in one place calls "the *mala mentis gaudia*—the pleasures of the mind which are intrinsically evil." These are "the dainties of Hell," the pleasures of having a grievance, or nursing a resentment, or fondling bitterness. Mrs. Fidget's "love" has developed an appetite for these hellish morsels. She has a sick relish for feeling ill-used and unappreciated. She has conditioned her soul to itch for being wounded—"anything will 'wound' a Mrs. Fidget"—and the scratching of that itch is one of the few remaining "joys" of her shriveled soul.[19]

Mrs. Fidget's sensitivity to "wounds," the ease with which she is hurt, is why she is so effective at making a martyr of herself. The intimacy of familial love makes it a prime candidate for the manipulation of those closest to us. This is, no doubt, how Mrs. Fidget got her family to "help" her. But it is important to remember that this tendency to manipulate is not restricted to maternal vampires "who cannot be caressed or obeyed enough."[20] It can infect an entire family, usually by substituting the faux virtue of unselfishness for the real virtue of love. Screwtape shows us how it works:

> This game is best played with more than two players, in a family with grown-up children for example. Something quite trivial, like having tea in the garden, is proposed. One member takes care to make it quite clear (though not in so many words) that he would rather not but is, of course, prepared to do so out of "Unselfishness." The others instantly withdraw their proposal, ostensibly through their "Unselfishness," but really because they don't want to be used as a sort of lay figure on which the first speaker practices petty altruisms. But he is not going to be done out of his debauch of Unselfishness either. He insists on doing "what the others want." They insist on doing what he wants. Passions are roused. Soon someone is saying "Very well then, I won't have any tea at all!" and a real quarrel ensues with bitter resentment on both sides. You see how it is done? If each side had been frankly contending for its own real wish, they would all have kept within the bounds of reason and courtesy; but just because the contention is reversed and each side is fighting the other side's battle, all the bitterness which really flows from thwarted self-righteousness and obstinacy and the accumulated grudges of the last ten

---

19 Lewis, *Letters to Malcolm*, 94.
20 Lewis, *The Four Loves*, 42.

years is concealed from them by the nominal or official "Unselfishness" of what they are doing or, at least, held to be excused by it. Each side is, indeed, quite alive to the cheap quality of the adversary's Unselfishness and of the false position into which he is trying to force them; but each manages to feel blameless and ill-used itself, with no more dishonesty than comes natural to a human.[21]

If you cannot recognize yourself and your relationships in this scene, then, as Lewis would say, "you are either a liar or a saint." Because unself-ishness primarily focuses on what we are going without rather than the good we are doing to others, it is easy for it to pat itself on the back, when it has only put a burden on the object of our "petty altruism." When this pat on the back is not echoed by the beneficiary of our unselfishness, we feel wounded. And this wound excuses whatever harsh words we say or manipulative tricks we pull.

If sin twists the maternal instinct so that a mother becomes a vampire, it warps the paternal instinct, turning a father into a brute. Fathers are par-ticularly prone to keeping their sons under their thumbs. The corruption of our familial gift-love, our need to be needed, means that we must always be the strongest, the wisest, the most well known. Any independence on the part of our children is crushed. We deliberately stunt their growth; we casually dismiss their opinions and thoughts. Lewis gives us a glimpse of this impulse, not in fatherhood, but in the form of Dr. Quartz, the teacher who pours himself into his students but cannot bear to see them become independent. At the first glimmer of resistance, of real maturity, he casts off his pupils (no doubt justifying his rejection because of their "disrespect and ingratitude"). He worked so hard to make his students fit to be his ri-vals, and then resented the moment of his success.[22]

This is the dark side of affection. To give, but to give grudgingly. To suffer for others, and to make sure that the others know it. To demand gratitude as a debt. To sacrifice our time for others, and then to hold it over their heads. To pout when we don't get our way, to sulk when we feel unappreciated, to prey upon the compassion of our families and dearest friends. To justify our possessiveness and tyranny on the grounds that we are doing our duty for the sake of others. What begins as a good desire to do things *for* others becomes, in the end, a craving to do things *to* others.

---

[21] Lewis, *The Screwtape Letters*, 156–57.
[22] Lewis, *The Four Loves*, 52.

What begins as a love that meets needs and bears burdens gradually and almost imperceptibly contorts our souls so that we demand to meet needs and bear burdens; we have no sense of ourselves apart from being the need meeters and burden bearers.

Friendship

Turning now to friendship, we discover how different it is from affection. Friendship is "the least natural of loves; the least instinctive, organic, biological, gregarious, and necessary. . . . Without Eros none of us would have been begotten and without Affection none of us would have been reared; but we can live and breed without Friendship."[23] Being unnecessary does not make it unimportant. Quite the contrary: "Friendship is unnecessary, like philosophy, like art, like the universe itself (for God did not need to create). It has no survival value; rather it is one of those things which give value to survival."[24]

Lewis accents the disembodied individuality of friendship: "It is an affair of disentangled, or stripped, minds. Eros will have naked bodies; Friendship naked personalities." Friendship for Lewis is high, almost intrinsically holy, "that luminous, tranquil, rational world of relationships freely chosen."[25] As a result, it is also quite rare, and thus underappreciated in the modern world. In fact, collectivism's push for "togetherness" in the modern world is hostile to friendship; it looks with suspicion on any love that causes people to withdraw from the herd in little twos and threes.

Friendship differs from Eros in another way. "Lovers are always talking to one another about their love; Friends hardly ever about their Friendship. Lovers are normally face to face, absorbed in each other; Friends, side by side, absorbed in some common interest."[26] In this way, friendship is always "about something"—some shared activity or common interest. Friendship arises when two people suddenly discover that they love the same thing in the same way. "What? You too? I thought I was the only one" is the typical expression of new friendship. Lewis discovered his first real friend this way. When he was about fifteen years old, a young boy named

---

[23] Ibid., 58.
[24] Ibid., 71. In one place, Lewis say that friendship "causes perhaps half of all the happiness in the world" ("The Inner Ring," in *The Weight of Glory and Other Addresses*, 157). It's also worth noting that one of the first things we learn about Eustace Clarence Scrubb is that he has no friends (Lewis, *The Voyage of the Dawn Treader*, 1).
[25] Lewis, *The Four Loves*, 70–71.
[26] Ibid., 61.

Arthur who lived near Lewis was ill; someone encouraged Lewis to visit him (though they were not friends at the time). Lewis accepted the invitation.

> I found Arthur sitting up in bed. On the table beside him lay a copy of *Myths of the Norsemen*. "Do you like that?" said I. "Do you like that?" said he. Next moment the book was in our hands, our heads were bent close together, we were pointing, quoting, talking—soon almost shouting— discovering in a torrent of questions that we liked not only the same thing, but the same parts of it and in the same way; that both knew the stab of Joy and that, for both, the arrow was shot from the North. Many thousands of people have had the experience of finding the first friend, and it is none the less a wonder; as great a wonder (pace the novelists) as first love, or even a greater. I had been so far from thinking such a friend possible that I had never even longed for one; no more than I longed to be King of England. . . . Nothing, I suspect, is more astonishing in any man's life than the discovery that there do exist people very, very like himself.[27]

This "You too?" is the hallmark of Lewis's view of friendship. In friendship, "Do you love me?" means "Do you see the same truth?"—or at least "Do you care about the same truth?"[28] And the glory of this experience is that it is not limited, like Eros, to two people. Adding a third person to a romantic relationship produces jealousy; Eros will not stand triangles for long. Friendship loves triangles and squares, even pentagons and hexagons. Lewis wonderfully draws out the power of adding friends: "In each of my friends there is something that only some other friend can fully bring out. By myself I am not large enough to call the whole man into activity; I want other lights than my own to show all his facets."[29]

Picture a gathering of friends: Becky, Jane, and Susan. Another friend, Ginny, comes along. No one makes Becky laugh like Ginny; no one makes Ginny so funny as Becky. And thus the whole circle of friends is enriched. The love of the three is augmented by the addition of the fourth.

In all of this discussion, Lewis is careful to distinguish a friend from an ally or a companion. An ally is one who "has your back," and certainly one's friends ought to be one's allies. But a friendship is different from an alliance. We need not experience the "You too?" with our allies. Likewise,

---

[27] Lewis, *Surprised by Joy*, 130–31.
[28] Lewis, *The Four Loves*, 71. "You will not find the warrior, the poet, the philosopher or the Christian by staring in his eyes as if he were your mistress: better fight beside him, read with him, argue with him, pray with him" (ibid.).
[29] Ibid., 61.

with companionship. Though that is most often what the modern world means by friendship, Lewis wants to make a distinction. Companionship occurs around a shared activity, one that is necessary for survival. This shared activity or mission demands planning and cooperation; thus, the people engaged in it must "talk shop." "This pleasure in cooperation, in talking shop, in the mutual respect and understanding of men who daily see one another tested" is what Lewis means by companionship. It occurs in schools, bars, golf clubs, mess halls, boardrooms, and offices, around innumerable activities and interests. But the relationship formed by companionship is not friendship; it is only the matrix of friendship. When two members of the team or tribe or club have the "You too?" moment, then the two are isolated from the larger team and become friends in the proper Lewisian sense. The shared activity, the common profession or recreation, is necessary to throw men together, but it does not of itself create friends. Friends share more than the common activity, "something more inward, less widely shared and less easily defined."[30]

Corrupted Friendship: The Lust for the Inner Ring

Now that we know what friendship is, we must attend to the ways in which it can go wrong. One danger is the one identified by Paul: "Bad company ruins good morals" (1 Cor. 15:33). Because friendship is always *about* something, it matters what that something is. Friendship "makes good men better and bad men worse."[31] Thieves and murderers can have the "You too?" moment about their thievery and murder. But there are more subtle dangers that Lewis identifies.

I noted above that friendship isolates us from the herd or group. Such isolation or secession can easily produce a form of corporate pride. Friends don't care that others find the object of their shared love to be silly or ridiculous. But the same impulse that allows them to be justly indifferent to the jeers of the crowd may also make them despise the crowd altogether. Their deafness to criticism fosters a sense of superiority. Our shared love of good literature may make us better judges of literature than the common man; but this truth (which we ought to contemplate only with great care) leads us to think that we are better in other ways as well. We may become a coterie, a self-appointed aristocracy. We may become patronizing to outsiders; one

---

30 Ibid., 66.
31 Ibid., 80.

of them asks a question and we glance at one another with a little laugh, metaphorically patting them on the head for their simplicity. "The glance and the laugh are . . . the audible and visible embodiment of a corporate superiority taken for granted and unconcealed."[32]

Such pride can easily turn a friendship into an Inner Ring. By Inner Ring, Lewis means a friendship that is "about almost nothing except the fact that it excludes."[33] This sort of "friendship" feeds on exclusivity. Though from the outside, all friendships look like Inner Rings, in a healthy friendship, the exclusivity is accidental. It's a by-product of "You too?" moments. But those in the grip of the Inner Ring move "from the innocent and necessary act of excluding to the spirit of exclusiveness . . . to the degrading pleasure of exclusiveness."[34] They build kingdoms in schools and in offices, on company softball teams and in book clubs, in the military and even in churches. Thus, alongside the official hierarchy of the institution, a separate hierarchy arises, built on the Inner Ring. The second system is invisible and fluid; you don't always know who's in and who's out. "There are no formal admissions or expulsions."[35] It is marked by informal slang, an allusive manner of conversation that acts as passwords for the insiders. You know you're inside one when you find yourself referring to an unidentified but identifiable group as "we" or "us." And you know that you're outside when you regularly refer to an unidentified but identifiable group as "they" or "them," or "so-and-so and his set." The word *clique* approximates the meaning. If the idea is still opaque, just recall the social system at your junior high or middle school, and it ought to become clear.

According to Lewis, the lust for the Inner Ring is one of the chief motivators of human action. "I believe that in all men's lives at certain periods, and in many men's lives at all periods between infancy and extreme old age, one of the most dominant elements is the desire to be inside the local Ring and the terror of being left outside."[36] He links the lust for the Inner Ring with worldliness.[37] And importantly, Lewis doesn't restrict Inner Rings to

---

[32] Ibid., 84.

[33] Ibid., 85.

[34] Lewis, *The Four Loves*, 86. "Your genuine Inner Ring exists for exclusion. There'd be no fun if there were no outsiders. The invisible line would have no meaning unless most people were on the wrong side of it. Exclusion is no accident; it is the essence" (Lewis, "The Inner Ring," in *The Weight of Glory and Other Addresses*, 156).

[35] Lewis, "The Inner Ring," in *The Weight of Glory and Other Addresses*, 144.

[36] Ibid., 146.

[37] Within the category of worldliness, Screwtape places "Worldly Vanities, the Choice of Friends, and the Value of Time" (Lewis, *The Screwtape Letters*, 59). In *Surprised by Joy*, Lewis describes the effect that

snobs, to hipsters, to the hangers-on who love to be around famous people, or to those who desperately try to keep up with the Joneses. Wherever there is friendship, there may become an Inner Ring. In fact, we may be immune to certain rings because we have an intense desire to enter some different ring. And it's the intensity of our desire that is the issue—"our longing to enter them, our anguish when we are excluded, and the kind of pleasure we feel when we get in."[38] For the heart of the Inner Ring is "the lust for the esoteric, the longing to be inside . . . the delicious sense of secret intimacy."[39]

Of course, the lust for the Inner Ring is insatiable; we are never satisfied in its fulfillment. If our chief desire is to be on the inside of the invisible line, then we will never be happy. "The circle cannot have from within the charm it had from outside."[40] Once we're in, the novelty wears off, and the ring we just entered loses its appeal. The only reason we don't wise up to this trick is that rings are often stacked inside each other, like onions or Russian nesting dolls.

Again, think of junior high or middle school. You come to the school from another town. You quickly identify the obvious rings in the school, usually by who sits with whom at lunch or what kind of clothing they wear. You select your target ring (or, if you're "lucky," perhaps a ring selects you). You learn the ropes; you jump through the invisible hoops, and soon you discover that you're in. The signal is given and you find yourself inside. But once inside, you discover how shallow the ring is. But you also discover something else. From the outside you thought that the ring consisted of the ten to fifteen cool kids in the school. But now, on the inside, you realize that there is actually a ring within a ring. And now you set to work on entering that one. In time, again you're successful, and you discover yet another ring, this time of only two or three people who are really inside. And, miracle of miracles, you get in that one as well. And then you discover more rings. The ringleader has an older brother; he himself is only a minor member of the older brother's set. But now that you're "best friends," you too can come along. And on and on it goes.

Of course, this is the best-case scenario. Most of us aren't so

---

an older boy at school had on him. "What attacked me through Pogo was not the Flesh (I had that of my own) but the World: the desire for glitter, swagger, distinction, the desire to be in the know. He gave little help, if any, in destroying my chastity, but he made sad work of certain humble and childlike and self-forgetful qualities which (I think) had remained with me till that moment. I began to labor very hard to make myself into a fop, a cad, and a snob" (68).

[38] Lewis, "The Inner Ring," in *The Weight of Glory and Other Addresses*, 149.

[39] Ibid., 151.

[40] Ibid., 155.

THE NATURAL LOVES

successful. We run into invisible walls we are never able to climb. We commit unpardonable sins that get us banished to the outer darkness. But whether we succeed or whether we fail, whether we mope on the outside or pass triumphantly further up and further in, two facts remain: (1) we are Inner Ringers, and (2) we are never truly happy. Either we're perpetually stung by the rejection or, having succeeded beyond our wildest dreams, we have peeled away the entire onion, and there is now nothing left.

But we might be unhappy for additional reasons. The things we had to do to gain entry into the various rings haunt our consciences.[41] We cut ties with the first real friend we made at the school in order to court friendship with the cool kids. And now we engage in small acts of unkindness, even cruelty, in order to propitiate the ring and enter the smaller circle. Worse still, we begin to take pleasure in the loneliness and humiliation of our former friends, those we've left outside. The deliciousness of being "in" salves (or is it sears?) our conscience and we quickly learn the ropes. We drop names of the important people to show that we too are important. We talk to fellow members of our ring in front of outsiders in order to feed on their envy. We learn the delight of tantalizing those on the border, only to deny them fruition. And worst of all, we do it so easily, so effortlessly. And we don't stop in middle school.

In describing these acts, Lewis doesn't believe that Inner Ringers are inherently more evil than everyone else. But he does think that "of all passions the passion for the Inner Ring is most skillful in making a man who is not yet a very bad man do very bad things." It's the desire to be welcomed by the ring that can lead us to make small compromises that set us on a dangerous and tragic trajectory. One of Lewis's key insights is that we are always sowing seeds of our future selves, and if we sow to the Inner Ring, there's a good chance that when harvest comes, we will be reaped as scoundrels—that peculiar kind of scoundrels who wonder how they ended up falling so far. In fact, the best way to grasp the lust for the Inner Ring would be to read Lewis's essay on the subject and then follow with the story of Mark Studdock in *That Hideous Strength*. A passage from the essay perfectly describes the choice that confronts Studdock again and again:

[41] In *Surprised by Joy* Lewis describes the negative effects of the all-consuming desire to be included in an exclusionary group. From this impulse, he argues, "all sorts of meanness flow; the sycophancy that courts those higher in the scale, the cultivation of those whom it is well to know, the speedy abandonment of friendships that will not help on the upward path, the readiness to join the cry against the unpopular, the secret motive in almost every action" (108).

To nine out of ten of you the choice which could lead to scoundrelism will come, when it does come, in no very dramatic colours. Obviously bad men, obviously threatening or bribing, will almost certainly not appear. Over a drink or a cup of coffee, disguised as a triviality and sandwiched between two jokes, from the lips of a man, or woman, whom you have recently been getting to know rather better and whom you hope to know better still—just at the moment when you are most anxious not to appear crude, or naïf or a prig—the hint will come. It will be the hint of something which is not quite in accordance with the technical rules of fair play; something which the public, the ignorant, romantic public, would never understand; something which even the outsiders in your own profession are apt to make a fuss about, but something, says your new friend, which "we"—and at the word "we" you try not to blush for mere pleasure—something "we always do." And you will be drawn in, if you are drawn in, not by desire for gain or ease, but simply because at that moment, when the cup was so near your lips, you cannot bear to be thrust back again into the cold outer world. It would be so terrible to see the other man's face—that genial, confidential, delightfully sophisticated face—turn suddenly cold and contemptuous, to know that you had been tried for the Inner Ring and rejected. And then, if you are drawn in, next week it will be something a little further from the rules, and next year something further still, but all in the jolliest, friendliest spirit. It may end in a crash, a scandal, and penal servitude; it may end in millions, a peerage, and giving the prizes at your old school. But you will be a scoundrel.[42]

Screwtape also describes the subtlety of the temptation. When Wormwood's "patient" makes friends with some worldly people, Screwtape asks,

Did he commit himself deeply? I don't mean in words. There is a subtle play of looks and tones and laughs by which a mortal can imply that he is of the same party as those to whom he is speaking. That is the kind of betrayal you should specially encourage, because the man does not fully realize it himself; and by the time he does you will have made withdrawal difficult.[43]

Like the earlier quotation, the choice is a small one. But the results, if Screwtape has his way, will be momentous. The man will begin to conform to the assumptions and views of this new ring. "He will be silent when he

---

42 Lewis, "The Inner Ring," in *The Weight of Glory and Other Addresses*, 153–54.
43 Lewis, *The Screwtape Letters*, 57–58.

ought to speak and laugh when he ought to be silent. He will assume, at first only by his manner, but presently by his words, all sorts of cynical and skeptical attitudes which are not really his."[44] Over time, he will become flippant, assuming (but never demonstrating) that virtue and nobility and other serious subjects are somehow ridiculous. (One thinks of what passes for late-night television and comedy these days.) This flippancy, though it bears a resemblance to true laughter, actually inoculates the man to God and joy. Indeed "it is a thousand miles away from joy: it deadens, instead of sharpening, the intellect; and it excites no affection between those who practice it."[45]

He will drift and begin to live a double life, looking down upon his worldly friends because they are not as spiritual as he is, and looking down upon his fellow Christians because they cannot comprehend the urbane and mocking world that he inhabits on weekends. He will inhabit two different rings and feel superior in both of them since he alone is the "complete, balanced, complex man." Even if the man realizes that he has compromised, he will continue to justify his friendships with the world-lings "on the ground that he is, in some unspecified way, doing these people 'good' by the mere fact of drinking their cocktails and laughing at their jokes."[46] He will imagine that he is being the salt of the earth at precisely the moment that he is losing his savor. He will believe that he is being the light of the world just as he is placing his lamp under the basket of worldliness.

Eros

Finally, we turn to examine Eros. Lewis begins by distinguishing between merely sexual desire and being "in love." The former he calls Venus, and he accents the bodily dimension of this appetite. The latter, while often mixed with Venus, is Eros proper, what today we might call romantic love. (For simplicity's sake, and because this is Lewis's own practice, I will write about Eros from the masculine side, with a man loving a woman; I trust female readers can make the necessary adjustments.)

Eros often begins with "delighted pre-occupation with the Beloved— a general, unspecified pre-occupation with her in her totality."[47] His is a

---

44 Ibid., 58.
45 Ibid., 67.
46 Ibid., 60.
47 Lewis, *The Four Loves*, 93.

contemplative love. A man in this state is not thinking about sex; he is thinking about a person. "If you asked him what he wanted, the true reply would often be, 'To go on thinking of her.'" Thus, we see a key difference between romantic love and sexual desire in their purest forms. Sexual desire wants a thing—sex, a sensuous bodily pleasure. Eros wants the beloved as a person. A man in the grip of lust does not, properly speaking, want a woman. "He wants a pleasure for which a woman happens to be the necessary piece of apparatus."[48] But Eros is different; it makes a man want not any woman but a particular woman—the beloved herself and not merely the pleasure she can give.

Drawing in our categories from Hedonics, Eros transforms a need-pleasure (the desire for sex) into the most appreciative of all pleasures. In the grip of Eros, we long to lose ourselves in the beloved. We want to somehow mingle with her, much as Milton's angels, with their bodies made of pure light, are able to totally embrace one another in a way that transcends our human capacities. So great is our love and desire for the beloved that we will forsake all other happiness for her sake. In this way, Eros can overwhelm our reason. We may know beyond a doubt that misery awaits us if we pursue our beloved; Eros still does not hesitate. "Better this than parting. Better to be miserable with her than happy without her. Let our hearts break provided they break together."[49] We would rather be unhappy with our beloved than happy on any other terms.

In calling forth this total commitment on our part, Eros displays a real splendor and grandeur, a real nearness to God by likeness. The willingness to bear any burden, pay any price, suffer any humiliation or pain in service of the one we love—this is a true picture of Love himself. In this way, just as creation helps us to understand what the word *glory* means (as we saw in chap. 11), so also Eros is one of the ways we come to understand what is meant by charity, or divine love. Whether we are talking about our love for God or our love for neighbor, Eros gives us experiential knowledge of the kind of love God calls us to have, a true image of divine things.

The proper end of Eros is marriage. The desire to completely mingle with our beloved is fulfilled when one man and one woman become one flesh. Sexual union is one (vital) dimension of the total union of husband and wife that makes them a single organism in the same way that a bow

[48] Ibid., 94.
[49] Ibid., 107.

and violin are one musical instrument.[50] This lifelong union is why divorce is such a horror; "it is more like having both your legs cut off than it is like dissolving a business partnership or even deserting a regiment."[51]

Two features of the relation between Eros and marriage are worth highlighting. First, Eros, in its intensity, loves to make promises. Lovers are always committing themselves to lifelong fidelity. They can't help it. Falling in love is so great an experience that we find ourselves unable to believe it is transitory. Eros has taken us outside ourselves—"it has made appetite itself altruistic, tossed personal happiness aside as a triviality and planted the interests of another in the centre of our being."[52] For those in the thrall of Eros, the idea that they could fall out of love is unthinkable; it is offensive even to suggest it. And so the promises flow effortlessly.

And also in vain. For however intense our feelings of Eros, we will not go on feeling them. "Eros is driven to promise what Eros of himself cannot perform."[53] But even though Eros cannot keep the promises himself, he is right to make them. It simply falls to us to keep them. We do so under the influence of a deeper, higher, and quieter love. This second type of love is not merely an intense feeling—"it is a deep unity, maintained by the will and deliberately strengthened by habit; reinforced by (in Christian marriages) the grace which both partners ask, and receive, from God."[54] Eros was the explosion that started the engine of marriage; it is the quieter love that is marriage's true fuel.

Second, I noted above that marriage creates a union between a man and a woman like the combination of a bow and violin. This stresses both their unity as one instrument (one flesh) and their substantial differences. A bow and a violin are very different things. So also are a husband and wife. In *The Four Loves*, Lewis accents this difference by stressing the representative dimension of Eros as it is expressed in the sexual union. In marital sex, the husband and wife each play a part. "In us all the masculinity and femininity of the world, all that is assailant and responsive, are momentarily focused."[55]

To some Christians, Lewis's reflections on the symbolic aspect of the marital union appear odd and confusing. For example, the symbolic or representative role played by the husband and wife Lewis calls "the Pagan

---

[50] Lewis, *Mere Christianity*, 104.
[51] Ibid., 105.
[52] Lewis, *The Four Loves*, 114.
[53] Ibid.
[54] Lewis, *Mere Christianity*, 109.
[55] Lewis, *The Four Loves*, 103.

Sacrament." By this, he does not mean that this representation is ungodly or sinful; rather, he is stressing that it is universal or natural. Even non-Christians throughout history have recognized the complementary differences between man and woman, and have sought to express and accent these differences in the marriage bed. Thus, the symbolism inherent in sexual union is a part of natural revelation; it is Deep Magic, woven into the fabric of the created order by God himself.

The whole point is that there is a natural mystery to marriage that even those outside the Christian faith recognize and celebrate. In the marriage act, "the lovers cease to be solely John and Mary; the universal He and She are emphasized."[56] The married couple put on their nakedness like ceremonial robes for a ritual. The husband represents man—initiative, responsibility, authority. In this ritual or masque, he plays the part of the Sky-Father. The wife, on the other hand, plays the part of woman—responsive, receptive, and submissive. She is the Earth-Mother. The physical union of a man and his wife is a picture of the union of heaven and earth—the Sky-Father waters the earth, and somehow the Earth-Mother brings forth fruit. So also the man plants his seed in the woman, and she bears the fruit of children. Or, again, the woman is a garden, a field. The man is the farmer who enters the garden to cultivate and enjoy its fruits. If this sort of language makes you blush or feel shy, that is all well and good. There is a great shyness about it. But let your imagination rest in the soil of the Song of Solomon and see if you do not begin to see what Lewis is gesturing at.

Lewis is aware that stressing the sacramental dimension of sexual union runs the risk of giving the marital act an undue and unhealthy gravity. We may take sex too seriously. What's more, given our sinfulness and selfishness, we may mistake the drama for reality. Thus, he stresses that the crown worn by the husband as the Sky-Father is a paper crown. A man must never truly arrogate to himself the sovereignty offered him by Venus in the marriage bed. He may play his part in the drama, but he must not strut or dominate in married life as a whole. Likewise, the extreme self-surrender of the woman is enacted in the ritual or drama; outside the marital act, the asymmetry or inequality of husband and wife is balanced by the reality that they are "two immortal souls, two free-born adults, two citizens."[57] This is important to Lewis. Legal and political equality is a

---

[56] Ibid., 104.
[57] Ibid., 103–4.

protection, given the pervasive reality of our sin and especially the way men have abused their natural prerogatives. But underneath this cloak of equality, the real inequalities remain. The authority and obedience that mark marriage are inherently good and beautiful.

Explaining the mystery is difficult; we are dealing with high matters indeed. But Lewis believes that the relation between husband and wife is marked by an inherent inequality. The man initiates; the woman responds. The man gives; the woman receives. Of course, even in receiving the man, the woman also gives to him. She gives herself. This is why Lewis uses the word "surrender." In the drama of sex, there is no equality; the relationship is asymmetrical. This does not mean (heaven forbid) that the man is better or superior. Presumably he is a better *man* than she is, but, of course, she is a better *woman* than he is. That's precisely the point; they are not interchangeable. Whatever mutuality occurs in the marital bed, it is not a strictly egalitarian one. There is a glorious asymmetry in the act, one that wise lovers can both enact and enjoy.

Gender and Sex

Before turning to the ways in which Eros can be twisted, let us explore one additional aspect of Lewis's view of the relation between the sexes. Lewis regards gender as something deeper and more fundamental than sex.

> Sex is . . . merely the adaptation to organic life of a fundamental polarity which divides all created beings. Female sex is simply one of the things that have feminine gender; there are many others, and Masculine and Feminine meet us on planes of reality where male and female would be simply meaningless.[58]

Male and female are faint and blurred reflections of a higher distinction between masculinity and femininity.

In the Space Trilogy, Lewis attempts to capture the quality of masculinity and femininity. The first novel takes place on Mars, the masculine planet, with its high, pointed mountains, its forests of stone, its cool weather and dangerous climate. The second takes place on Venus, the feminine planet, with its warm oceans, its soft, floating islands, its luxuriant vegetation. But the quality of masculinity and femininity is not restricted

---

[58] Lewis, *Perelandra*, 172.

to the geography and climate of the planets themselves. Lewis attempts to display this fundamental polarity in his description of Malacandra and Perelandra, the two angelic beings who govern Mars and Venus.

As purely spiritual beings, Malacandra and Perelandra could not be male or female; they were sexless and lacked all physically defined sexual differences. Nevertheless, Malacandra was masculine, and Perelandra feminine. Malacandra was like rhythm, providing the steady, foundational beat beneath music. Perelandra was melody, running atop the rhythm and giving the music its memorable beauty. Or, again:

> Malacandra seemed to him to have the look of one standing armed, at the ramparts of his own remote archaic world, in ceaseless vigilance, his eyes ever roaming the earthward horizon whence his danger came long ago. "A sailor's look," Ransom once said to me; "you know . . . eyes that are impregnated with distance."[59]

Masculinity is oriented outward to the horizon in a posture of protection and provision. There is a cold hardness about masculinity; Malacandra stood with a spear in his hand, ready to defend those in his charge from enemies. Perelandra, on the other hand, opened inward, as if her eyes were "the curtained gateway to a world of waves and murmurings and wandering airs, of life that rocked in winds and splashed on mossy stones and descended as the dew and arose sunward in thin-spun delicacy of mist."[60] She glowed with a warm splendor, and her palms were open as if to receive. Again, the mysteries of gender and, flowing from them, of the male and female sex are not easily grasped through explanations. Far better to imaginatively experience them through immersion in Lewis's imagery and language in his Space Trilogy.

Corrupted Eros: Pornography and Justified Promise Breaking

We turn now to the ways in which Eros can go wrong. In the interests of space, I'll limit myself to four of these ways—two that are corruptions of the sexual desire, and two that are corruptions of Eros proper. Screwtape describes the ways hellish propaganda has distorted our sexual "taste," by which he means the standards of beauty and desirability in a given society.

---

59 Ibid.
60 Ibid.

The distortions differ from generation to generation; the paragon of beauty in the Jazz Age was not the same as that of the 1960s, which differed again from that of the 1990s. The common thread in these distortions was the falseness and impossibility of the standard. In Lewis's day this was accomplished by propping up and pinching back the women to make them look slimmer or firmer than they really were. In our day, Photoshop, lighting, and computers achieve the same result. The whole goal is to direct men's desires toward something that does not exist—"making the role of the eye in sexuality more and more important and at the same time making its demands more and more impossible."[61] Thus, Screwtape unpacks the demonic strategy inherent in pornography.

But the corruption of the sexual desire doesn't stop with the distortion of the female image. Pornography is a stepping stone to the evil of masturbation, which Lewis regards as evil because it takes an appetite designed to lead us outside ourselves (first to a spouse, and then to children and grandchildren) and turns it back on itself. Masturbation "sends the man back into the prison of himself, there to keep a harem of imaginary brides." And the longer a man lives in this prison, the harder it is for him to escape. A man in the grip of such lusts has enormous difficulty in pursuing and uniting with a real woman. The harem in his head (or on his computer) is "always accessible, always subservient, calls for no sacrifices or adjustments, and can be endowed with erotic and psychological attractions which no real woman can rival." In the imaginary film that plays in his head or on his screen, "he is always adored, always the perfect lover." In fact, the desire to be adored and admired as a "real man" is often as much a motive for pursuing the pornographic as any biological or bodily appetite. But this fantasy makes no demands on his selfishness; "no mortification [is] ever imposed on his vanity." The imaginary harem, in the end, simply becomes the medium through which a man increasingly adores himself.[62]

Screwtape goes on to describe a second corruption of the sexual desire. He notes that most men are haunted by a terrestrial and an infernal Venus. In other words, there are two idealized women that captivate the imagination of a man. Desire for the *terrestrial* Venus is more or less natural, and its tendency, as we saw above, is to lead to marriage (though it can be exploited

---

[61] Lewis, *The Screwtape Letters*, 120. Of course, the same distortion can happen in the female perception of men as well, whether in terms of physical attractiveness or, more often, in terms of the impossible standards set through movies, books, and television.

[62] Lewis to Keith Masson, March 6, 1956, in *Collected Letters*, 3:758.

by leading a man to illicitly desire his neighbor's wife). But the desire for the *infernal* Venus is a brutal desire; there is a "tang" in the flavor; the man is captivated by the "visible animality, or sulkiness, or craft, or cruelty"[63] in the face of the woman. This is the grotesque desire a man has for a prostitute or porn star, and it can be twisted beyond recognition into something profoundly ugly and perverse.

The sulkiness or cruelty that draws a man to the infernal Venus is due to the modern tendency to take Venus so seriously. For Lewis, the solemnization of sex, in both its Christian and unbelieving forms, is ludicrous and destructive. Lewis points to our advertisements as evidence of the wrong kind of seriousness; they portray sex in terms of "the rapt, the intense, the swoony-devout."[64] Whatever kind of gravity sex is intended to have (and Lewis admits that it is a serious business), we have chosen the wrong kind. We have removed the gaiety and laughter from sex, scrubbed the mirth off of Aphrodite's face.

The result is that modern society is practically obsessed with sex. Under the guise of bringing sex out of the closet and treating it like any other appetite, we have actually given it a centrality and privilege that we would never give to our other appetites. We know that our other impulses must be bridled. "Absolute obedience to your instinct for self-preservation is what we call cowardice; to your acquisitive impulse, avarice. Even sleep must be resisted if you're a sentry. But every unkindness and breach of faith seems to be condoned provided that the object aimed at is 'four bare legs in a bed.'"[65] We have allowed our sexual appetite to grow ludicrous and excessive; we are oversexed and obsessed with sex. We feel that we have a right to sexual happiness. As a result "the sexual motive is taken to condone all sorts of behaviour which, if it had any other end in view, would be condemned as merciless, treacherous and unjust."[66] And because we are trying to draw water from a broken cistern, we find that the satisfaction promised is illusory. Venus, in her warped and idolatrous form, cannot make good on her promises, even as the treachery we committed in pursuing her and the misery and pain that resulted are all too real.[67]

---

[63] Lewis, *The Screwtape Letters*, 121.

[64] Lewis, *The Four Loves*, 98.

[65] Lewis, "We Have No 'Right to Happiness,'" in *God in the Dock*, 320.

[66] Ibid.

[67] In particular, Lewis notes that in a sexualized society that tolerates widespread infidelity, women are almost always the greatest losers. They are generally more monogamous (even for biological reasons) and thus they are more often the victims of betrayal rather than the perpetrators.

A society in which conjugal infidelity is tolerated must always be in the long run a society adverse to women. Women, whatever a few male songs and satires may say to the contrary,

But this is not just a problem for sexual desire. In fact, Lewis thinks that a wrong desire for sex, while clearly immoral and destructive, cannot wreak the same kind of havoc as the exaltation of Eros. Much of the standard dissatisfaction in marriage is due to "the false belief that the blend of affection, fear, and desire which they call 'being in love' is the only thing that makes marriage either happy or holy."[68] We come to believe that Eros really did intend to make good on the promises he made; that it is possible to experience "being in love" in a permanent fashion. When reality finally sets in, we are primed and ready to abandon our former love for a newer model.

As we saw earlier, Eros at his most godlike makes his greatest demands. And it is then that he is most dangerous, producing tragic adulteries, cruel abandonments, and even murder and suicide. His demands feel overwhelming; his decrees irresistible. We say that we "can't help falling in love." In such moments, we can move from revering our beloved to revering Eros himself. We idolize romantic love and justify all manner of evil in its name. Lovers excuse their betrayals with the words "Love made us do it." A man who says that his fear or anger made him break trust or betray a friend speaks differently. The latter is ashamed even as he makes his excuse. "Love made us do it" is less of an appeal to extenuating circumstances and more of an appeal to authority. Being in love justifies the act; in fact, there may be a hint of boasting, defiance, even martyrdom in the words.

> The pair can say to one another in an almost sacrificial spirit, "It is for love's sake that I have neglected my parents—left my children—cheated my partner—failed my friend at his greatest need." These reasons in love's law have passed for good. The votaries may even come to feel a particular merit in such sacrifices; what costlier offering can be laid on love's altar than one's conscience?[69]

Eros, thus exalted as a god, becomes a demon, and as a demon, be-

---

are more naturally monogamous than men; it is a biological necessity. Where promiscuity prevails, they will therefore always be more often the victims than the culprits. Also, domestic happiness is more necessary to them than to us. And the quality by which they most easily hold a man, their beauty, decreases every year after they have come to maturity, but this does not happen to those qualities of personality—women don't really care twopence about our *looks*—by which we hold women. Thus in the ruthless war of promiscuity women are at a double disadvantage. They play for higher stakes and are also more likely to lose. I have no sympathy with moralists who frown at the increasing crudity of female provocativeness. These signs of desperate competition fill me with pity. (Ibid., 321–22)

[68] Lewis, *The Screwtape Letters*, 108–9.
[69] Lewis, *The Four Loves*, 113.

comes destructive. The desire for the beloved takes on a morbid form. Like corrupted affection, exalted Eros becomes unduly possessive and imperialistic. The lovers seek to conquer each other, to absorb without being absorbed, to make the other person in his or her totality a reflection of oneself. The other person becomes a mirror in which we see our own greatness and glory. We use others, assimilate them, and make them extensions of ourselves. What normal lovers might utter in jest—"I could eat you"—takes on an ominous tone. Eros, in this exaggerated and morbid form, bears a great resemblance to hatred, as lovers in the grip of corrupted Eros become increasingly jealous, exacting, and resentful.

CHAPTER 14

DIVINE LOVE

Putting the Natural
Loves in Their Place

In *The Four Loves*, Lewis's overall aim is to show that charity—love for God—must govern all our natural loves. Our loves must be "ordered," to use Augustine's term. Lewis's method is to distinguish and describe the three natural loves and then to show how they go wrong. However, in the final chapter, he attempts to ground this self-destruction of the natural loves in their failure to be properly subjected to charity. Now that I too have distinguished, described, and illustrated the natural loves and their corruptions, I want to show how, for Lewis, divine love reorders and guides the natural loves to their proper end.

We begin with God's love itself. God is love, and his love is necessarily a gift-love. God has no needs; this is an essential truth of the Christian faith. No constraint led him to create the world. He was not lonely, nor was he bored. In himself, he lived at home in the happy land of the Trinity, and he lived there in complete and utter contentment. His creation of the world was a free overflowing of his own generosity. "God, who needs nothing, loves into existence wholly superfluous creatures in order that He may love and perfect them."[1]

As the Maker of heaven and earth, God "implants in us both Gift-loves

---

[1] Lewis, *The Four Loves*, 127.

and Need-loves."[2] As we have seen, the gift-loves are images of divine love; they show us, in part, what God's love is like. Our need-loves, however, are not resemblances of God. Rather, they are correlatives; they are the creaturely answer to the fundamental divine gift-love. Our need-loves are recognitions of our own real poverty.

From this natural starting point, we've seen how the lower loves can go wrong; they can aspire to deity, setting themselves up as rivals to God, with the result that they become demonic. But it need not be so. Instead, the lower loves are meant to be governed by God's love. We must put first things first. But this can easily be misunderstood. We might wrongly think, as Augustine apparently did, that great grief at the loss of an earthly good is evidence of an inordinate love. To sob uncontrollably at the death of a friend would show that we loved the person too much. The way to avoid such inordinate loves, then, would be to refuse to give our hearts to anything but God. In other words, "do not let your happiness depend on something you may lose." Lewis rightly notes that this sort of safety-first attitude is more Stoic than Christian.[3] Jesus wept over Jerusalem and at the tomb of Lazarus. Paul says that he would have had "sorrow upon sorrow" if Epaphroditus had died (Phil. 2:27). He had unceasing anguish in his heart because his Jewish brethren were cut off from their Messiah (Rom. 10:1). Whatever else Christian love may be, it is not safe from sorrow.

Love demands vulnerability. Apart from such vulnerability, our hearts grow hard and stiff.

> Love anything, and your heart will certainly be wrung and possibly be broken. If you want to make sure of keeping it intact, you must give your heart to no one, not even to an animal. Wrap it carefully round with hobbies and little luxuries; avoid all entanglements; lock it up safe in the casket or coffin of your selfishness. But in that casket—safe, dark, motionless, airless—it will change. It will not be broken; it will become unbreakable, impenetrable, irredeemable.

We will not preserve our love for God by suppressing and resisting all love for creatures. The road of safety first, the road of no risk of tragedy, leads

---

[2] Ibid.

[3] Ibid., 120. In *Till We Have Faces*, the Fox, who is a Stoic, articulates the same basic perspective. When Psyche is taken for the Great Offering, the Fox weeps over the loss and then expresses his shame: "To love, and to lose what we love, are equally things appointed for our nature. If we cannot bear the second well, that evil is ours" (86).

only to damnation. "The only place outside Heaven where you can be perfectly safe from all the dangers and perturbations of love is Hell."[4]

But Augustine's solution goes wrong in another way as well. It treats our natural loves as though they are *inherently* in competition with our love for God. In this view, love is a zero-sum game: the more you love creatures, the less you can love God. Love for one replaces or cancels out love for the other. Ironically, it is Screwtape who gives voice to the zero-sum view. He calls it the philosophy of hell: "'To be' *means* 'to be in competition.'"[5] But this is not what Lewis means by inordinate loves. Inordinate is not a quantitative term, as though we are loving lower things "too much" in any absolute, measurable sense. Rather, when our loves are out of order, it is because we love earthly things too much *in proportion* to our love for God. But in that case, the issue is not the greatness of our earthly loves; it is the smallness of our love to God. Moreover, this is not first and foremost about the comparative degrees of warm feelings toward God and creatures (though such issues do enter the discussion). Rather, "the real question is, which (when the alternative comes) do you serve, or choose, or put first? To which claim does your will, in the last resort, yield?"[6] This is what Jesus meant by the call for his disciples to hate father and mother, husband and wife, children and life (Luke 14:26). It has to do with ultimate allegiance, deepest desire and affection, fundamental loyalty. As we saw in an earlier chapter, first things must come first. And God is the first of first things.

Four Gifts of Rightly Ordered Love

So, if putting God first isn't fundamentally a matter of suppressing, denying, or rejecting earthly loves in every sense, what does it mean? If we place God at the center of our loves, what will happen to us? Or, put another way, if gift-loves and need-loves are natural, what happens when grace restores and transforms nature? Lewis mentions four gifts that God graciously gives us when divine love, or charity, orders our natural loves.

First, *we share in God's own gift-love*. Our natural gift-loves are directed toward objects we find lovable in themselves. Under the influence of charity, we are enabled to love the unlovable—the ugly, the proud, fools and tyrants, even our enemies. Evil men know how to give good gifts to their

4 Lewis, *The Four Loves*, 121.
5 Lewis, *The Screwtape Letters*, 106.
6 Lewis, *The Four Loves*, 122–23.

own children, but it is the sons of God who pray for their persecutors, who return blessing in the face of cursing, who do good to those who do evil, who give a cup of cold water to their enemies in distress (Matt. 5:44; Rom. 12:14, 20–21).

Second, *God enables us to love him with his own gift-love.* Not that we give him anything that isn't already his.

Who has given a gift to [the Lord],
    that he might be repaid? (Rom. 11:35)

Instead, we willingly offer to God by grace what is already his by right. We render back to him what he has freely given to us. "Our wills are ours to make them Thine."[7] And, as Jesus taught us, one of the ways that we give to God is by giving to the poor and needy in the name of Christ. "As you did it to one of the least of these my brothers, you did it to me" (Matt. 25:40).

Third, *God does not merely exalt and transform our gift-loves; he also glorifies our need-loves.* He gives us a supernatural need-love of himself. "Like a river making its own channel, like a magic wine which in being poured out should simultaneously create the glass that was to hold it, God turns our need of Him into Need-love of Him."[8] He doesn't create the need; that is already there by nature. Instead, he gives us a full recognition, a sensible awareness, even a glad acceptance of our utter bankruptcy before him. This is "the joy of total dependence," the true humility that we explored in an earlier chapter, in contrast to the subtle and vain idea that we have something on our own, some truly native luminosity, to commend us to God. When God turns the fact of our need into the reality of a need-love, we become "jolly beggars." We part with our last claim to intrinsic freedom, worth, and power, and discover that the only freedom, worth, and power worth having is that which is ours only because it is (in another sense) not ours.[9]

Finally, *God gives us a need-love of others.* That is, he enables us to receive with gladness the charity of others. Most of us are willing to accept charity from God; he is so high above us that we feel the propriety of his gift. But when his gift comes to us through the hands of a fellow creature, we balk. "We want to be loved for our cleverness, beauty, gen-

---

[7] Ibid., 127.
[8] Ibid., 129.
[9] Ibid.

erosity, fairness, usefulness."[10] We find it incredibly difficult to be loved in the face of our poverty, sinfulness, and ugliness. Lewis's illustration of this point is apt:

> Suppose yourself a man struck down shortly after marriage by an incurable disease which may not kill you for many years; useless, impotent, hideous, disgusting; dependent on your wife's earnings; impoverishing where you hoped to enrich; impaired even in intellect and shaken by gusts of uncontrollable temper, full of unavoidable demands. And suppose your wife's care and pity to be inexhaustible. The man who can take this sweetly, who can receive all and give nothing without resentment, who can abstain even from those tiresome self-depreciations which are really only a demand for petting and reassurance, is doing something which Need-love in its merely natural condition could not attain.[11]

To receive in this way is often harder (and, in a certain respect, more blessed) than to give. To receive charity not merely from God but from God in another person; to receive it by this channel with gladness and gratitude, without putting on airs; to be so at home in our poverty and indigence that we can receive such charity without (in the manipulative sense) "taking advantage of" such charity—this is a transformation of the soul that only grace can accomplish.

Such is the larger picture of the way charity transforms our loves. But, as Lewis would say, we must always bring things down to brass tacks. The remainder of this chapter will attempt to show what this transformation of the natural loves by divine love looks like "on the ground." As before, we begin with familial affection.

Affection Put Right

In a short article entitled "The Sermon and the Lunch," Lewis offers a starting point for a program of improving home life.[12] This is a renovation of the domestic affections that can only be accomplished when charity reigns. I've adapted and filled out the program that he suggests.

The first thing we must do is recognize that familial love must be converted. The home, like all other areas of human life, is fallen and therefore

---

[10] Ibid., 132.
[11] Ibid.
[12] Lewis, "The Sermon and the Lunch," in *God in the Dock*, 282–86.

must be redeemed. This means, first of all, that it must die. "Every natural love will rise again . . . but none will rise again until it has been buried." This death means fundamentally submitting our familial affection to God, not merely in word but also in deed. "You cannot love a fellow-creature fully till you love God."[13] And God, according to Lewis, is eminently patient; he will work with whatever germ of desire for him you have. Thus, Pam's brother Reginald, her solid guide in *The Great Divorce*, tells her that she will become solid enough for Michael to perceive her when she learns "to want Something Else besides Michael. I don't say 'more than Michael,' not as a beginning. That will come later." Pam is treating God as a means to Michael; her love for God is a stepping stone to her love for her son. This is precisely backward. Thus, the first step—her first choice—must simply be to separate her love for God from her love for Michael. She must learn "to want God for His own sake."[14] This will begin to deliver her from the ravenous, possessive love she has had for her son. Put another way, love for God must govern our love for our family.[15]

Second, we must recognize that familial love is often the greatest enemy of familial happiness. This is because our ownership in our familiars makes us react in ways we would never react to strangers. Blunders that would be quickly forgiven if they were committed by outsiders receive no quarter in those whom we "care" about. Their attachment to us makes us more impatient with them. The same impulse that leads us to defend our family against outsiders also leads us to criticize our family members when they embarrass us. In both cases, our claim in them and upon them is what we rise to defend.

Third, we must beware lest the principal attraction of the home—that we can let our hair down and "be ourselves"—should become a justification for sin. In a number of places, Lewis describes "the domestic Rudesby," the member of the family who abuses the intimacy and affection that allows us

---

[13] Lewis, *The Great Divorce*, 105.
[14] Ibid., 98.
[15] That something must govern the natural loves is obvious from the beginning of *The Four Loves*. However, Lewis is characteristically shrewd in how he introduces the divine governor. He paints in caricatures and extremes, showing the corrupt tendencies of natural loves. He does so, knowing that his audience will likely object. "Why stress these marginal cases? A little common sense, a little give and take, prevents their occurrence among decent people." The introduction of common sense and decency is important. It shows that, whatever else we may say about the happiness of family love, it only produces this happiness "if there is common sense and give and take and 'decency.'" In other words, only if something more, and other, than Affection is added." Something else must hold the reins, or "Affection will 'go bad on us'" (53–55). Lewis's apologetic strategy is to introduce the need for a governor under the name of common sense, and then eventually show that what we call "common sense" is actually charity, love for God, and that this alone is the true governor of affection (and all the natural loves).

to "say anything to one another." Familial affection does let down its hair; formal politeness is unnecessary once we've retired to the glorious refuge called home. But the Rudesby, in a twisting of logic, says, "Affection takes liberties. I am taking liberties. Therefore, I am being affectionate." If we object to the Rudesby's "liberties"—his hurtful remarks, his biting words, his abuse of his intimate knowledge—he will take offense. Even worse, he may take revenge. "He then sometimes avenges himself by getting on his high horse and becoming elaborately 'polite.' The implication is of course, 'Oh! So we are not to be intimate? We are to behave like mere acquaintances? I had hoped—but no matter. Have it your own way.'"[16]

What the Rudesby forgets is that the private sphere has its own manners, as much as the public sphere does. "Home life has its own rule of courtesy—a code more intimate, more subtle, more sensitive, and therefore, in some ways more difficult, than that of the outer world." Both forms of courtesy are built on the same principle—don't give any preference to yourself; put others' interests before your own. The public form of this principle may involve formal rules and rituals, whereas the private may not. But this is not because the principle has been abandoned at home. It is simply that there "you must have the reality which that ritual represented." "Those who leave their manners behind them when they come home from the dance or the sherry party have no real courtesy even there. They were merely aping those who had."[17]

Fourth, when we speak of the unguarded comfort of home, we must be careful what we mean. When we say that home is the place where we can "be ourselves," we cannot demand unfettered freedom to do what we'd like. We must remember who we are. "There is nowhere this side of heaven where one can safely lay the reins on the horse's neck. It will never be lawful simply to 'be ourselves' until 'ourselves' have become sons of God."[18]

Fifth, we must learn to love the moment when we become unnecessary to our children and students. "The hour when we can say 'They need me no longer' should be our reward."[19] This is what all our efforts should be tending toward. "The proper aim of giving is to put the recipient in a state where he no longer needs our gift. . . . We must aim at making ourselves superfluous." Fathers should labor so that their sons surpass them. Teachers should

---

[16] Ibid., 44.
[17] Ibid., 43.
[18] Lewis, "The Sermon and the Lunch," in *God in the Dock*, 286.
[19] Lewis, *The Four Loves*, 50.

work so that their students become their peers, critics, and even rivals. And this must be a happy moment. "We should be delighted when it arrives, as the fencing master is delighted when his pupil can pink and disarm him."[20] Or, since most readers don't fence, we might say: as the father is delighted when his son can finally beat him at basketball, or chess, or (fill-in-the-blank). Affection in its gift-love form must learn to desire the good of the object, even if that good comes from somewhere else.

In *Perelandra* Lewis gives a great image of the joy of being surpassed. The Oyarsa of Perelandra rejoices to give up her rule and authority over the beasts and birds and lands of Venus when Tor and Tinidril grow old enough to take their places as king and queen of that planet. It is her glory to decrease, to give way, to relinquish her place to the one for whom it was prepared. Even the beasts of Perelandra bear witness to this truth. The great singing beasts of Perelandra have no milk and therefore cannot suckle their young. So their whelps are nursed by the she-beasts of another kind. Until the young singing beast is weaned, it is subject to the beautiful but silent foster mother. But when it is grown, it leaves her and becomes the most beautiful and delicate of beasts. And the foster mother wonders at its song. Maleldil designed this relationship so that "from the habits of these two beasts much wisdom will come into the minds of my King and my Queen and their children."[21] Parents and teachers too must learn this wisdom.

Finally, if we are to preach the goodness and happiness of domesticity and familial affection, we must take our call seriously. Home life is difficult; it is not a panacea or magical charm. If it is to be a means of grace, that grace will be channeled through what Lewis calls "rules." Not rules in a legalistic sense, but rules in the sense of a *regula*, a way of life, an ordering and structuring of relationships so that the home is not tyrannized by the most selfish and manipulative member. And this *regula* can work only if it is rooted in something greater than the home.

I think we catch a glimpse of this "something greater" in Lewis's depiction of the solid people in *The Great Divorce*. Whenever the solid people are about to deliver a painful truth to a ghost, they inevitably do so with mirth and laughter. At the point in the story where Len confronts the big ghost who is always demanding his rights and comments that the big man was not a decent man on earth, we read, "Mirth danced in his eyes as he said

[20] Ibid., 51.
[21] Lewis, *Perelandra*, 168.

it."[22] Reginald tells his sister, Pam, that she ought not to have tried to live on the memory of Michael after his death; this turned the past into a tyrant. "It was Egyptian—like embalming a body." Pam attempts to manipulate Reginald with the sulks.

> "Oh, of course. I'm wrong. Everything I say or do is wrong, according to you." "But of course!" said the Spirit, *shining with love and mirth so that my eyes were dazzled*. "That's what we all find when we reach this country. We've all been wrong! That's the great joke. There's no need to go on pretending one was right! After that we begin living."[23]

When Sarah Smith tells her husband to get rid of his great, ugly doll, the tragic persona that he'd used for years to manipulate her, we read that "merriment danced in her eyes."[24]

The consistency of this pattern—hard truth delivered with mirth and laughter—is meant to show us something about how our closest relationships ought to work. Heaven's joy, as we will explore in more detail later, is invulnerable to hell's manipulation. Pam tells her brother that she believes in a God of love (in her twisted sense of the term). Reginald points out that at that moment she has no love for him or for her own mother. Pam seizes upon this and thinks that she has hurt Reginald. His response is essential. "'Lord love you!' said the Spirit with a great laugh. 'You needn't bother about that! Don't you know that you can't hurt anyone in this country?'"[25]

This is the invulnerability of heaven. The saints cannot be hurt by the manipulation of the damned. They are no longer subject to the tyranny of their loved ones' grievances. This is heaven's *regula*, and Lewis shows it to us so that it can, in some measure, work its way back into our earthly lives. This invulnerability, this protection against manipulation by the perpetually aggrieved, flows from the joy of being forgiven. Rooted and grounded in the love of God, we are freed to love manipulators without being manipulated. We may not yet be able to rebuke them with our mirth and laughter; we are, after all, still in our pilgrim condition. We can be wrong and we can be hurt. But if the grace of God defines us, then we can live with Mrs. Fidget and Dr. Quartz with patience and longsuffering, and, if not a twinkle in the eye, at least a twinkle in the soul.

---

22 Lewis, *The Great Divorce*, 29.
23 Ibid., 102.
24 Ibid., 126.
25 Ibid., 104.

Friendship Put Right

What effect does charity have on friendship? To begin, charity solidifies one of the fundamental goods of friendship. As a young boy at school, Lewis learned the potency of a band of brothers standing against tyranny. In his autobiography, he provocatively calls one of the horrific schools he attended "Belsen," after the Nazi concentration camp. The headmaster (who eventually proved to be insane) was a tyrant—cruel, despotic, and erratic. The schoolboys' only solace was each other. It was there that Lewis learned one of the formative lessons of his life.

> To this day the vision of the world which comes most naturally to me is one in which "we two" or "we few" (and in a sense "we happy few") stand together against something stronger and larger. England's position in 1940 was to me no surprise; it was the sort of thing that I always expect. Hence while friendship has been by far the chief source of my happiness, acquaintance or general society has always meant little to me, and I cannot quite understand why a man should wish to know more people than he can make real friends of.[26]

The bonds forged in the face of such unjust cruelty are why governing authorities are always suspicious of friendship. "Every real Friendship is a sort of a secession, even a rebellion . . . a pocket of potential resistance" against public opinion. Friendship in this sense is a bulwark against tyranny, whether of the monarchical or democratic variety. The common taste or vision of friends strengthens opinions that we otherwise hold timidly.

> Alone among unsympathetic companions, I hold certain views and standards timidly, half ashamed to avow them and half doubtful if they can after all be right. Put me back among my Friends and in half an hour—in ten minutes—these same views and standards become once more indisputable. The opinion of this little circle, while I am in it, outweighs that of a thousand outsiders.[27]

When grace augments friendship, it produces the church, in which the common vision shared by Christians leads us to care exclusively for the love of the brethren and to stop our ears to the opinion of the pagan society all around us. In other words, empowered by divine love, we to-

---

[26] Lewis, *Surprised by Joy*, 32–33.
[27] Lewis, *The Four Loves*, 79.

gether strengthen weak hands and feeble knees. The church is a society of friends gathered around a common taste for the gospel of Christ, a thick and resilient community that cares nothing for the scorn of the wicked. It's no accident that the clarity and boldness of the church in the book of Acts emerges from a community devoted to apostolic preaching and committed to meeting each other's needs.

Second, given that friendship is such a chief source of happiness, one of the ways we love others with charity is by cultivating friendships among other people. I don't mean that we should try to be friends (in the technical Lewisian sense) with everyone; that is quite simply impossible. Instead, we ought to be in the business of midwifing friendships. We do so by being alert to the interests and loves of those around us. We know their tastes, hobbies, and loves sufficiently, so that when we come across someone who shares the same tastes, we can make a match. Lewis notes that true and deep friendships are quite unlikely. "A few years' difference in the dates of our births, a few more miles between certain houses, the choice of one university instead of another, posting to different regiments, the accident of a topic being raised or not raised at a first meeting—any of these chances might have kept us apart." But, as Christians, we know that when we make a friend, "a secret Master of Ceremonies has been at work."[28] What appears to be happenstance is actually providence. Knowing this, if we are to love our neighbors as ourselves, then it perhaps behooves us, as we have opportunity, to assist the Master of Ceremonies in at least creating the possibility of friendship by throwing people together, making introductions, and doing what we can so that as many people as possible can have the "You too?" moment.

Third, the chief danger of friendship is the encouragement of the lust for the Inner Ring. Under the influence of grace, we find ourselves able to endure being outside the Inner Ring. We don't obsess about the worldlings and their success. Instead, we simply seek to love God and then love others. Like the Narnians in *The Horse and His Boy*, we should be ready to be friends with anyone who is friendly, and not give a fig for anyone who isn't. And if we somehow find ourselves inside an ugly Inner Ring, one built on exclusion, we should labor to tear down the invisible wall and to erase the invisible line. We should blow up the hidden boundaries by embracing those on the outside, no matter how awkward a hug that might be.

---

28 Ibid., 89.

There's a great scene in the film *42*, a movie about Jackie Robinson, in which the Southern-bred shortstop Pee-Wee Reese puts his arm around Jackie before the start of a game, knowing that his racist friends and family are in attendance, and says, "Thank you, Jackie, for letting my family see who I really am." Charity strengthens friendship with divine grace so that we can resist the pull of the world's approval.

Finally, charity enables us to be alive to God's purposes in friendship.

> [Friendship] is the instrument by which God reveals to each the beauties of all the others. They are no greater than the beauties of a thousand other men; by Friendship God opens our eyes to them. They are, like all beauties, derived from Him, and then, in a good Friendship, increased by Him through the Friendship itself, so that it is His instrument for creating as well as for revealing.[29]

Eros Put Right

To restore Eros to its proper place, we must begin with its subjugation. Eros, at its highest, sounds like a god. It demands unconditional obedience. Thus, the first step is to shatter this demand. Eros, like any of the natural loves, can be judged by something outside of itself. And in this case, Eros must bow very low indeed. Our romantic feelings are to be evaluated by what will seem to be very prosaic and simple means—justice, honesty, loyalty, and the keeping of promises. When Eros exalts itself to the heights and attempts to justify infidelity, unchastity, or some other evil, we must bring it back to brass tacks. "But you made vows. You said, 'Till death do us part.'" Or "you are even now unwilling to make vows; you wish to enjoy love's fruit (sexual pleasure) without entering through love's gate (marriage)." Resisting Eros's demands for total commitment is the first step in putting it back on its proper footing.

The humbling of Eros necessarily includes the humbling of Venus. Our sexual desires must be subjected to a higher power as much as anything else. Venus's humbling ought to produce at least two effects on us. First, in marriage, we are freed from viewing sex with the wrong kind of seriousness. We refuse to dehumanize ourselves by solemnizing and divinizing sex. Instead, we learn to freely laugh along with Venus. We recognize that God gave us bodies at least in part because he has a sense of humor, that

---

banishing play from the marriage bed is the surest way to let in a false goddess, and thus we are able to enjoy the comic relief provided by Venus.

> She herself is a mocking, mischievous spirit, far more elf than deity, and makes game of us. When all external circumstances are fittest for her service she will leave one or both the lovers totally indisposed for it. When every overt act is impossible and even glances cannot be exchanged—in trains, in shops, and at interminable parties—she will assail them with all her force. An hour later, when time and place agree, she will have mysteriously withdrawn; perhaps from only one of them. What a pother this must raise—what resentments, self-pities, suspicions, wounded vanities and all the current chatter about "frustration"—in those who have deified her! But sensible lovers laugh. It is all part of the game; a game of catch-as-catch-can, and the escapes and tumbles and head-on collisions are to be treated as a romp.[30]

What married couple can't identify with the self-pity, wounded vanity, and frustration that bubbles up in response to the fickleness of our sexual desires? And what couple doesn't need to hear that the sensible response to such inconveniences is to laugh? Might it not be that, for some of us, one of the chief obstacles to marital happiness is that we've grown old and forgotten to have fun?

The second effect of humbling Venus is the blossoming of self-control. None of our appetites can be given free rein, least of all, the sexual appetite. Our bodily passions must be bridled, like a horse. This is precisely the picture Lewis paints in *The Great Divorce*. One of the ghosts has a red lizard on his shoulder. The lizard, which represents the ghost's lusts and sexual appetite, is constantly whispering in the ghost's ear. The ghost is conflicted about the lizard: on the one hand, he is embarrassed by the lizard's lewd talk; on the other hand, the talk titillates and delights him. Because he knows that the lizard's talk is inappropriate in heaven, the ghost is planning to leave. He is stopped by a bright angel who offers to silence the lizard. The ghost initially accepts the angel's offer, but then recoils when he realizes that the angel intends to kill the lizard. Like Augustine before his conversion, the ghost has an attitude that essentially says, "Give me chastity, but not yet."

In the ensuing conversation, the ghost repeatedly makes excuses for his unwillingness to allow the angel to kill the lizard: he needs time to

---

[30] Ibid., 100.

consider the offer; he is not feeling well; he prefers the gradual process rather than the quick death; he is afraid that killing the lizard will kill him. For his part, the angel is persistent; his one question, which he asks over and over, is "May I kill it?" and he repeatedly reminds the ghost of the finality of the Choice: "This moment contains all moments."[31] As the ghost's resolve weakens, the lizard begins to bargain for its life, promising to behave and warning the ghost that he will no longer be a real man if he allows the angel to kill it. In the end, the ghost relents and gives the angel permission, whimpering, "God help me. God help me."[32] The angel breaks the back of the lizard, as the ghost screams in agony and pain.

Then, in a moment, two great changes occur. The ghost begins to grow solid; he turns into a strong, bright, golden-headed man. At the same time, the lizard too undergoes a transformation: "What stood before me was the greatest stallion I have ever seen, silvery white but with mane and tail of gold. It was smooth and shining, rippled with swells of flesh and muscle, whinneying and stamping with its hoofs. At each stamp the land shook and the trees dindled."[33] Immediately, the solid man mounts the great stallion and rides joyously and swiftly toward the great mountains of heaven. And while they head into the sunrise, the narrator hears heaven and nature sing a song of glorious anticipation.

The death and resurrection of sexual desire is a microcosm of the restoration of all natural loves and appetites. God intends to rule man's appetites and loves through his redeemed and obedient will. On earth, all lower natures are our enemies, rebellious and opposed to our wills; in glory, they will be our servants—"obedient fire in your blood and heavenly thunder in your voice."[34] Lower natures long for us to overcome them so that they can become their true selves. And we overcome them through self-denial, self-control, and taking up our cross to follow Christ. Yes, our sexual appetites must die, but in God's world, faithful death leads to resurrection. "Lust is a poor, weak, whimpering, whispering thing compared with that richness and energy of desire which will arise when lust has been killed."[35]

> To shrink back from all that can be called Nature into negative spirituality
> is as if we ran away from horses instead of learning to ride. There is in our

[31] Lewis, The Great Divorce, 109.
[32] Ibid., 110.
[33] Ibid., 111–12.
[34] Ibid., 113.
[35] Ibid., 114.

present pilgrim condition plenty of room (more room than most of us like) for abstinence and renunciation and mortifying our natural desires. But behind all asceticism the thought should be, "Who will trust us with the true wealth if we cannot be trusted even with the wealth that perishes?" Who will trust me with a spiritual body if I cannot control even an earthly body? These small and perishable bodies we now have were given to us as ponies are given to schoolboys. We must learn to manage: not that we may some day be free of horses altogether but that some day we may ride bare-back, confident and rejoicing, those greater mounts, those winged, shining and world-shaking horses which perhaps even now expect us with impatience, pawing and snorting in the King's stables. Not that the gallop would be of any value unless it were a gallop with the King; but how else—since He has retained His own charger—should we accompany Him?[36]

Of course, it's not only Venus that must be humbled; Eros himself must learn to bow. Our romantic love, as much as our sexual appetite, must find its place in submission to God. Again, this submission has two key implications. First, in addition to the natural symbolism of sexuality—the pagan sacrament that I highlighted earlier—Lewis reminds us that rightly ordered Eros partakes of an even higher mystery. The natural and complementary asymmetry in the marital act is extended and transformed into the whole of marriage. A husband is the head of his wife, just as Christ is the head of the church. If nature places a paper crown on man's head in the act of marital love, then grace places on his head a crown of thorns. For this is what Christian headship means—that a husband gives himself for his bride in order that she might be pure and holy (Eph. 5:25–27). Christian headship means that a husband has the great privilege of dying first. What's more, this sacrifice is to be endured with joy and gladness of heart. As King Lune says about kingship, "This is what it means to be a king: to be first in every desperate attack and last in every desperate retreat, and when there's hunger in the land (as must be now and then in bad years) to wear finer clothes and laugh louder over a scantier meal than any man in your land."[37] Or, as I've taken to paraphrasing him, "This is what it means to be a man—first in, last out, laughing loudest."

Of course, it is not only husbands who face suffering and sacrifice in marriage; the way of the cross is expected of wives as well (and many have

---

36 Lewis, *Miracles*, 266.
37 Lewis, *The Horse and His Boy*, 223.

trodden it). However, while there is a deep common thread in the sacrifices of a husband and a wife, the forms of their sacrifices differ. A husband gives himself up as a man, as the head. A wife gives herself as a woman, as the body. The husband's sacrificial love for his wife is to be met with the wife's fitting honor to her husband. His initiative is met with her response; his protection and provision is met with her glad submission. And thus marriage itself is caught up in the Great Dance.

But I mentioned two implications of humbling Eros. A humbled Eros recognizes its own insufficiency. Humbled Eros knows that a marriage does not live on Eros alone. In fact, for Lewis, Eros is like the dive that gets us into the water; it is not what enables us to swim. The good but temporary thrill of Eros gives way to something else. Falling in love is something that happens to us; being in love and remaining in love is something that we do as grace strengthens and trains us. As a passion, Eros cannot preserve itself; but it can be an incentive to the deeper and more permanent love. Eros, in the intensity of its passion, makes great promises; but marital love, governed by divine love and empowered by divine grace, keeps them.

Conclusion

We end where we began. Natural loves are good, but they are holy only when God's hand is on the rein.[38] "There is but one good; that is God. Everything else is good when it looks to Him and bad when it turns from Him."[39] Like a garden that cannot weed itself, natural loves do not have within themselves the resources to secure their own permanence or to keep themselves from internal corruptions. Apart from the love of God, affection and Eros grow tyrannical, possessive, and jealous; friendship becomes exclusive and proud. What's more, "the higher and mightier it is in the natural order, the more demoniac it will be if it rebels."[40]

This is easy for us to forget. The great natural loves are such strong images of divine love, so close in their resemblance to God who is love, that we easily mistake like for same. It's easy to think that we've brought our loves to God when what we've actually done is stamped our selfish, tyrannical loves with a divine imprimatur. Do not pass this by without some serious soul-searching. Lewis may display this corruption most frequently and viv-

---

[38] Lewis, *The Great Divorce*, 100.
[39] Ibid., 106.
[40] Ibid.

idly in the corrupt and possessive form of maternal love. But the key is to see the principle and the pattern at work in those cases, and then to make the necessary adjustments in our own. We must witness the excuses, the self-justifications, the twisted affection, the impossible demands and martyr complexes, the self-righteous anger and fondled bitterness, and then learn to recognize the same in ourselves. And then, like the ghost with the lizard, we must ask God to kill it. Not to manage it, or curb it, or manipulate it. Not to tame it, or massage it, or quarantine it. Our natural loves must be converted; they must die.

But we must not forget the true lesson of the red lizard. "If the risen body even of appetite is as grand a horse as ye saw, what would the risen body of maternal love or friendship be?"[41] Yes, the great natural loves become the great demons that devour others and destroy us, but the inverse is true as well. The greater the natural glory of our loves, the greater their glorification after they have died. "Every natural love will rise again and live forever in this country: but none will rise again until it has been buried."[42] And ultimately this death and resurrection happen in the presence of God. "When God arrives (and only then), the half-gods can remain."[43] When God is the sun at the center of our solar system, all the planets orbit properly.

> We were made for God. Only by being in some respect like Him, only by being a manifestation of His beauty, loving-kindness, wisdom or goodness, has any earthly Beloved excited our love. It is not that we have loved them too much, but that we did not quite understand what we were loving. It is not that we shall be asked to turn from them, so dearly familiar, to a Stranger. When we see the face of God we shall know that we have always known it. He has been a party to, has made, sustained and moved moment by moment within, all our earthly experiences of innocent love. All that was true love in them was, even on earth, far more His than ours, and ours only because His. In Heaven there will be no anguish and no duty of turning away from our earthly Beloveds. First, because we shall have turned already; from the portraits to the Original, from the rivulets to the Fountain, from the creatures He made lovable to Love Himself. But secondly, because we shall find them all in Him. By loving Him more than them we shall love them more than we now do.[44]

---

[41] Ibid., 115.
[42] Ibid., 105.
[43] Lewis, *The Four Loves*, 119.
[44] Ibid., 139.

There is no total renunciation in the Christian life. The natural loves must die, but they die in order to be raised and transfigured. Jesus, and all in him, is mine. In his presence, they grow strangely bright. In becoming wholly his, they become wholly themselves. And in becoming themselves, they make us both whole and holy. They make us truly human.

CHAPTER 15

HELL

The Outer Darkness

I began this book by noting the centrality of the Choice in Lewis's writings. In every choice, we are turning the central part of us, the part that chooses, into something a little different from what it was before. And our choices add up. Small battles have great effects.

> Good and evil both increase at compound interest. That is why the little decisions you and I make every day are of such infinite importance. The smallest good act today is the capture of a strategic point from which, a few months later, you may be able to go on to victories you never dreamed of. An apparently trivial indulgence in lust or anger today is the loss of a ridge or railway line or bridgehead from which the enemy may launch an attack otherwise impossible.[1]

As we near the end of this book, it is worth taking a step back to see the two possible outcomes of this great war. As we've seen, reality confronts us with an absolutely final either–or.

> Taking your life as a whole, with all your innumerable choices, all your life long you are slowly turning this central thing either into a heavenly creature or into a hellish creature: either into a creature that is in harmony with God, and with other creatures, and with itself, or else into one

[1] Lewis, *Mere Christianity*, 132.

that is in a state of war and hatred with God, and with its fellow-creatures, and with itself. To be the one kind of creature is heaven: that is, it is joy and peace and knowledge and power. To be the other means madness, horror, idiocy, rage, impotence, and eternal loneliness. Each of us at each moment is progressing to the one state or the other.[2]

In *That Hideous Strength*, Dimble notes that the universe "is always hardening and narrowing and coming to a point. . . . Good is always getting better and bad is always getting worse."[3] In a sense, heaven and hell are eating into merry Middle Earth from opposite sides. So we'd do well to consider the two final and irrevocable alternatives: willed and unalterable union with God or the black fire of self-imprisonment.[4] We cannot adequately treat the Christian life without attending to the next life. After all, once we admit that we are eternal creatures, eternity must loom large in our minds. We cannot and must not keep it in the background. As Lewis asks, "If that other world is once admitted . . . how can 'the rest of Christianity'—what is this 'rest'?—be disentangled from it?"[5]

But before we look at the final separation, let's take a moment to explore Lewis's view of purgatory.

Purgatory

First, though he does not often speak of it, Lewis does seem to embrace some version of purgatory. His most extended reflections on it come in his final book, *Letters to Malcolm*, and he explicitly says that much of his thinking on the particulars of the afterlife are only guesses. Before we can understand what Lewis does say, we must first note what he rejects.

First, purgatory is not a second chance to embrace Christ after death. Some have mistakenly concluded that Lewis believes in such a second chance because of the conversions of ghosts in *The Great Divorce*: the ghost with the red lizard asks for his lusts to be killed, and he is transformed into a solid man with the stallion (and other ghostly conversions are alluded

---

[2] Ibid., 92.
[3] Lewis, *That Hideous Strength*, 281.
[4] "But though freedom is real it is not infinite. Every choice reduces a little one's freedom to choose the next time. There therefore comes a time when the creature is fully built, irrevocably attached either to God or to itself. This irrevocableness is what we call Heaven or Hell. Every conscious agent is finally committed in the long run: i.e., it rises above freedom into willed, but henceforth unalterable, union with God, or else sinks below freedom into the black fire of self-imprisonment" (Lewis to Joyce Pearce, July 20, 1943, in *Collected Letters*, 2:585).
[5] Lewis, *Letters to Malcolm*, 120.

to). But according to the guide in the novel, these are not, strictly speaking, second chances. Rather, we are witnessing the characters' fundamental choices through the lens of a vision in a dream. Thus, the decisions in the story might be thought of as echoes of choices made long ago. They might equally be thought of as anticipations of choices to be made at the end of all things. But both answers are misleading. As the guide says, "Ye cannot fully understand the relations of choice and Time till you are beyond both. And ye were not brought here to study such curiosities."[6] Thus, Lewis's somewhat odd views of eternity and time, coupled with the fact that the novel is an imaginative supposal in the form of a dream, complicate any attempt to view the decisions in *The Great Divorce* as second chances. What Lewis wrote about *The Screwtape Letters* could equally apply to *The Great Divorce*: "Its purpose was not to speculate about diabolical life [or the particulars of the afterlife] but to throw light from a new angle on the life of men."[7]

More importantly, as Lewis well knows, the traditional doctrine of purgatory concerns the fate of the saved souls after death, not the fate of the unsaved. And here Lewis rejects three additional views of purgatory that have appeared in the history of the church. First, he rejects any notion of transaction or bargain in relation to time spent in purgatory. In his view, the Reformers were right to reject the Romish doctrine in the sixteenth century. Indulgences were (and are) an abomination. Second, he rejects the view that purgatory is simply temporary hell, with devils tormenting us as retributive punishment. Third, he rejects the view that purgatory's pains are tortures that keep us from remembering God as we ought to do.

Instead, Lewis seems to embrace a more traditional, Dante-inspired vision of purgatory. Instead of a retributive punishment, purgatory is a purification initiated at the request of the departed saint. "The saved soul, at the very foot of the throne, begs to be taken away and cleansed."[8] Lewis is thus pushing against any notion that we will somehow keep our filth in heaven—as though, apart from purgation, we would have smelly breath and rags dripping mud all over the streets of gold. Of course, no Protestant believes that we retain such filth. We are indeed purged and cleansed, but, for most Protestants, the purging is instantaneous. We shed the body of death and the soul's corruption when we shuffle off this mortal coil. Thus, the reference in Hebrews 12:23 to "the spirits of the righteous made perfect."

---

6 Lewis, *The Great Divorce*, 71.
7 Lewis, *The Screwtape Letters*, xl.
8 Lewis, *Letters to Malcolm*, 108.

Lewis likewise demands this cleansing, but because of church tradition and his own experience, he assumes that all cleansing involves suffering and time. "I never believed before—I thought it immensely improbable—that the faithfulest soul could leap straight into perfection and peace the moment death has rattled in the throat."[9] Of course, suffering is not the purpose of purgatory; it is a by-product. To draw an analogy to the dentist's chair, death is like the pulling of a tooth, and the astringent rinse afterward is the purgation. Its purpose is to cleanse, but, as Eustace would say, it hurts like billy-oh. Again, "no nonsense about merit" or indulgences and the like.

At this point, Lewis offers a creative resolution to the difference between the Protestant instantaneous cleansing and the Roman Catholic extended purgation. Lewis suggests that, while the blessed dead are not in a timeless state, they may experience time differently. Time might, for saints and angels, "have thickness as well as length," on analogy with our experiences where "time slows down" and we are able to notice many things at once.[10] Thus, a reconciliation between the Protestant view of instantaneous cleansing at the point of the saint's death and Lewis's view of purgation through (but not for) suffering is possible. What, from the standpoint of the living, is instantaneous is, from the inside, an actual length of time—or better, a "width" of time, since that moment is "thick." Our awareness of the passions of the flesh forever dying, of "Brother Ass" spending his final breath, of the soul's remaining inward curve being finally straightened, will be to us more than an earthly moment. Our sensitivity to it will be such that its thickness, if translated into temporal terms, will be *as though* we spent an age being undragoned.

Apply Lewis's view to the death of the patient at the end of *Screwtape*. The patient apparently dies in a bombing during the blitz. He instantly puts off sin and the Devil. "There was a sudden clearing of his eyes (was there not?) as he saw you for the first time, and recognised the part you had had in him and knew that you had it no longer."[11] In this moment, it was "as if a scab had fallen from an old sore, as if he were emerging from a hideous, shell-like tetter, as if he shuffled off for good and all a defiled, wet, clinging garment."[12] The patient sees (and sheds) Wormwood's influence. He recog-

9 Lewis, *A Grief Observed*, 42.
10 Lewis, *Letters to Malcolm*, 109.
11 Lewis, *The Screwtape Letters*, 184.
12 Ibid. It's worth noting that later Screwtape mentions the possibility that the patient still may have pains in his future. This could be a reference to purgatorial pains; it may also be a reference to the severe ardors and steep exertions of heaven.

nizes the angelic spirits who had haunted him his whole life. More than that, he sees Christ himself, wearing the form of a man, and falls down prostrate before him. When contemplated from the outside, this final stripping, this complete cleansing, is instantaneous. But perhaps when enjoyed from the inside, that instant has so much thickness that it is felt by the patient to be five hundred years.

All of this is, of course, speculative, as is most of our knowledge of what happens to us when we die. But even if it were true, how does the notion of "thick Time" and post-death cleansing relate to Lewis's similar embrace of prayers for the dead? For, even if the departed soul experiences a thick moment of time that to him is five hundred years, to us on earth the cleansing is immediate. Thus, to pray that God would cleanse our departed loved one and bring him nearer to himself seems superfluous. These are good questions and, in the end, may overthrow Lewis's entire position. In a different sort of book, I might have taken the time to explore the question further. But my main goal has been to make his view comprehensible and to show its bearing on the Christian life. To that end, Lewis notes in his letters that he sometimes prays for the dead simply out of long habit. Whatever we may say about purgatory and the usefulness of such prayers, we ought to be challenged by this. Do I pray for anyone so consistently and fervently that his or her death would cause a noticeable disruption in my petitionary life?

Hell

When it comes to the subject of hell, we must begin with a simple fact: Lewis really believes in it. Against liberal demythologizers, Lewis asserts that, however unpalatable hell might be to the modern mind, the doctrine "has the full support of Scripture, and, specially, of Our Lord's own words; it has always been held by Christendom; and it has the support of reason." We have no right to water down the truth and remove "the darker elements" of Christianity so as to turn it into a religion of pure consolation.[13] To reject hell is to attempt to tame God, and a tame God is just a wish fulfillment dream and a fantasy. The rejection of hell often smothers the hope of heaven. "I have met no people who fully disbelieved in Hell and also had a living and life-giving belief in Heaven."[14] At the same time, when

---

[13] Lewis, *The Problem of Pain*, 120.
[14] Lewis, *Letters to Malcolm*, 75.

he discusses hell, his aim is not to make the doctrine tolerable; how could anyone wish to tolerate such a doctrine? Rather, his aim is either to show that it is moral (that is, that God is just in consigning some of his creatures to final ruin) or, addressing our wills and consciences, to make us feel its reality so that we will turn from our sins and avoid it.

True to his view of theology, Lewis notes that we must not confuse the reality of hell with the imagery used to communicate to us about it. The imagery is varied, and it is difficult—based on our own present experience—to see how one reality might encompass all the symbols and imagery the Bible uses to tell us about hell. Lewis notes three in particular: punishment, destruction, and banishment. All three symbols are meant to suggest something unspeakably horrible. "Any interpretation which does not face that fact is, I am afraid, out of court from the beginning."[15] I'll return to these three scriptural images in a moment. For now, I want to explore a central tension in Lewis's account of hell. Put simply, is hell God-inflicted or self-inflicted? In other words, are people cast into hell by a righteous and vengeful God, or is hell something that we do to ourselves by remaining in our own self-centeredness and rebellion?

Most often, Lewis treats hell as something self-inflicted. Hell is the name we give to the final, rebellious reaction against goodness. In this way of thinking, goodness (or God) simply is itself; it (he) does not change. What makes the difference is our response to him.

> God is the only comfort, He is also the supreme terror: the thing we most need and the thing we most want to hide from. He is our only possible ally, and we have made ourselves His enemies. Some people talk as if meeting the gaze of absolute goodness would be fun. They need to think again. They are still only playing with religion. Goodness is either the great safety or the great danger—according to the way you react to it. And we have reacted the wrong way.[16]

We catch a glimpse of this principle in the final Screwtape letter. When the patient dies, he comes into the presence of Christ and experiences it as "cool light," caught up in a world of transfinite delights. On the other hand, Wormwood experiences the divine presence as "blinding, suffocating fire," as a choking and paralyzing sensation that comes from encountering the

---

15 Lewis, *The Problem of Pain*, 127.
16 Lewis, *Mere Christianity*, 31.

"deadly air that breathes from the heart of Heaven."[17] God's presence is the same; what differs is the condition of the recipient.[18]

Or, again, Lewis insists that "the doors of Hell are locked on the *inside.*"[19] "There are only two kinds of people in the end: those who say to God, 'Thy will be done,' and those to whom God says, in the end, '*Thy* will be done.' All that are in Hell, choose it. Without that self-choice there could be no Hell."[20] When we reject God, he grants our wish; he leaves us alone.[21] He allows us to remain as we are, on the trajectory that we have freely chosen. And this is not a comfort. "The characteristic of lost souls is 'their rejection of everything that is not simply themselves.'"[22] We become egoists, attempting to devour others, to turn them into appendages of ourselves. Our capacity for good is quenched; the world shrinks around us, until death removes our last contact with something other than the self. "He has his wish—to lie wholly in the self and to make the best of what he finds there. And what he finds there is Hell."[23] This is what Lewis means when he suggests that "Hell is a state of mind." "Every state of mind, left to itself, every shutting up of the creature within the dungeon of its own mind—is, in the end, Hell."[24] In such a state, all that we're left with is our own envy, prurience, resentment, loneliness, and self-conceit. Nothing to take us out of ourselves; no distractions to divert our minds. Only the endless gnawing ache, forever curving inward on itself. "It's not a question of God 'sending' us to Hell. In each of us there is something growing up which will of itself *be Hell* unless it is nipped in the bud."[25]

And there's the rub. According to Lewis, God does not *send* anyone to hell. Is hell thus *purely* self-inflicted? Or can we say that God, in his justice, actually *casts* the wicked into the lake of fire, into outer darkness? Lewis does embrace this truth; he begins his chapter on hell in *The Problem of Pain* with "the conception of Hell as a positive retributive punishment inflicted

---

[17] Lewis, *The Screwtape Letters*, 187.
[18] The same is true of Orual's encounter with the rams in *Till We Have Faces*. In one recounting of the vision, the rams sense some intruder and lower their terrible heads to charge and overwhelm an enemy (299). In another recounting of the same vision, the rams knock Orual flat. But, she notes: "They were not doing it in anger. They rushed over me in their joy—perhaps they did not see me—certainly I was nothing in their minds. I understood it well. They butted and trampled me because their gladness led them on; the Divine Nature wounds and perhaps destroys us merely by being what it is. We call it the wrath of the gods" (284).
[19] Lewis, *The Problem of Pain*, 130.
[20] Lewis, *The Great Divorce*, 75.
[21] Lewis, *The Problem of Pain*, 130.
[22] Ibid., 125.
[23] Ibid., 124–25.
[24] Lewis, *The Great Divorce*, 70.
[25] Lewis, "The Trouble with 'X' . . . ," in *God in the Dock*, 155.

by God."[26] In eternally judging such a sinner, God does not leave the rebel wholly alone; he plants the flag of truth and justice in the horribly rebellious soul (much to the pain and torment of the rebel). The misery of the damned here is essentially a by-product; the real aim of hell is the emphatic assertion of truth, of reality, of joy.

Moreover, as we saw in an earlier chapter, Lewis explicitly embraces the view that God has "hot wrath" against sinners. He rejects the modern demythologized notion that God's anger is simply "what inevitably happens to us if we behave inappropriately towards a reality of immense power."[27] God is no live wire that we blunder against; hell is not an inadvertent electrocution. Rather, God is a consuming fire. He will burn up all that is opposed to him. And if all we are is opposition, if all that remains of us is hostility and enmity to him, then in burning that up, he will burn us up as well.

For his own part, Lewis believes that in the long run, the two conceptions—hell as self-inflicted and hell as God-inflicted—mean the same thing. Hell is both a sentence inflicted by a just Judge and the simple result of the fact that men prefer darkness to light. "We are therefore at liberty to think of this bad man's perdition not [merely?] as a sentence imposed on him but as the mere fact of being what he is."[28] And after death, all that is left of the bad man is his badness. This is difficult for us to understand, but Lewis tries to help us through George MacDonald, the Scottish guide in *The Great Divorce*. Normally we can distinguish a bad man from his badness. His badness is the twisting or corruption of who and what God made him to be. But imagine that this distinction collapses—that the badness, in a sense, swallows up the man. If that were to happen, the man would, in essence, cease to be a man.

But badness here is too abstract. MacDonald instead uses the example of a grumbling old woman. He says that the main question in her case is whether she is a grumbler or only a grumble. A grumbler can be saved; the woman can turn from her grumbling and become human again. But if she has collapsed into her grumbling, if the grumble has swallowed up her humanity, then what is left can only be swept away.

> The whole difficulty of understanding Hell is that the thing to be understood is so nearly Nothing. But ye'll have had experiences . . . it begins with

---

26 Lewis, *The Problem of Pain*, 124.
27 Lewis, *Letters to Malcolm*, 96.
28 Lewis, The *Problem of Pain*, 124.

a grumbling mood, and yourself still distinct from it: perhaps criticising it. And yourself, in a dark hour, may will that mood, embrace it. Ye can repent and come out of it again. But there may come a day when you can do that no longer. Then there will be no you left to criticise the mood, nor even to enjoy it, but just the grumble itself going on forever like a machine.[29]

Lewis is attempting to thread a tight needle. On the one hand, hell is real. The damned are really damned. And from within, from the perspective of the rebels, hell is practically endless; that is why we see millions and millions of miles of empty, futile houses in the Grey Town.[30] In hell, people are always moving away from each other; they cannot stand the presence of other beings, so they cut themselves off from all contact. They shut themselves in their own tiny prisons of resentment and anger and lust. On the other hand, from the perspective of reality, hell is nearly nothing. It is only a crack in heaven's sidewalk. It is smaller than a pebble of the earthly world, smaller than an atom of heaven. However big it may seem to those inside, in reality,

all loneliness, angers, hatreds, envies and itchings that it contains, if rolled into one single experience and put into the scale against the least moment of the joy that is felt by the least in Heaven, would have no weight that could be registered at all. . . . If all Hell's miseries together entered the consciousness of yon wee yellow bird on the bough there, they would be swallowed up without trace, as if one drop of ink had been dropped into that Great Ocean to which your terrestrial Pacific itself is only a molecule.[31]

Hell is the darkness outside, "the outer rim where being fades away into nonentity."[32]

Or, coming back to the three biblical images of hell mentioned earlier—punishment, destruction, and banishment: We've explored some of what is meant by punishment. Lewis captures the horror of banishment well in commenting on Jesus's words "I never knew you; depart from me" (Matt. 7:23):

In some sense, as dark to the intellect as it is unendurable to the feelings, we can be both banished from the presence of Him who is present

---

29 Lewis, *The Great Divorce*, 77–78.
30 Ibid., 9–10.
31 Ibid., 138–39.
32 Lewis, *The Problem of Pain*, 129.

everywhere and erased from the knowledge of Him who knows all. We can be left utterly and absolutely outside—repelled, exiled, estranged, finally and unspeakably ignored.[33]

The finality of this exile—the door slamming shut, the futility of our knocking, the terror of being totally and unendingly forgotten—is what accounts for its horror. Then there is destruction, which means "the unmaking, or cessation, of the destroyed." But, in our experience, all destruction turns the thing destroyed into something else. A burnt log becomes gases, heat, and ash. So also with humans. "To enter hell, is to be banished from humanity. What is cast (or casts itself) into hell is not a man: it is 'remains.'"[34]

We catch a glimpse of what Lewis means in Weston's disintegration in *Perelandra*. After he becomes the Unman, the demonic power animating Weston's body sometimes allows vestiges of Weston's consciousness to come out. What comes out is nonsensical gibbering and irrational babbling. Weston is no longer a man; the light has gone out. All that is left of his decaying psychic energy is shattered and scattered. He can't form coherent thoughts; he feels that they are taking off his head. He has passed through the rind and into "the positive and self-consuming Death." His humanity has been utterly eaten away. "Only a ghost was left—an everlasting unrest, a crumbling, a ruin, an odor of decay."[35]

So, then, it is true that Lewis believes that hell is both God-inflicted and self-inflicted. However, his accent clearly falls on the self-inflicted side. He worries that the Christian tradition has overemphasized the punishment to the exclusion of the self-wrought destruction and banishment into nothing. For my own part, I often worry about the opposite. A self-inflicted hell is palatable to us in our present condition; as Lewis himself acknowledges, the notion that God actively judges sinners eternally is the most unpalatable and repellant form of the doctrine. The notion that God would, in complete and total justice, not merely *permit* us to decay into ourselves but actually *cast us* into outer darkness—at this, we balk. But this is in fact the way the Bible speaks. According to our Lord, we will not simply drift away from his presence; we will be thrown, hurled with a ferocity that will shock us with its total rejection. Hell will be the trash heap of the cosmos.

---

[33] Lewis, "The Weight of Glory," in *The Weight of Glory and Other Addresses*, 41.
[34] Lewis, *The Problem of Pain*, 128.
[35] Lewis, *Perelandra*, 111. The same unrest, mental breakdown, and overwhelming fear appears again in chap. 13 when Weston reemerges to talk with Ransom.

At the same time, I do think Lewis's emphasis is needed. We need multiple images to grasp the horror of hell, just as we need multiple images to grasp the glory of union with Christ. Therefore, we ought to embrace the truth that hell is *both* God-inflicted and self-inflicted. The danger comes when we use one image to cancel or minimize the other. Instead, we must labor to hold them both, to believe them both, to preach them both, to fear them both.

Lewis and the Prophet Joel

In the course of my writing this book, our church had a series of sermons through the Minor Prophets. I was assigned the book of Joel. Unlike its predecessor Hosea, Joel does not focus on the grossness of Israel's sin—the ingratitude, the transgressing of covenants, the whoredom and unfaithfulness of God's people. Instead, it dwells almost exclusively on the coming judgment on the day of the Lord. Imminent judgment in Joel's day consists of two main elements: agricultural devastation and military conquest. Drought, pestilence, and wildfires devastate crops. Locusts devour the harvest. The fruit of the land is cut off, and famine overtakes the land. What's more, the judgments come one after another. The cutting locust gives way to the swarming locust, followed by the hopping locust. What the drought doesn't take, the pestilence finishes off. There's not even time to catch your breath.

And then, in the midst of the agricultural devastation, the barbarian army appears on the horizon, like a pack of lions with gnashing teeth and sharp claws. Those fires that devastated the crops? The army starts them. Its chariots rumble like thunder. Barriers and defenses are no protection against the invaders. They scale walls. They climb into windows. They are uncountable and unstoppable. This hostile horde is single-mindedly devoted to Israel's destruction. And the clincher is that this army, which is hell-bent on destruction, is led by none other than God himself.

> The LORD utters his voice
>> before his army. (Joel 2:11)

How do we make this real in the twenty-first-century West? We don't fear famines and apocalyptic droughts; we are entertained by them on the big screen. Barbarian hordes from the north have no reality for us;

elsewhere in the world, people do fear those things. In numerous countries, pillaging, kidnapping, torture, and murder are real dangers. But when
we hear about them, they feel distant and purely hypothetical, like a dream
or, again, something out of the movies. Thus, our imaginations need help,
and Scripture provides the images we need.

But there's another problem. To the degree that we do seriously reckon
with these horrors and seek to imagine ourselves in those situations, we
invariably cast ourselves as the victims. We are the hungry children with
sunken eyes and empty bellies. We are the innocent villagers fleeing before
the army of orcs. Thus, to say that such a fate might be merited, that we
might actually *deserve* the famine and the orcs, is outrageous to our ears.
We can't imagine we've done anything that could warrant fire, pestilence,
famine, and conquest. However much we may be aware of our failures and
sins, to unleash orcs and goblins upon us would be massive overkill on
God's part. Mass murderers, rapists, terrorists—perhaps they deserve such
a fate. But not us. We're good people. Or at least nice people. We try to be
kind to others. We love our families and friends. We tolerate our enemies.
How could God possibly inflict this great and awesome day upon us?

Two answers may help. The first is that we don't have a sufficiently
serious view of our sins. We have forsaken God, rejected God, turned away
from God. We have not served him with joyfulness and gladness of heart for
all the abundance he supplies us. If we cannot grasp the great outrage that
it is for a creature, one who was made by God and for God, to completely
reject, ignore, and disobey him, we'll never understand God's judgment. If
he has made us, and if he has given us life and breath and everything, if all
that we have has come from his hand, and if we've responded with such
callousness, ingratitude, grumbling, and disobedience, and if we continue
to pursue sin despite his blockades, what else could our crimes deserve? Put
another way, the first answer to our troubled imaginations is that we need
to seriously reflect on a book like Hosea.

But Lewis suggests a second answer. We are the hungry child and the
innocent villager, yes. But we are also the drought, the locust, the barbarian. The army that Yahweh leads against us consists of the inhuman and
decayed versions of ourselves. And the day of the Lord, the final one to
which all the historical ones have pointed, is the moment when our inhuman self catches the villager, when the locust that we are devours the
last grain of our wheat. Picture that final moment—you with your back

against the wall, the undeterred eye of the locust, the brute, the gnawing emptiness that is drought fixed firmly upon you. It closes in; you recoil in absolute and unremitting terror. Then what? The imagination fails. What would the devouring be like? Perhaps it would not be like anything. Perhaps the comparison fails because to the one experiencing it, the reason and imagination that might have made the comparison, has failed. The light has gone out.

Or maybe that's too far. Can we really claim that the light ever goes completely out? Are those in hell really simply "remains," beings that once were human but now are not? For my own part, I couldn't go so far. The Bible does suggest something like that trajectory; in Romans 1, Paul seems to define the wrath of God *as* the giving over of human beings to their sin and corruption. Hell then would be the final giving over, the end and fulfillment of that depraved trajectory. But that is just what the Bible gives us—a trajectory. An ever-increasing descent into nothingness and evil. Just as heaven is an everlasting journey further up and further in to unending joy and being and reality, hell is an everlasting fall further down and farther out to eternal misery and nonbeing and unreality. To return to Joel's images, perhaps hell is simply the devouring, with no sense of the damned ever being finally devoured. Perhaps the damned exist (we dare not call it living) in that endlessly recurring moment when the cutting locust, the gnawing emptiness, the inhuman brute that bears our own likeness begins to devour us. As the Scripture says, the worm does not die, and the fire is not quenched (Mark 9:48). The fire consumes; it is ever-consuming, but nothing is ever finally consumed. Endless death, as Augustine said, is endless dying. The horror is real and everlasting.

In the end, our imaginations fail us. However horrible hell might be, we cannot out-describe it. We may miss the mark, but it will not be because we have overstated hell's horror. But perhaps, with the help of Lewis and Joel, we've made a little more progress in seeing the end of our great Choice. For this is the whole reason for exploring hell in the first place. "In all discussions of Hell we should keep steadily before our eyes the possible damnation, not of our enemies nor our friends (since both these disturb the reason) but of ourselves. This chapter is not about your wife or son, nor about Nero or Judas Iscariot; it is about you and me."[36]

---

[36] Lewis, *The Problem of Pain*, 131.

CHAPTER 16

HEAVEN

Further Up and Further In

Of all the chapters that I've set myself to write, this one may be the hardest. Lewis's writings on heaven are so moving, so vivid, so profound, that doing anything more than quoting them feels futile, even wrong. I felt the same way when I wrote my book on Narnia: it's better to simply encourage readers to revisit the last two chapters of *The Last Battle* and journey with the Narnians "further up and further in," as they impossibly climb waterfalls, run faster than they ever imagined possible, and slowly come to the recognition that though they have left Narnia, they have actually come home; or to experience the solidity and reality of the green plains in *The Great Divorce*. Some of the magnificent passages in "The Weight of Glory" and *The Problem of Pain* will likely make an impression that I can only hope to muddle and confuse. But in the end, I think this chapter is necessary. To labor to make Lewis's account of hell understandable and imaginable but then withhold the same effort concerning heaven would be false to Lewis's vision of the Christian life. And so, with much fear and trembling (as well as much hope in God's help), let us speak about heaven.

Longing for Heaven

We must first remember that heaven and hell are not strictly parallel. They are opposites, but they are *asymmetrical* opposites. Hell is nearly nothing, the place where being fades away into nonentity. It was not, as Jesus said, made for man. Heaven, on the other hand, "is reality itself. All that is fully real is Heavenly."[1] It is "the home of humanity and therefore contains all that is implied in a glorified human life."[2] "To enter heaven is to become more human than you ever succeeded in being on earth."[3] Heaven is our proper home; it is where we belong. As Jewel the unicorn says when he arrives in real Narnia: "I have come home at last! This is my real country! I belong here. This is the land I have been looking for all my life, though I never knew it till now."[4]

Some of Lewis's best prose seeks to capture this "looking for" heaven. He describes it as "our desire for our far-off country."[5] This is the phenomenon that we explored in chapter 10, on Joy, the inconsolable longing, the pleasing pain, the unsatisfied desire that is more desirable than any satisfaction. It shows up in countless ways in Lewis's writings. Here it is toward the end of *The Voyage of the Dawn Treader*:

> And suddenly there came a breeze from the east, tossing the top of the wave into foamy shapes and ruffling the smooth water all round them. It lasted only a second or so but what it brought them in that second none of those three children will ever forget. It brought both a smell and a sound, a musical sound. Edmund and Eustace would never talk about it afterward. Lucy could only say, "It would break your heart." "Why," said I, "was it so sad?" "Sad!! No," said Lucy.[6]

Lewis often describes it in musical terms. When the patient dies in *Screwtape*, he discovers "that central music in every pure experience which had always just evaded memory was now at last recovered."[7] In "The Weight of Glory," it is "the echo of a tune we have not heard."[8] Or, again, picking up the breeze imagery, one catches a whiff of the longing in the arrival of the Oyarsa of Perelandra in *That Hideous Strength*, as a summer breeze, laden with unimaginable scents, blows through the room: "A soft tingling and shivering as of foam and breaking bubbles ran over their flesh. Tears ran down Ransom's cheeks. He alone knew from what seas and what islands

[1] Lewis, *The Great Divorce*, 69.
[2] Lewis, *The Problem of Pain*, 129.
[3] Ibid., 127–28.
[4] Lewis, *The Last Battle*, 196.
[5] Lewis, "The Weight of Glory," in *The Weight of Glory and Other Addresses*, 29.
[6] Lewis, *The Voyage of the Dawn Treader*, 237.
[7] Lewis, *The Screwtape Letters*, 186.
[8] Lewis, "The Weight of Glory," in *The Weight of Glory and Other Addresses*, 31.

that breeze blew."[9] The breeze wakes the inconsolable wound in Ransom and Merlin, and they both ache at this touching.

Yet again, in *The Dawn Treader*, Lewis tries to capture the longing when Lucy reads the wonderful story in the magician's book. As she does, she forgets that she is reading at all. "She was living in the story as if it were real, and all the pictures were real too. When she had got to the third page and come to the end, she said, 'That is the loveliest story I've ever read or ever shall read in my whole life. Oh, I wish I could have gone on reading it for ten years.'"[10] Discovering that she can't reread the story (the demand for "encore" never works), she is heartbroken, and even more so when she realizes that she can't even remember what the story was about. But "ever since that day what Lucy means by a good story is a story which reminds her of the forgotten story in the Magician's Book." More importantly, when she meets Aslan, she asks if Aslan will ever tell her that story again. He responds, "Indeed, yes, I will tell it to you for years and years."[11]

Of this longing for our true home, Lewis says, "There have been times when I think we do not desire heaven; but more often I find myself wondering whether, in our heart of hearts, we have ever desired anything else." This desire is no mercenary desire; no bribery is involved. Heaven is the proper reward for the saved soul, since what God does in saving us is to "fit us for Heaven" by stoking the longing for our true home.[12]

Of course, as we've seen throughout this book, this longing can settle on false objects. We can refuse the holiday at the sea and insist on playing with our mud pies in the slums. We can mistake the means through which the desire comes for the source and end of the desire itself. When we do, we find (eventually) that the desire dies. If we insist on trying to satisfy the longing by drinking from the earthly fountains, the whole thing goes wrong. We become disillusioned, disobedient, and set on the path to misery. For Lewis, this is why suffering is such a mercy to the Christian. Suffering shatters the illusion that all is well in the world. "Pain insists upon being attended to. God whispers to us in our pleasures, speaks in our conscience, but shouts in our pain: it is His megaphone to rouse a deaf world."[13] Pain and suffering shatter our self-sufficiency and self-reliance;

---

9 Lewis, *That Hideous Strength*, 320.
10 Lewis, *The Voyage of the Dawn Treader*, 154–55.
11 Ibid., 158.
12 Lewis, *The Problem of Pain*, 149.
13 Ibid., 91.

they remind us how weak we truly are. They are reminders that "here we have no lasting city" (Heb. 13:14). The mixture of pleasure and pain, joy and sorrow that we encounter in this life is a severe mercy from the hand of a loving Father.

> The settled happiness and security which we all desire, God withholds from us by the very nature of the world: but joy, pleasure, and merriment, He has scattered broadcast. We are never safe, but we have plenty of fun, and some ecstasy. It is not hard to see why. The security we crave would teach us to rest our hearts in this world and oppose an obstacle to our return to God: a few moments of happy love, a landscape, a symphony, a merry meeting with our friends, a bathe or a football match, have no such tendency. Our Father refreshes us on the journey with some pleasant inns, but will not encourage us to mistake them for home.[14]

Nevertheless, while we must not mistake pleasures for joy, pleasures are "the far off and momentary coruscations" of the God who is Joy himself. More than that, they are promises. They compel us to ask, "What would it be to taste at the fountain-head that stream of which even these lower reaches prove so intoxicating?" For this is what we are promised: "The whole man is to drink joy from the fountain of joy."[15]

Longing to Join the Dance

In our present condition, this joy is nearly unimaginable. That is why descriptions of heaven must so often be guarded by negations (e.g., there will be no sex or marriage in heaven). But this is not because heaven is empty; it is because it is so full that our earthly joys are not strong enough to bear its weight. "We must believe—and therefore in some degree imagine—that every negation will only be the reverse side of a fulfilling."[16] Lewis's essay on transposition is devoted entirely to showing how this impossible imagining is to be done.

But we can say more about this longing and ache. In "The Weight of Glory," Lewis says that the longing that strikes us when we catch the scent of the far-off country contains the longing to be noticed, accepted, and welcomed by Someone. We pine to be treated as more than strangers in this

---

14 Ibid., 116.
15 Lewis, "The Weight of Glory," in *The Weight of Glory and Other Addresses*, 44.
16 Lewis, "Transposition," in *The Weight of Glory and Other Addresses*, 109.

universe, to be acknowledged, "to meet with some response, to bridge some chasm that yawns between us and reality." This, of course, is the inverse of hell's banishment and exile. For the promise of heaven is that God will mark us; he will notice us. He will call us in, welcome us, receive us. Not only will we be fully known (that is true of us already); we will *know* that we are known.

But we don't merely want to see and be seen. We also long to be "taken into the dance." We ache "to be united with the beauty we see, to pass into it, to receive it into ourselves, to bathe in it, to become part of it." At present, we know ourselves to be on the wrong side of the door. "We cannot mingle with the splendours we see. But all the leaves of the New Testament are rustling with the rumour that it will not always be so. Some day, God willing, we shall get *in*."[17]

What does it mean to be thus taken into the dance, to get fully and finally in? Again our imaginations fail us. But in using the image of the Great Dance, Lewis is attempting to wed total and spontaneous freedom and joy with the most intricate and beautiful order—so intricate that it must be labor; so free that it cannot be laborious. From one angle, we can say that it is obedience. We humans "become as perfect in voluntary obedience as the inanimate creation is in its lifeless obedience." But lest obedience have all the hard, dutiful connotations that it has now, we must picture it as a game or play.

> Heaven is leisure . . . but pretty vigorous too as our best leisure really is. Man was created "to glorify God and enjoy Him forever." Whether that is best pictured as being in love, or like being one of an orchestra who are playing a great work with perfect success, or like surf bathing, or like endlessly exploring a wonderful country [like true Narnia?] or endlessly reading a glorious story [like Lucy and the magician's book]—who knows? Dante says Heaven "grew drunken with its universal laughter."[18]

Lewis defends this apparent trivializing of heaven by reminding us that

> dance and game are frivolous, unimportant down here; for "down here" is not their natural place. Here, they are a moment's rest from the life we were placed here to live. But in this world everything is upside down.

17 Lewis, "The Weight of Glory," in *The Weight of Glory and Other Addresses*, 42.
18 Lewis to Mrs. Johnson, May 25, 1957, in *Collected Letters*, 3:856, interpolations mine.

> That which, if it could be prolonged here, would be a truancy, is likest that which in a better country is the End of ends. Joy is the serious business of Heaven.[19]

Pleasures (and even pains) initiate us into the eternal rhythm of self-giving, but it is only there that we actually experience its true reality. "For the Eternal Word also gives Himself in sacrifice; and that not only on Calvary. For when He was crucified He 'did that in the wild weather of His outlying provinces which He had done at home in glory and gladness.'"[20]

In heaven, we will always be giving away what we are receiving and thereby receiving more than we've been given. This eternal self-giving is a different sort of eternal dying from that found in hell. It is "a continual self-abandonment—an opening, an unveiling, a surrender, of itself."[21] This increasing self-surrender may even have its own ardors and exertions; the journey further up and further in may have its own delightful severities and steep ascents.[22]

The Resurrection of the Body

We must not forget that it is the whole man who will drink from the fountain of joy. Our full selves, including our bodies, will join the Great Dance. As we saw in chapter 7, the beauties of nature may be a secret that God has shared with man alone; the beasts don't love sunsets; and angels, while loving all things, including colors, presumably have no retinas with which to enjoy them. It falls to man, the rational animal that straddles the line between the world of spirit and the world of matter, to praise God for the beauties of nature. And so the resurrection of the body is crucial.

Lewis admits that he cannot fathom how exactly this resurrection will happen. He doubts that it can simply mean the reanimation of our corpses; the material pieces that make up our bodies are reused again and again after our deaths, now as fertilizer, then as the parts of cows, then again in some other human beings. Indeed, even in this life, our bodies cycle through the material components many times before we die. Thus, resurrection does not demand the reattachment of the soul to those precise pieces of matter that we possessed at the moment of our deaths.

---

[19] Lewis, *Letters to Malcolm*, 92.
[20] Lewis, *The Problem of Pain*, 157.
[21] Ibid., 156.
[22] Lewis, *Letters to Malcolm*, 108.

Instead, in speculating about the nature of the resurrection, Lewis argues that the key is not the material components (though he insists that matter will be and must be involved); rather, "what the soul cries out for is the resurrection of the senses."[23] It is through the senses that we turn matter into soul; the physical world of matter strikes our senses, and then our minds perceive and know it, thus making it, in some manner, soulish. Physics tells me that sunbeams are waves or particles or some such thing; the best descriptions the scientists offer are in equations and numbers. But whatever light really is, as far as we are concerned, we only know it as it strikes our eyes and then is translated, in some mysterious process, into knowledge in the soul. It is light thus translated that we call beautiful, that Milton hailed as holy, and that Lewis explores in the short story "A Man Born Blind." Therefore, Lewis speculates, what really must be raised is this power of turning matter into soul.

Lewis sees an echo and anticipation of the resurrection of the senses in memory. In our present condition, we have the ability, however feeble and intermittent, to raise dead sensations from the grave. A song, a smell, a word triggers a memory, and immediately we're transported back to that earlier time; or perhaps that earlier experience, in its own dim way, is present to us again. And as we saw in chapter 10, memory often glorifies these earlier experiences.

In *Surprised by Joy*, Lewis recalls a time when his brother made a toy garden out of some moss and twigs on a biscuit tin. He writes, "I do not think the impression was very important at the moment, but it soon became important in memory."[24] That momentary glimpse of beauty in his boyhood was "a whisper which memory will warehouse as a shout."[25] In other words, memory *glorifies* the original experience. In the hands of memory, the experience is transfigured, its true import unfurled and manifested. Again, this is perhaps the heavenly counterpart to the hellish descent from grumbler to grumble. Just as happy experiences are glorified in memory and thus anticipate the resurrection, so also by endlessly revolving on injustices done to us, by turning over and over in our minds the bitterness of our past, we begin to roll down a hill that will eventually carry us over the cliff into the endless abyss of the outer darkness.

Of course, this power of memory isn't the same as the resurrection. In

---

23 Ibid., 121.
24 Lewis, *Surprised by Joy*, 7.
25 Lewis, *Letters to Malcolm*, 122.

glory, we will do more than remember our earthly lives. But it is a pointer to resurrection. The remembered past offers the first weak beginnings of the glorification of the senses; one day that glorification will burst into nature with a shout. When our sensory bodies are raised, all creation will rise with us and in us, including beasts and birds and the hills that enchanted us as children. Lewis was agnostic about whether all dogs go to heaven, but he certainly believed that beloved pets will be raised with (and, in some mysterious way, "in") their masters. Just as we become our true selves when we are raised in Christ, so our dogs and cats will become fully themselves in our resurrection.[26] They too must join the Great Dance.

The new heavens and new earth will not simply be a copy of the present creation. Nor will they be a substitute or replacement. They will be "the same, yet not the same, as this." Their relationship to our present experience will be like a flower's to its root, like a diamond's to the coal whence it comes.

> Then the new earth and sky, the same yet not the same as these, will rise
> in us as we have risen in Christ. And once again, after who knows what
> aeons of the silence and the dark, the birds will sing and the waters flow,
> and lights and shadows move across the hills, and the faces of our friends
> laugh upon us with amazed recognition.[27]

By seeing in memory the early stirrings of resurrection, Lewis suggests another way in which the glorified state will surpass this world. At present, our experiences are ours; that is, they are private. Even two people who are present for the same event will experience it in very different ways. Thus, our memories can only be communicated to others imperfectly, with words. But, Lewis suggests, a day is coming when we may perhaps be able to share not only our present experiences but also our glorified memories. The fields in which we played as children have been bulldozed to make way for a shopping center; they exist now only in our recollections. In glory, might we not be able to take others for a walk in them?

The Resurrection of the Body of Christ

The possibility of sharing our experiences with others leads us into another dimension of Lewis's vision of heaven. The Christian hope is not merely

---

[26] See Lewis's extended discussion of the issue in chap. 9 of *The Problem of Pain*.
[27] Lewis, *Letters to Malcolm*, 123.

the resurrection of the body but also the resurrection of the body of Christ, that is, the church. The church is one body, with many members, and these many members are different so that each can know and praise God in his or her own unique way. For each individual's relationship to God is unique. "If all experienced God in the same way and returned Him an identical worship, the song of the Church triumphant would have no symphony, it would be like an orchestra in which all the instruments played the same note."[28]

God loves different notes. He loves harmony. That's why he created us all as unique characters.

> Your soul has a curious shape because it is a hollow made to fit a particular swelling in the infinite contours of the Divine substance, or a key to unlock one of the doors in the house with many mansions. . . . Your place in heaven will seem to be made for you and you alone, because you were made for it.[29]

Put another way, each man has a secret which God shares with him only. There are some things about God that each person sees better than everyone else. And yet each man also seeks to share that secret with others. This attempt at sharing our secret with others is continuously successful and yet never complete. "Heaven is a city, and a Body, because the blessed remain eternally different: a society, because each has something to tell all the others—fresh and ever fresh news of the 'My God' whom each finds in Him whom all praise as 'Our God.'"[30] The eternal progress of heaven— the further up and further in—happens (at least partially) through hearing what others see of God from their own unique vantage points. Heaven is the place where we learn to love as others love without ceasing to be ourselves. As we become more united to God, we also become more united to each other. But this union with each other doesn't result in a single identity or conformity. In being joined together we become more alike and more ourselves. Our hearts will swell as each of us tells his fellows about "My God," and then we all praise him afresh as "Our God."

To draw this into the theme of this book, "true personality lies ahead." The self which we possess now is only a parody or shadow or first attempt at it. And this true personality is not something we attain by our efforts

---

28 Lewis, *The Problem of Pain*, 155.
29 Ibid., 152.
30 Ibid., 155.

but something we receive as a gift. And it will come to us "when we occupy those places in the structure of the eternal cosmos for which we were designed or invented." Each of us has a place in the Great Dance.

> As a color first reveals its true quality when placed by an excellent artist in its pre-elected spot between certain others, as a spice reveals its true flavor when inserted just where and when a good cook wishes among other ingredients, as the dog becomes really doggy only when he has taken his place in the household of man, so we shall then first be true persons when we have suffered [i.e., allowed] ourselves to be fitted into our places.[31]

Of course, being fitted into place means we must submit to being molded. We might even be called to cut off a hand or gouge out an eye. The self must die if it is to live. "The crucifixion of the natural self is the passport to everlasting life." We give up attempts to establish our own value and instead *receive* value from the One who made us and redeemed us. Our true personality, our true self, our real value lies in union with Christ. We "share the victory by being in the Victor." And not just in the Victor, but in the Victor's body. "As organs in the Body of Christ, as stones and pillars in the temple, we are assured of our eternal self-identity and shall live to remember the galaxies as an old tale."[32] We find our real selves in Christ, in his body, in love, in joy.

Sarah Smith of Golders Green

One scene in *The Great Divorce* brings together a number of these themes: heaven as being in love, hell as almost nothing, the new creation as raised up in the redeemed, and, most importantly for our purposes, the relevance of this for the Christian life. In chapter 14, I mentioned the invulnerability of heaven. The solid people in *The Great Divorce* are immune to the manipulations of the damned. The most extended proof of this point occurs at the end of the book, in the conversation between Sarah Smith of Golders Green and her husband, Frank.

Sarah arrives on the scene in grand, heavenly style. She is attended by angels who scatter heavenly flower petals at her feet and musicians who sing glorious music. She is surrounded by young men and women, boys

---

[31] Lewis, "Membership," in *The Weight of Glory and Other Addresses*, 173.
[32] Ibid.

and girls whom she loved on earth and who thereby became, in a sense, her children. Cats, dogs, birds, and horses also follow her. As we saw earlier, animals find their place in relation to man. "Every beast and bird that came near her had its place in her love. In her they became themselves. And now the abundance of life she has in Christ from the Father flows over into them."[33] The unbearable beauty of her face and the splendor of her train lead the narrator to mistake her for Mary the mother of Jesus. But in reality, she is a simple saint who has loved those around her with a love that comes from God himself.

Out on the green plain, she meets her husband, Frank. Or, rather, she meets the remains of Frank. Not only is he a wispy ghost, but his personality has split into two—a short, dwarfish ghost that represents Frank's shriveled, cold, damp self, as well as a tall, theatrical ghost that Frank projects to others. The dwarf leads the theatrical ghost (the Tragedian) on a chain and for much of the conversation is unable to take his eyes off it. On earth, Frank was notoriously manipulative; he wielded the pity and compassion of others as a weapon to serve his own ends, all while viewing himself as a tragic hero and martyr. His grand acts of unselfishness included allowing his wife to use the last stamp in the house when he needed to mail a letter, a memory he has apparently been holding on to for all these years. His journey to heaven is apparently motivated by the desire to see his great suffering praised and echoed in the sadness and misery of his wife over his absence.

For her part, Sarah sees through the facade, refusing even to address the Tragedian. What's more, as a glorified saint, she is invulnerable to his manipulations. She expresses happiness at his arrival and kisses him on his head. She asks his forgiveness for the wrongs she did to him on earth. He expectantly asks her if she has missed him, hoping to see his worth reflected in her great misery over his absence. When he discovers that she has not been unhappy at all (how could she be, in heaven?), he is deeply offended. He measures love by the degree of unhappiness when the beloved is gone. Her love for him is measured by her need of him. But Sarah now has no needs. She is *in love*, and now loves truly. She wants him, but does not need him.

At the news that he is not needed, the Tragedian launches into a rant of despair and theatrical agony. But Sarah will have none of it. She rebukes the

---

[33] Lewis, *The Great Divorce*, 119.

big ugly doll, the persona he uses to manipulate her, and tells Frank to look at her and drop the chain. True to form, she does so with "merriment [dancing] in her eyes." Her "rebuke" is a big joke, and she is inviting the dwarf to share it. But the dwarf struggles hard against Joy. Her laughter and mirth do reach him, and for a moment he sees the absurdity of the Tragedian. But it is all against his will. He clings tightly to the chain, and flings her words back in her face. He is unable to conceive of someone wanting him without needing him. And so he resolves to return to hell and attempts again to wield pity as a weapon. "It is nothing to you that I go back to the cold and the gloom, the lonely, lonely streets."[34]

Sarah objects and tells him to stop talking like that. He seizes on her objection as evidence that he can play on her compassion and send her on a guilt trip. But again she corrects him, telling him to stop acting, that his blackmail will do no good. Pity can be used that way on earth, as when a child who has done wrong sulks in his room until his family relents and comes to comfort him. In the Shadowlands, misery can hold joy hostage through pity. But not in heaven. Heaven's Joy is incapable of being manipulated by hell's blackmail. Sarah can no longer pay the ransom. Frank can, if he chooses, make himself wretched, but he cannot communicate his wretchedness. "Everything becomes more and more itself." Good becomes better, evil becomes worse. Light becomes brighter, and darkness fades further into nothingness. And while the light is able to swallow up the darkness, the darkness cannot infect the light. Sarah is now fully and finally in love, and therefore she cannot love a lie. "The Happy Trinity is her home: nothing can trouble her joy."[35]

Finding Ourselves in the Happy Land of the Trinity

We were made to come home to the happy land of the Trinity, to take our place in the Great Dance. Everything in our present experience is whispering this possibility. The Choice of ways lies before us. God or self. Joy or misery. Heaven or hell. Aslan is telling us all the time the way into true Narnia. "The call is not only to prostration and awe; it is to a reflection of the Divine life, a creaturely participation in the Divine attributes which is far beyond our present desires. We are bidden to 'put on Christ,' to become

---

[34] Ibid., 130.
[35] Ibid., 134. The song that the angels and young people sing after the encounter is essentially a rendering of Psalm 91.

like God."[36] For in becoming like God, we become our true selves. "Our real selves are all waiting for us in Him."[37] "We shall be true and everlasting and really divine persons only in Heaven, just as we are, even now, coloured bodies only in the light."[38] I can think of no better way to close this chapter than Lewis's own conclusion to his chapter on heaven in *The Problem of Pain*:

> The golden apple of selfhood, thrown among the false gods, became an apple of discord because they scrambled for it. They did not know the first rule of the holy game, which is that every player must by all means touch the ball and then immediately pass it on. To be found with it in your hands is a fault: to cling to it, death. But when it flies to and fro among the players too swift for eye to follow, and the great master Himself leads the revelry, giving Himself eternally to His creatures in the generation, and back to Himself in the sacrifice, of the Word, then indeed the eternal dance "makes heaven drowsy with the harmony." All pains and pleasures we have known on earth are early initiations in the movements of that dance: but the dance itself is strictly incomparable with the sufferings of this present time. As we draw nearer to its uncreated rhythm, pain and pleasure sink almost out of sight. There is joy in the dance, but it does not exist for the sake of joy. It does not even exist for the sake of good, or of love. It is Love Himself, and Good Himself, and therefore happy. It does not exist for us, but we for it. The size and emptiness of the universe which frightened us at the outset of this book, should awe us still, for though they may be no more than a subjective by-product of our three-dimensional imagining, yet they symbolise great truth. As our Earth is to all the stars, so doubtless are we men and our concerns to all creation; as all the stars are to space itself, so are all creatures, all thrones and powers and mightiest of the created gods, to the abyss of the self-existing Being, who is to us Father and Redeemer and indwelling Comforter, but of whom no man nor angel can say nor conceive what He is in and for Himself, or what is the work that He "maketh from the beginning to the end." For they are all derived and unsubstantial things. Their vision fails them and they cover their eyes from the intolerable light of utter actuality, which was and is and shall be, which never could have been otherwise, which has no opposite.[39]

---

36 Lewis, *The Problem of Pain*, 46–47.
37 Lewis, *Mere Christianity*, 225.
38 Lewis, "Membership," in *The Weight of Glory and Other Addresses*, 174–75.
39 Lewis, *The Problem of Pain*, 158–59.

CHAPTER 17

ORUAL'S CHOICE

Discovering Her True Face

This final chapter will focus on one of Lewis's final works, *Till We Have Faces*. If you haven't read it, or its story is not relatively fresh in your mind, I strongly urge you to read the novel first and then return to this chapter. What I have to say here is really designed to prompt a second (or third or fourth) reading and (I fear) would ruin a first reading, since the reader would be unable to not know what I have to say. Part of the brilliance of this novel is the way your perception of what is happening changes as the book progresses. A reader who knows the ending before picking up the book for the first time will be robbed of the gift of surprise.

Lewis regarded *Till We Have Faces* as "far and away" his best book (even though he recognized that many critics and most of the population did not share his assessment). A friend of mine (and fellow Lewis lover) described the book as "grey." According to him, it lacks the sparkle of Lewis's other fiction. I think there is truth in that assessment, and yet the mundane and muted dullness of much of the book is intentional. *Till We Have Faces* is a thick novel; many themes in Lewis's thought are woven into its pages. For example, the tension between reason and imagination runs throughout the novel. It is expressed as a contrast between Greek thought and pagan mysteries, between philosophy and poetry, between clear religion and thick religion. Lewis's view of mythology—those good but twisted dreams given to pagans in the time before Christ—also finds ample expression in the novel. The novel itself is a retelling of the myth of Cupid and Psyche, and the literary relationship between the original myth and Lewis's reworking merits careful study.

As interesting as these other themes are, I will focus on what I take to be the central dimension of this story—the life and struggle of Orual, the novel's main character. The book itself is written as Orual's autobiography. It contains two parts; the longer part is Orual's accusation and complaint against the gods, and the shorter, concluding part is almost an appendix that transforms the entire story. For my part, I've structured this chapter accordingly, briefly laying out Orual's story as she presents it in part 1, and then revisiting the same story in light of the revelations in part 2. In doing so, I confess some reluctance; I'm attempting to make explicit what Lewis has accomplished implicitly in the story itself.

Orual's Complaint

As noted above, part 1 is Orual's autobiographical complaint against the gods, especially against Ungit (the barbarian name for Aphrodite or Venus) and Ungit's son (the barbarian Cupid). Orual is the daughter of the king of Glome, a small, fictional barbarian kingdom east of Greece. At the beginning of the story, the king has no male heir; only two daughters (Orual and Redival), whom he essentially despises and neglects. For their part, the girls are fearful of their erratic and violent father, especially after the death of their mother. In due time, the king acquires a Greek slave, whom he dubs "the Fox," and sets him to tutor his daughters until a son is born. The Fox is a Stoic: while he has a nostalgic love for Greek poetry, he thinks the poets breathe lies about the gods. He views all nature as an unbroken whole, with the soul being a kind of spark of divinity in every man. The Fox exalts reason and rejects the pagan and poetic view of Hades and the afterlife, as well as the notion that the gods are jealous of humans. He is also wise and shrewd as a counselor to the king, and he has a deep love for his pupils (who affectionately call him "Grandfather").

Orual also loves the Fox and his Greek wisdom. Redival, on the other hand, is obsessed with boys and trivialities, and therefore rejects the Fox's teaching. Soon, the king remarries in hopes of gaining a son, but his new wife dies in childbirth, bearing a beautiful daughter named Psyche. Psyche "made beauty all round her. When she trod on mud, the mud was beautiful; when she ran in the rain, the rain was silver. When she picked up a toad—

she had the strangest and, I thought, unchanciest love for all manner of brutes—the toad became beautiful."[1] Orual falls instantly in love with her and essentially becomes her mother. For Orual, Psyche is the beginning of all her joys and the object of all her loves. "I wanted to be a wife so that I could have been her real mother. I wanted to be a boy so that she could be in love with me. I wanted her to be my full sister instead of my half sister. I wanted her to be a slave so that I could set her free and make her rich."[2] These are the happiest times of Orual's life—when she and Psyche and the Fox are always together.

For her part, Redival envies Psyche; she mocks her, despises her, and tattles on her. It is Redival who ruins the good times. One day she catches the common people worshiping Psyche as a goddess, and this puts great fear into Orual. What will Ungit do if she discovers that a mortal is stealing worship from her? The danger escalates when a plague breaks out. At first, the people believe that Psyche has a healing touch, and she is regarded as a kind of savior. Later, the fickle crowds come to believe that Psyche's touch spreads the disease, and she is deemed the Accursed. At the same time, Glome suffers a great famine and drought, as well as conflict with her neighbors. The priest of Ungit believes these great evils are the result of some great transgression and calls for Psyche to be sacrificed to Ungit's son, the god of the Grey Mountain. The king acquiesces to the sacrifice in order to save his own kingdom, but Orual and the Fox are distraught. Despite their best efforts, Psyche is doomed to be left on the mountain, either to be devoured by a Shadowbrute or to be married to Ungit's son (or perhaps both; the sacred stories are very mysterious in that way).

For her part, Psyche faces death with courage and nobility. In fact, when Orual visits her the night before the Great Offering, Orual is almost saddened by Pscyhe's stability and bravery in the face of death. She wants to comfort Psyche, and yet it is Psyche who comforts her. In fact, Psyche gives her own testimony to Lewis's notion of Joy. In her happiest moments, when faced with the beauties of nature, she had a kind of longing for death.

> And because it was so beautiful, it set me longing, always longing. Somewhere else there must be more of it. Everything seemed to be saying, Psyche come! But I couldn't (not yet) come and I didn't know where I was

---

[1] Lewis, *Till We Have Faces*, 22.
[2] Ibid., 23.

to come to. . . . The sweetest thing in all my life has been the longing—
to reach the Mountain, to find the place where all the beauty came from.[3]

Her composure frustrates and embitters Orual, so that the two sisters part
on troubled terms.

After Psyche is left on the mountain, Orual resolves to bury what's left
of her. She enlists Bardia, a good man and the captain of the king's guard,
to aid her in her journey up the Grey Mountain. But when they arrive at the
top, they discover, wonder of wonders, that Psyche is alive and living in apparent health and happiness in a valley on the Grey Mountain. She claims
that she was rescued from her bonds by the god of the West wind and carried to a palace where she was married to the god of the Grey Mountain.
The joy of the reunion is cut short when Psyche attempts to show Orual her
palace and discovers that Orual cannot see it at all. As far as Orual can tell,
Psyche is imagining things or pretending. Orual is horrified by Psyche's
insistence on the reality of the house. She doesn't know whether Psyche is
mad or telling the truth, nor does she know which would be worse. She tries
to convince Psyche to leave the mountain, but Psyche refuses to leave her
husband and her home. Once again, the sisters part on troubled terms, with
Orual reeling from the new Psyche, and Psyche promising to do whatever
she can to help Orual see and believe the gods.

Before Orual leaves the mountain, however, she has a momentary
glimpse of the god's house. She sees the grey palace in all its solid grandeur. But as quick as a flash, the palace vanishes from sight, and Orual is
left again with her doubts. In her heart, she rages against the gods who tan-
talize humans with riddles and mockery, and who refuse to speak plainly.
Upon returning to Glome, Orual attempts to make sense of the situation.
Bardia believes that Psyche has indeed been married to a god, but the god is
really the monstrous Shadowbrute, which explains why he comes to Psyche
at night and forbids her to see his face. The Fox, on the other hand, rejects
the divine explanation and instead believes that an outlaw has deceived
Psyche into believing that he is a god and that they are living in a palace.
Either way, Orual resolves to rescue Psyche from the clutches of the god or
the Brute or the outlaw. She returns to the mountain, overcoming her own
doubts about whether she should leave Psyche in her apparent happiness,
and threatens to commit suicide if Psyche will not listen to her. Psyche

---

[3] Ibid., 74–75.

relents and agrees to take a light into her bed chamber in order to look upon her husband's face (Orual believes this will prove that her husband is a monster or a vile man). Psyche reluctantly exposes the god, who then sends her into exile and leaves Orual with the ominous words, "You also shall be Psyche."

For a while, Orual lives in fear of what the god might do to her. But in time, she settles back into life. She grows closer to Bardia, who treats her more and more like a man—teaching her to fight with a sword and ride horseback. Meanwhile, she harbors a hidden love for him and a hidden jealousy against Bardia's wife. Upon her return, Orual veils herself at all times, creating a mystery about her appearance for the rest of her life. When the king dies after an accident, Orual shrewdly navigates the politics of the palace and the surrounding kingdoms in order to become queen. She rescues a neighboring prince from his evil brother, challenging the brother to single combat and defeating him. From then forward, she resolves to "queen it," locking up Orual deep inside of her, driving all of the softness and femininity out of her, and cultivating a hard but joyless strength. She becomes a great queen, mysterious and awful behind her veil. With the help of her three trusted counselors—the Fox, Bardia, and Arnom (the high priest of Ungit)—she does many great deeds. Though she still harbors a secret love for Bardia, she knows that she can never have him. Instead, she busies herself with improving Glome—freeing slaves, improving the mines, building a library, and refining the laws of the kingdom. Her busyness hides her pain and sorrow and loneliness.

She grows old in this manner, until one year, when on a journey to a neighboring country, she comes across a small temple dedicated to a new deity—Istra, which is the barbarian word for *Psyche*. As the priest tells the story of how Psyche became a goddess, Orual is shocked to hear the story of her own life, but twisted and distorted in terrible ways. In the priest's version of the story (which is essentially the same as the classical myth of Cupid and Psyche), Psyche has two jealous sisters, who intentionally ruin her happiness because they envy her palace and divine marriage. Orual is deeply offended by the lies of the gods and, at that moment, resolves to write her complaint in order to set the story straight. Her final accusation against the gods reads:

> They gave me nothing in the world to love but Psyche and then took her from me. But that was not enough. They then brought me to her at such

a place and time that it hung on my word whether she should continue in bliss or be cast out into misery. They would not tell me whether she was the bride of a god, or mad, or a brute's or villain's spoil. They would give no clear sign, though I begged for it. I had to guess. And because I guessed wrong they punished me—what's worse, punished me through her. And even that was not enough; they have now sent out a lying story in which I was given no riddle to guess, but knew and saw that she was the god's bride, and of my own will destroyed her, and that for jealousy. As if I were another Redival. I say the gods deal very unrightly with us. For they will neither (which would be best of all) go away and leave us to live our own short days to ourselves, nor will they show themselves openly and tell us what they would have us do. For that too would be endurable. But to hint and hover, to draw near us in dreams and oracles, or in a waking vision that vanishes as soon as seen, to be dead silent when we question them and then glide back and whisper (words we cannot understand) in our ears when we most wish to be free of them, and to show to one what they hide from another; what is all this but cat-and-mouse play, blindman's buff, and mere jugglery? Why must holy places be dark places?

I say, therefore, that there is no creature (toad, scorpion, or serpent) so noxious to man as the gods. Let them answer my charge if they can. It may well be that, instead of answering, they'll strike me mad or leprous or turn me into beast, bird, or tree. But will not all the world then know (and the gods will know it knows) that this is because they have no answer?[4]

Unraveling Orual

Part 2 of Orual's story is written a few weeks after she completed part 1. It is an addendum. But it doesn't simply add to the story; in many ways it changes the story. Part 1 is true; Orual is an honest narrator (at least, she attempts to be). But there is more to the story, and in part 2, she relates how the rest of the story comes crashing in on her, and how she comes to truly know herself for the first time. Thus, the whole purpose of part 2 is to make us rethink everything we've read in part 1, to see Orual in a whole new light.

Rereading the first lines of part 1 again in light of the ending, we realize that Orual's story has, in many ways, been a book about the four loves. "I am old now and have not much to fear from the anger of *gods*.

---

[4] Ibid., 249–50.

I have no *husband* nor *child*, nor hardly a *friend*, through whom they can hurt me."[5] What four relationships define Orual's life? Her angry and bitter relationship with the gods, her unrequited romantic love for Bardia, her motherly affection for Psyche, and her deep friendship with the Fox. In a letter, Lewis wrote that Orual is "an instance . . . of human affection in its natural condition: true, tender, suffering, but in the long run, tyrannically possessive and ready to turn to hatred when the beloved ceases to be its possession."[6]

It is through writing her complaint that Orual comes to see herself more clearly. As she says at the beginning of part 2, "I know so much more than I did about the woman who wrote it."[7] Writing has forced her to sift and sort her memories and motives. Coupled with coincidental (or rather, providential) conversations and events, she slowly comes to realize how twisted and ugly her loves are. Taking these four relationships in turn, we'll see divine love eventually conquer the savage and selfish loves that lie beneath the surface of part 1.

Orual and Bardia

We begin with her hidden, romantic love for Bardia. After Bardia dies, Orual laments that, as queen, she is unable to show the depth of her affection for him. She grieves that she was never able to tell him that she loved him. But in seeking to comfort Bardia's wife, Ansit, she discovers the true nature of her love.

Orual's relationship with Bardia had always been bittersweet—Bardia clearly respected and trusted Orual, but he did so because he treated her like a man. Thus, Orual's simultaneous grief and pleasure when Bardia teaches her to ride horseback and fence with swords. Bardia's return to his wife after "the day's work is over" pops the bubble of Orual's happiness after her triumph over the prince of Phars.[8] In her drunken loneliness, Orual harbors the impossible dream that Bardia is her husband (and Psyche their child). But her love for Bardia is not merely sad and lonely; it is also filled with jealousy and possessiveness. As seen in her anger when the Fox insults Bardia (but not when Bardia insults the Fox),[9] her instant hatred of

---

[5] Ibid., 3, italics mine.
[6] Lewis to Clyde Kilby, October 2, 1957, in *Collected Letters*, 3:831.
[7] Lewis, *Till We Have Faces*, 253.
[8] Ibid., 222.
[9] Ibid., 196.

Bardia's wife before she even meets her ("a very vile woman,"[10] "that petted thing,"[11] that "doll or scold of a wife"[12]), her prim courteousness and secret relish when she discovers that Ansit might be jealous of her[13]—Orual's love for Bardia is all the more fierce and possessive for its being unrequited and secret.

All of this comes tumbling out in her conversation in Ansit's house. Ansit not so subtly accuses Orual of working Bardia to death. The two women discover their mutual jealousy (and share a moment of mutual grief when they realize they each loved Bardia). More than that, Orual comes to realize that her love for Bardia had been the same kind of love as that of the gods which she so detests. She had devoured Bardia. The early rising to get started on the day's work, the constant (and sometimes needless) labor, subtly encouraging other men to mock Bardia for his faithfulness to Ansit—all of these Orual had done and justified on account of her loneliness. Like Ungit who steals the fruitful years of the virgins in her house and robs the common people of their wealth through sacrifices, Orual had taken and taken and given nothing in return. And she had had the audacity to call it love. As Ansit says:

> Yours is Queen's love, not commoners'. Perhaps you who spring from the gods love like the gods. Like the Shadowbrute. They say the loving and the devouring are all one, don't they? . . . You're full fed. Gorged with other men's lives, women's too: Bardia's, mine, the Fox's, your sister's—both your sisters.'[14]

Yes, she had loved Bardia, but as she realizes, "A love like that can grow to be nine-tenths hatred and still call itself love."[15] And so, in Orual, we again see the twisted face of corrupt Eros.

Orual and the Fox

But not just corrupt Eros. Orual's friendship with the Fox is twisted too. The Fox is a wonderful friend and mentor to Orual—faithful, loyal, willing to say the hard truth no matter what. He seeks to live up to his ideals of

---

10 Ibid., 146.
11 Ibid., 153.
12 Ibid., 149.
13 Ibid., 232–33.
14 Ibid., 264–65.
15 Ibid., 266.

friendship. "One of his maxims was that if we cannot persuade our friends by reasons we must be content 'and not bring a mercenary army to our aid.' (He meant passions.)"[16] When Orual returns from her second meeting with Psyche, the Fox refuses to press her and guilt her into revealing the secret of how she persuaded Psyche to use the lamp to reveal her lover. "Friends must be free," he says. To manipulate her into revealing it—to use "love" as a tool to get what he wants—that would kill friendship, raising a greater barrier between them than the secret itself. And of course, the grand irony of the Fox's words is that Orual has just come from manipulating Psyche in precisely this manner. Psyche agrees to take the lamp into the god's bed-chamber only because Orual threatens to kill herself. Like the Tragedian in *The Great Divorce*, Orual uses Psyche's love and pity for her as a weapon to get her way. And this, the Fox says, is the one thing friends must not do. It is "wrong to weep and beg and try to force you by your love. Love is not a thing to be so used."[17]

But Psyche is not the only victim of Orual's manipulations. After she becomes queen, Orual gives the Fox his freedom. She does this out of love and affection for him. But when she realizes that he plans to use his freedom to return to the Greeklands, she is distraught that he would even consider leaving. She wallows in self-pity, lamenting that no one loves her.

> "Fool!" said I to myself. "Have you not yet learned that you are that to no one? What are you to Bardia? as much perhaps as the old King was. His heart lies at home with his wife and her brats. If you mattered to him he'd never have let you fight. What are you to the Fox? His heart was always in the Greeklands."[18]

And even though she says none of this to the Fox, she can't help but pull on his heart strings: "'Grandfather!' I cried, no Queen now; all Orual, even all child. 'Do they mean you'll leave me? Go away?'"[19] The Fox, to his credit, decides to remain in Glome out of love for Orual, but one can't help but feel that guilt at Orual's distress kept him from returning to his own family in Greece. And so, even though her love for the Fox isn't as jealous and possessive as her love for Bardia, again we see that Orual's friend-love is also corrupt. Her love is real and tender, but it is also selfish and self-pitying.

16 Ibid., 177–78.
17 Ibid., 204.
18 Ibid., 209.
19 Ibid., 207–8.

Orual and Psyche

And so we turn to the last of the natural loves, and the one that dominates Orual's life. Her love for Psyche is essentially mother-love; it is real and deep, but even in part 1 we can see the twisting of her affection for her younger sister. The three conversations between them—in the prison room, after the Great Offering, and the final one before Psyche is exiled—show, in ways subtle and overt, how tyrannical and possessive her mother-love is.

Orual visits Psyche in prison in hopes of comforting her as a mother does her child; instead, Psyche comforts her and this reversal makes "its own little eddy of pain";[20] Orual is cheered again only when Psyche reverts to her childlike state, calling Orual "Maia" and crying in her lap. In addition, Orual feels a fierce possessiveness of Psyche; she bristles whenever Psyche speaks of her love for the Fox. Corrupt affection needs to be needed; the growth and maturity of the beloved is a threat to be resisted at all costs. Orual begrudges Psyche her independence; she is injured by the solace Psyche receives from her hopes of life after death. With horror, Orual begins to realize that Psyche has sources of strength beyond what Orual can give her. For Orual, to be loved is to be needed, and Psyche no longer needs her (at least, not in the same way she did as a child). Thus, in Orual's mind, Psyche is cruel and has a heart of iron and stone. Her maturity, stability, independence, and hope in the gods put a rift between the two sisters; Psyche no longer "belongs" to Orual, and this knowledge breeds bitterness amidst Orual's love.

Their reunion after the Great Offering is initially euphoric. Psyche alive! Though Orual is confused and skeptical of Psyche's story, she pushes aside those feelings and simply rejoices to have her beloved back. Yet even here, in the midst of her happiness, she chafes when Psyche praises her for having done such a good job in raising her, as if those days were old and gone, as if Orual is no longer needed. But the real rift between them, which began in the prison, opens wider when Orual is unable to see Psyche's palace. Orual is horrified and grieved by the distance between them. She is revolted by the unspeakable joy on Psyche's face and rages in her heart against the gods who stole her beloved. But this rage eventually falls upon Psyche, as Orual realizes that Psyche's ultimate allegiance is now elsewhere. Psyche refuses to leave the mountain and her husband. She rebuff's Orual's attempts to rule her like a tyrannical mother. "'Dear Maia, I am a wife now. It's no longer you that I must obey.' I learned then how one can hate those

---

[20] Ibid., 67.

one loves."[21] Again, Psyche's independent will and happiness shatter Orual's world; there is now a deep and permanent cloud between them.

In the final meeting, Orual has come on a mission—to persuade Psyche that her unseen husband is either a monster or a villain. Orual appeals to her importance to Psyche—she is all the mother, father, and kin that Psyche has. We witness Orual's true vision of herself—the sole, burdened, resolute caregiver, responsible to guide and protect little Psyche. But Psyche is unmoved by Orual's appeals, and Orual is again shocked at Psyche's stability and maturity, even as Orual herself rants and raves in her anger. And then Orual threatens to kill herself if Psyche will not obey, and Psyche sees the true nature of Orual's mother-love.

> You are indeed teaching me about kinds of love I did not know. It is like looking into a deep pit. I am not sure whether I like your kind better than hatred. Oh, Orual—to take my love for you, because you know it goes down to my very roots and cannot be diminished by any other newer love, and then to make of it a tool, a weapon, a thing of policy and mastery, an instrument of torture—I begin to think I never knew you. Whatever comes after, something that was between us dies here.[22]

This is Orual's maternal affection: possessive, tyrannical, easily injured, willing to lie and manipulate to get its way, determined to keep the beloved a child, desperate to be needed, nursing the grievance that she alone, of all people, truly loves Psyche. But all of these corruptions of natural love flow from Orual's hatred of the gods. To this we now turn.

Orual and God

Throughout her life, Orual feared and hated the gods because they hide in dark places, speak in riddles, refuse to reveal their desires clearly, and send prosperity in order to set people up for a fall. But in her final days, Orual realizes that her hatred runs deeper than that. Standing before the divine judge in her final vision, she realizes that her grand accusation against the gods is really a vile scribble, a snarling and savage complaint.

In truth, she hated the gods because they stole Psyche from her, and she hated Psyche because she was so stolen. Psyche had willingly responded to the overtures of the god of the mountain and been granted unspeakable joy.

---

[21] Ibid., 127.
[22] Ibid., 165.

As Orual reads her own spiteful complaint, she admits that she was given the same offer as Psyche. Psyche always had a longing for death, a desire to find the place where all joy came from. Later, on her way to bury Psyche, the beauty of the world offers Orual herself the same joy. "Why should your heart not dance?"[23] But Orual slams the door—her sadness, her self-pity, her ugliness so define her that she will not let Joy in.

So also, during the two girls' lives, when the gods give them a glimpse of their reality. In a flash, Psyche sees the West wind as it carries her to the god's palace; in a similar flash of lightning, Orual sees the god's palace while kneeling at the river. Psyche follows the tantalizing glimpse and is nourished by the god. Orual rejects her momentary glimpse of the palace as another indecipherable riddle. She wants the gods to reveal themselves to her on her own terms; thus, her desperate but demanding prayers for a sign. Again and again, Orual refuses to answer the call of Joy. She fights to keep that door shut. She wants (or says she wants) proof. But when she is offered it in the form of Psyche's obvious health and strength on the mountain, she screams, "I don't want it. I hate it. Hate it, hate it, hate it. Do you understand?"[24] She dallies with the idea that the gods might hide themselves from humans because they are too beautiful (as the story of Anchises and Aphrodite suggests), but in the end she pushes that thought aside, until the gods dig it out of her in the divine courtroom.

These contrasts appear throughout the story. What's more, Orual is aware of them. She both loves Psyche intensely and is intensely jealous of her. Psyche is more beautiful than Orual and eventually is physically stronger.[25] Psyche's joy and strength, like that of the bright spirits in *The Great Divorce*, are invulnerable to manipulations. It is "full of pity yet in a way so pitiless."[26] Orual's strength, on the other hand, grows hard and joyless. Psyche's love expands: her love for the god makes her love Orual more. Orual's love constricts, so that in the end, her love is no different from hatred. And the increasing contrast breeds greater and greater rivalry. Even after Psyche is gone, Orual feels threatened. When faced with the prospect of death in her single combat, she fears that she will cower and that Psyche will surpass her in everything—courage, beauty, favor of the gods, strength. When the Fox considers returning to the Greeklands,

---

23 Ibid., 96.
24 Ibid., 124.
25 Ibid., 103.
26 Ibid., 124.

Orual sulks, "If [Psyche] were still with us, he would stay. It was Psyche he loved. Never me."[27]

All of these things—Orual's hatred of the gods, her self-pity, her jealousy of Psyche and Ansit, her twisted love of Bardia—appear again and again in part 1 in her imagination and dreams. Her dreams about "cruel Psyche," in which Psyche mocks her, hates her, and steals every good thing from her, are not merely the ravings of her fever; they are her true self bubbling up from beneath. She fondles the thought of her own funeral—Psyche "weeping and repenting of all her cruelties," Bardia crying bitterly.[28] Everyone would love her once she were dead. She relishes midnight fantasies in which Ansit is dead, Bardia is seeking her love, and she makes him beg her forgiveness before granting his request. Her whole life has been defined by her self-pity, so much so that she is completely blinded to her sister Redival's loneliness and sadness at being cast aside by the arrival of the Fox and Psyche.

In the final chapters, Orual discovers that she is Ungit—ugly, greedy, devouring, and demanding. "Glome was a web—I the swollen spider, squat at its center, gorged with men's stolen lives."[29] She is a tortured tangle of contradictions: tyrannically possessive of Psyche yet incredibly jealous of her as well; desperate to be loved yet fiercely independent; full of both love and hate for all those close to her. In Orual, we see how easily our best desires can be corrupted, how the highest of our loves can become the most evil. In the presence of the gods, Orual comes face-to-face with the demon within. For the first time, she says what she really means, and she issues this profound warning:

> When the time comes to you at which you will be forced at last to utter the speech which has lain at the center of your soul for years, which you have, all that time, idiot-like, been saying over and over, you'll not talk about joy of words. I saw well why the gods do not speak to us openly, nor let us answer. Till that word can be dug out of us, why should they hear the babble that we think we mean? How can they meet us face to face till we have faces?[30]

But Orual is not only Ungit. She is also Psyche, and therein lies the hope, not only for her but for all of us. We all are born into the house of

---

[27] Ibid., 209.
[28] Ibid., 170.
[29] Ibid., 276.
[30] Ibid., 294.

Ungit. "We want to be our own," without God interfering with us and shattering our little kingdoms. We are all fiercely possessive of what we think is ours. We are cravers who love to say, "My own. Mine. Mine." Our natural loves, in their various ways, have become demons.

But the gospel gives us a way out. As Orual discovers, pagan mystery religions and Greek philosophy both had parts of the truth. But the gospel is both thick *and* clear. Psyche catches a glimpse of this truth while tied to the tree—she observes that Fox has seen something true about the greatness of the divine nature, but also that the priest is right that blood and sacrifice are necessary to get to God. In the story, set as it is in the pre-Christian world, we only catch the glimpse. But in the gospel, we see the reality. Myth becomes fact. This has been the whole purpose of Lewis's myth—to enable us to experience "as concrete what can otherwise be understood only as an abstraction."[31] And this also accounts for the utter inadequacy of this chapter. Explanation and abstraction have their place; hopefully they will enrich your next reading of the story. But myth transcends explanation. "What flows into you from the myth is not truth but reality (truth is always *about* something, but reality is that *about which* truth is), and, therefore, every myth becomes the father of innumerable truths on the abstract level."[32]

There are many other truths to explore in *Till We Have Faces*. The best way to do so would be to take what you've learned from this chapter and reread the novel. But for now, I'll close with this one.

The glimpses of God and the gospel and ourselves that appear in this story don't just give us information. They issue a call to us: "Die before you die."[33] Orual dies; she is stripped and exposed, and her true word dug out of her shriveled soul. But she is not left in the courtroom to get what she deserves. Mercy triumphs over judgment. And like her, we must answer this call. We must die before we die. We must be unmade so that we also can be Psyche. We must become no one so that we can become truly human. We must turn away from our narrow, selfish, and self-pitying dreams and plans and instead come into the presence of the true and better Cupid, the greater God of love. He is the answer. Before his face, our questions die away. In his presence, not only our vices but even our virtues are burned away. He is fullness of Joy and at his right hand are pleasures forevermore.

---

[31] Lewis, "Myth Became Fact," in *God in the Dock*, 66.
[32] Ibid.
[33] Lewis, *Till We Have Faces*, 279.

CONCLUSION

As this book concludes, I'm very mindful of the wealth of material on the Christian life in Lewis that I've left untouched. Rereading through Lewis's books, essays, and letters in the course of my revisions has reinforced my deep appreciation of Lewis but also reminded me how many of his insights have to go uncommented on in this book. For readers who desire to chase down some of these insights, I'll include a few suggestions here.

1. Teaching through *That Hideous Strength* in an undergraduate class, I was struck by the subtle confidence in God shown by the Dimbles. For instance, when Mrs. Dimble stays the night with Jane Studdock, she pauses to say her prayers.[1] No pretense, no awkwardness (at least on her part), no attempt to hide it or to make more of it than necessary. She is simply a Christian woman, and a Christian woman prays before bed, regardless of who is watching. Her actions essentially say: "Prayer is the most normal thing in the world. How could I not speak to the God who has saved me? I will neither compel you to join me, nor feel shy or awkward about doing something that is as natural to me as breathing." There is a quality in her obedience at that point that I find eminently compelling and worthy of imitation.

2. Men and women are different, and this difference manifests itself in the different ways we tend to define love. Men tend to think that love means not giving trouble to others. Women tend to think that it means taking trouble for others.[2] Lewis's experience was that "men are more likely to

---

[1] Lewis, *That Hideous Strength*, 75.
[2] "Another great help, where the parties concerned are male and female, is the divergence of view about Unselfishness which we have built up between the sexes. A woman means by Unselfishness chiefly taking trouble for others; a man means not giving trouble to others. As a result, a woman who is quite far gone in the Enemy's service will make a nuisance of herself on a larger scale than any man except those whom Our Father has dominated completely; and, conversely, a man will live long in the Enemy's camp before he undertakes as much spontaneous work to please others as a quite ordinary woman may do every day. Thus while the woman thinks of doing good offices and the man of respecting other people's rights,

hand over to others what they ought to do themselves, and women more likely to do themselves what others wish they would leave alone. Hence both sexes must be told 'Mind your own business,' but in two different senses!"[3] Elsewhere, he writes:

> I have often had the fancy that one stage in Purgatory might be a great big kitchen in which things are always going wrong—milk boiling over, crockery getting smashed, toast burning, animals stealing. The women have to learn to sit still and mind their own business: the men have to learn to jump up and do something about it. When both sexes have mastered this exercise, they go on to the next.[4]

3. Bringing the two previous ideas together, Mother Dimble's remarks on marriage are worth hours of reflection, touching as they do on the relationship between nature, culture, sexuality, gender, stories, liturgies, and obedience to God. They appear in a brief conversation with Jane that runs as follows:

> "Some of what he says, or what the Masters say, about marriage does seem to me to be a lot of fuss about something so simple and natural that it oughtn't to need saying at all. But I suppose there are young women nowadays who need to be told it."
> "You haven't got much use for young women who do, I see."
> "Well, perhaps I'm unfair. Things were easier for us. We were brought up on stories with happy endings and on the Prayer Book. We always intended to love, honor and obey, and we had figures and we wore petticoats and we liked waltzes . . . "[5]

Unpacking the thick truth embedded in that little interchange would be very worthwhile in a very confused age.

4. God has given human beings the gift of rhythms. The four seasons, rhythms of feasting and fasting, the church calendar with special days—all of these give voice to our love of both change and permanence. Holy days (and even holy places) are "focal points or reminders." They keep our belief in God's omnipresence and transcendence from becoming mere sentiment

each sex, without any obvious unreason, can and does regard the other as radically selfish" (Lewis, *The Screwtape Letters*, 154).
[3] Lewis to Mary Willis Shelburne, September 3, 1962, in *Collected Letters*, 3:1366.
[4] Lewis to Mary Willis Shelburne, July 31, 1962, in *Collected Letters*, 3:1361.
[5] Lewis, *That Hideous Strength*, 165–66.

and abstraction. At the same time, these focal points are meant to remind us that "every bush (could we perceive it) [is] a Burning Bush."[6]

5. The difficulty of prayer reveals a lot about us.

> Prayer is irksome. An excuse to omit it is never unwelcome. When it is over, this casts a feeling of relief and holiday over the rest of the day. We are reluctant to begin. We are delighted to finish. While we are at prayer, but not while we are reading a novel or solving a cross-word puzzle, any trifle is enough to distract us.[7]

Nevertheless, dutiful prayers, hard prayers offered in deep obedience, in the sorrowful absence of devotional feeling, may be the most valuable to God. They come from deep within us, and show, in a way suited to our pilgrim condition, who we really are (and what we are really becoming).

6. Running with the theme of the present book, an in-depth examination of the conversions of both Mark and Jane Studdock would be very illuminating. Mark's conversation involves the renunciation of his Inner Ring-ishness and occurs through an encounter with what he calls "the Normal." Jane's involves a deep wrestling with her marriage to Mark, her conflicted relationship to her own sexuality and gender, a preference for "Nice People" over "Nasty People," and her encounter with God's kind of community at St. Anne's. In both cases, though the pathways differ, Mark and Jane must eventually come into the presence of God and be changed.[8]

Other themes could be added, and this book would run on and on like the mountains in true Narnia. But I want to end where we began—with the four facts we explored in the first chapter: (1) you are here and now; (2) God is here and now; (3) God demands all of you; and (4) therefore, every minute of every day, you are confronted with the Choice. Here is Lewis again on those first two truths:

> If there is a God, you are, in a sense, alone with Him. You cannot put Him off with speculations about your next door neighbours or memories of

---

[6] Lewis, *Letters to Malcolm*, 75.
[7] Ibid., 113.
[8] For a wonderfully perceptive essay on this theme, see Gavin Ortlund, "Conversion in C. S. Lewis's *That Hideous Strength*," *Themelios* 41, no. 1 (2016): 8–19.

what you have read in books. What will all that chatter and hearsay count (will you even be able to remember it?) when the anaesthetic fog which we call "nature" or "the real world" fades away and the Presence in which you have always stood becomes palpable, immediate, and unavoidable?[9]

You are alone in God's presence. And, for most of us, this creates a certain kind of caution in the soul. We are wary lest, in God's presence, we get carried away and lose our heads. We don't want to come out into our ordinary lives having made any resolutions or commitments that will prove inconvenient or burdensome. We know what sorts of promises we can make in the grip of spiritual enthusiasm. Like Lewis, our recurrent temptation is "to go down to the sea and there neither dive nor swim nor float, but only dabble and splash."[10] We want to preserve some area of our lives upon which God has no claim, some realm of "our own" with which he has nothing to do.

But there is no such area. God claims all, and while he is very merciful and will forgive many failures, he will accept no deliberate compromise. "Failures will be forgiven; it is acquiescence that is fatal, the permitted, regularised presence of an area in ourselves which we still claim for our own."[11] The line in our hearts that separates our old selves from our new selves that God is creating must be a fighting line, not a permanent frontier fixed by agreement with the world, the flesh, and the Devil.[12] "There's no bargaining with Him."[13] God is not claiming this much of our time or that much of our attention. He is not even claiming all of our time and all of our attention. He is claiming *us*, ourselves, the totality of who and what we are. That is his claim.

And it doesn't matter what diverts us from surrendering to his claim; all roads that do not lead to life ultimately lead to death.

"If you have not chosen the Kingdom of God, it will make in the end no difference what you have chosen instead." Those are hard words to take. Will it really make no difference whether it was women or patriotism, cocaine or art, whisky or a seat in the Cabinet, money or science? Well, surely no difference that matters. We shall have missed the end for which we are formed and rejected the only thing that satisfies.[14]

9 Lewis, *Mere Christianity*, 217.
10 Lewis, "A Slip of the Tongue," in *The Weight of Glory and Other Addresses*, 187.
11 Ibid., 192.
12 Lewis, *Letters to Malcolm*, 31.
13 Lewis, "A Slip of the Tongue," in *The Weight of Glory and Other Addresses*, 190.
14 Ibid., 190–91.

Given our tendency to shrink back from God's total demand and our nearly perpetual attempt to preserve our own autonomy, we might be tempted to despair. What hope can we have of making any progress? I close this book with two truths from Lewis that I hope will encourage you to daily lay down your arms and take up your cross.

The first truth is this: "What God does for us, he does in us."[15] Our own efforts may always suffer under "this fatal reservation," this desire to play it safe and to temper God's total demands. But God is not deterred by our weakness, failures, and sin. He is relentless. And we will know that he is working within us because our wills will increasingly align with his. This process—of God overcoming my resistance and bringing me into greater union with himself—"will appear to [us] to be the daily or hourly repeated exercises of [our] own will in renouncing [the "My Own"] attitude, especially each morning, for it grows all over [us] like a new shell each night."[16] And these small acts of the will have great effects.

> Good and evil both increase at compound interest. That is why the little decisions you and I make every day are of such infinite importance. The smallest good act today is the capture of a strategic point from which, a few months later, you may be able to go on to victories you never dreamed of. An apparently trivial indulgence in lust or anger today is the loss of a ridge or railway line or bridgehead from which the enemy may launch an attack otherwise impossible.[17]

The second truth is that ultimately all of God's demands are rooted in his love. "He claims all, because He is love and must bless. He cannot bless us unless He has us. When we try to keep within us an area that is our own, we try to keep an area of death. Therefore, in love, He claims all."[18] Lewis learned this from his wife, Joy.

> Long ago, before we were married, [Joy] was haunted all one morning as she went about her work with the obscure sense of God (so to speak) "at her elbow," demanding her attention. And of course, not being a perfected saint, she had the feeling that it would be a question, as it usually is, of some unrepented sin or tedious duty. At last she gave in—I know how

---

15 Ibid., 191.
16 Ibid.
17 Lewis, *Mere Christianity*, 132.
18 Lewis, "A Slip of the Tongue," in *The Weight of Glory and Other Addresses*, 190.

one puts it off—and faced Him. But the message was, "I want to give you something" and instantly she entered into joy.[19]

As Aslan says in *The Magician's Nephew*, "Oh Adam's sons, how cleverly you defend yourselves against all that might do you good!"[20] God desires to give us himself. "He can give that only insofar as our self-affirming will retires and makes room for Him in our souls."[21] And this is a real gift. Yes, we must do our duties. We must bear our crosses. God demands all. But he also gives all, for he is a giver, and he has nothing to give but himself.

So we end where we began. "Begin where you are." You are here and now. God is here and now. God demands all (because he wishes to give you all). So turn to him. Turn to Christ and give yourself up to him. Only then will you begin to have a real self. Only in his presence can you ever hope to become fully human.

The Choice is yours.

---

[19] Lewis, *A Grief Observed*, 46–47. Joy describes her own conversion experience in similar words: "All my defenses—the walls of arrogance and cocksureness and self-love behind which I hid from God—went down momentarily and God came in. . . . There was a Person with me in that room, directly present to my consciousness—a Person so real that all my previous life was by comparison a mere shadow play" (quoted in Devin Brown, *A Life Observed: A Spiritual Biography of C. S. Lewis* [Grand Rapids: Baker, 2013], 29).
[20] Lewis, *The Magician's Nephew*, 183.
[21] Lewis, "A Slip of the Tongue," in *The Weight of Glory and Other Addresses*, 189.

LEWIS WORKS CITED

The Abolition of Man. New York: HarperOne, 2001.

Christian Reflections. Edited by Walter Hooper. New York: HarperOne, 1980.

The Collected Letters of C. S. Lewis. Vol. 1, *Family Letters, 1905–1931*. Edited by Walter Hooper. New York: HarperOne, 2004.

The Collected Letters of C. S. Lewis. Vol. 2, *Books, Broadcasts, and the War, 1931–1949*. Edited by Walter Hooper. New York: HarperOne, 2004.

The Collected Letters of C. S. Lewis. Vol. 3, *Narnia, Cambridge, and Joy, 1950–1963*. Edited by Walter Hooper. New York: HarperOne, 2007.

The Collected Poems of C. S. Lewis. Edited by Walter Hooper. London: Fount, 1994.

An Experiment in Criticism. San Francisco: HarperOne, 2012.

The Four Loves. New York: Mariner, 1971.

God in the Dock: Essays on Theology and Ethics. Edited by Walter Hooper. Grand Rapids: Eerdmans, 1970.

The Great Divorce: A Dream. San Francisco: HarperOne, 2001.

A Grief Observed. New York: HarperOne, 1996.

The Horse and His Boy. New York: HarperCollins, 2010.

Image and Imagination. San Francisco: HarperOne, 2014.

The Last Battle. New York: HarperCollins, 2010.

Letters to Malcolm: Chiefly on Prayer. San Diego: Harcourt, Brace, 1992.

Lilies That Fester. New York: Mariner, 2012.

The Magician's Nephew. New York: HarperCollins, 2010.

Mere Christianity. San Francisco: HarperOne, 2001.

Miracles: A Preliminary Study. San Francisco: HarperOne, 2001.

On Stories and Other Essays on Literature. New York: Harvest, 2002.

Out of the Silent Planet. New York: HarperCollins, 2012.

Perelandra. New York: HarperOne, 2012.

A Preface to Paradise Lost. New York: Oxford University Press, 1961.

Present Concerns. Edited by Walter Hooper. San Diego: Harcourt Brace Jovanovich, 1986.

The Problem of Pain. San Francisco: HarperOne, 2001.

Reflections on the Psalms. New York: Harvest Books, 1986.

The Screwtape Letters. Annotated ed. San Francisco: HarperOne, 2013.

Selected Literary Essays. Edited by Walter Hooper. San Francisco: HarperOne, 2013.

The Silver Chair. New York: HarperCollins, 2010.

Surprised by Joy. New York: Houghton Mifflin Harcourt, 1966.

That Hideous Strength. New York: HarperOne, 2012.

Till We Have Faces: A Myth Retold. New York: Harcourt, Brace, 1980.

The Voyage of the Dawn Treader. New York: HarperCollins, 2010.

The Weight of Glory and Other Addresses. San Francisco: HarperOne, 2001.

The World's Last Night. New York: Harcourt, 1986.

GENERAL INDEX

SCRIPTURE INDEX

WISDOM FROM THE PAST FOR LIFE IN THE PRESENT

Theologians on the Christian Life

AUGUSTINE
by GERALD BRAY

BAVINCK
by JOHN BOLT

BONHOEFFER
by STEPHEN J. NICHOLS

CALVIN
by MICHAEL HORTON

EDWARDS
by DANE C. ORTLUND

LEWIS
by JOE RIGNEY

LLOYD-JONES
by JASON MEYER

LUTHER
by CARL R. TRUEMAN

NEWTON
by TONY REINKE

OWEN
by MATTHEW BARRETT &
MICHAEL A. G. HAYKIN

PACKER
by SAM STORMS

SCHAEFFER
by WILLIAM EDGAR

SPURGEON
by MICHAEL REEVES

WARFIELD
by FRED G. ZASPEL

WESLEY
by FRED SANDERS

The Theologians on the Christian Life series provides accessible introductions to the great teachers on the Christian life, exploring their personal lives and writings, especially as they pertain to the walk of faith.

Visit crossway.org/TOCL for more information.